Contemporary Party Politi

Contemporary Party Politics

Robin T. Pettitt

First published 2014 by
PALGRAVE MACMILLAN

Palgrave Macmillan in the UK is an imprint of Macmillan Publishers Limited,
registered in England, company number 785998, of Houndmills, Basingstoke,
Hampshire RG21 6XS.

Palgrave Macmillan in the US is a division of St Martin's Press LLC,
175 Fifth Avenue, New York, NY 10010.

Palgrave Macmillan is the global academic imprint of the above companies
and has companies and representatives throughout the world.

Palgrave® and Macmillan® are registered trademarks in the United States,
the United Kingdom, Europe and other countries

ISBN: 978-0-230-23779-7   hardback
ISBN: 978-0-230-23780-3   paperback

This book is printed on paper suitable for recycling and made from fully
managed and sustained forest sources. Logging, pulping and manufacturing
processes are expected to conform to the environmental regulations of the
country of origin.

A catalogue record for this book is available from the British Library.

A catalog record for this book is available from the Library of Congress.

Printed in China

Til min Regnbue

Contents

List of Figures

List of Tables

Acknowledgements

One does not complete a project such as this without incurring considerable debt. On the academic side I would like to gratefully acknowledge the work of several anonymous reviewers who have commented on the text at various stages from proposal to final draft. They have undoubtedly helped improve the manuscript significantly. I would also like to thank the people at Palgrave Macmillan for encouraging me in my endeavours. I owe particular thanks to Steven Kennedy for seeing the book through its early stages and to Stephen Wenham for seeing it through to completion. Stephen Wenham in particular has been very tolerant of my many broken deadlines.

I would also like to thank Pascal Perrineau and CEVIPOF – Paris for hosting me during some of my most productive months working on the book. Rejane Senac facilitated my initial introduction to CEVIPOF for which I am very grateful. Odile Gaultier-Voituriez was ever helpful in getting me access to key pieces of literature.

Most importantly I need to thank my family for their tolerance and forgiveness – especially Rainbow Murray for her love and support throughout the slow birth of this book. Jeg elsker dig. Speaking of slow births, it would not do to neglect the most important development during the making of this book: the arrival of my beautiful daughter Alicia Hope Murray-Pettitt. This book will not mean very much to you for the foreseeable future – but at least there will be one more thing in the house for you to gnaw on.

Chapter 1

Introduction

Political parties are the most important organisations in modern democratic states. That is the simplest and most straightforward reason for reading, and indeed writing, a book dedicated to the study of political parties. There are many reasons why parties are important. If we want to know why so few women become legislators; if we want to know why one person and not another gets to lead a country; or how much of a choice we have on the ballot paper, we need to look to political parties for most of our answers. The importance of political parties is captured by Schattschneider's oft quoted claim that 'modern democracy is unthinkable save in terms of parties' (1942, p. 1). No modern democracy has been made to work without political parties. Modern democracy is party democracy. One of the few attempts to build a 'no-party democracy', Uganda, is really little more than a thinly veiled one-party state and struggles to live up to most definitions of democracy.

The dominance of parties in the modern world is also illustrated by the fact that, not only do they sit at the centre of all democratic countries; they are also a feature of many non-democratic systems. There are two major examples of this. The first is Communist single-party states, most notable the former Soviet Bloc in Eastern Europe and the Soviet Union. In these countries the only party allowed to exist was the Communist Party. The Communist Party sat at the centre of all political power and reached far into people's lives. It was therefore a tool used by Communist leaders for political and social control of the population. Even today a Communist Party dominates political life in the world's most populous nation, The People's Republic of China.

The second example is the Ba'ath Party in Iraq and Syria. As with the Communist Parties in the Soviet Bloc and China, the Ba'ath Party was the only legal party in Syria and Iraq and used as a way of controlling all aspects of the state.

It could even be argued that understanding political parties is now more important than ever. With the end of the Cold War there was a major expansion of democratic government. Many military dictatorships and Communist single-party states became multi-party democracies, vastly increasing the number of political parties in the world. Indeed, with the end of the Cold War, liberal democracy, which is also party

1

democracy, was seen as having seen off its final competitor (Communism) for the position of most desirable political system. The future, argued people like Francis Fukuyama, belonged to liberal (party based) democracies. If the future is indeed in the hands of liberal democracies, then understanding the organisations at the heart of this political system must be a prime concern.

Indeed, when looking around the world, there are only a handful of countries, such as Saudi Arabia and the Central African Republic, that do not have political systems based around political parties. The fact that so few countries have political systems devoid of parties in some form underlines the importance of this type of organisation. In short, political parties are at the heart of all democratic and a great many non-democratic countries.

The fact that political parties should be such a dominant feature of both democratic and non-democratic systems of government is hardly surprising. Political parties organise people with roughly similar viewpoints and give them a 'label' (that is, the party's name). Under that label, parties then present a programme for what they want to do should they acquire power. This gives voters, the media and other observers a way of judging what political trends are moving in a society. Imagine a parliament of several hundred members, without parties. It would be well neigh impossible to establish a working majority for a government. Voters would have a difficult time judging who was responsible for certain actions, and therefore faced with a difficult task when deciding whom to support at an election.

Further, political parties provide a critical link between citizens and governments through their membership organisations. Political parties have both a civil society element (the membership organisation) and a government element (parliamentarians and ministers). Through that they can give their leaders a level of popular legitimacy that personal individual rule would find it difficult to match. This works both in democratic multi-party democracies and in one-party authoritarian regimes. Even if there is no democratic element in a country's system, dictators have often found it expedient to at least pretend to have popular legitimacy through a party organisation.

Political parties are the vehicles through which both voters and campaigners can be mobilised behind some cause – which in turn is key to winning elections in democratic countries. Indeed, Michels wrote that:

[a] class which unfurls in the face of society the banner of certain definite claims and which aspires to the realization of a complex of ideals [...] needs an organization. Be the claims economic or be they political, organization appears the only means for the creation of a collective

will. Organization [...] is the weapon of the weak in their struggle with the strong (1915, p. 21)

In other words if people who do not have significant personal resources want to achieve their aims, the best way of doing so is through collective action in the form of an organisation.

Now, obviously such political organisations need not take the form of a political party. Trade unions, single issue organisations, terrorist groups and rebel armies are all examples of organisations pursuing 'certain definite claims'. However, in a democratic polity the most effective and direct way of realising a 'complex of ideals' is by gaining control of the levers of government power. That means succeeding in getting elected to legislative assemblies or other positions of power, which in turn is most easily done through a political party. Nowhere in the democratic world do independents – politicians without party affiliation – dominate elected positions. Instead, political parties do. As Aldrich (2011, p. ix) writes 'for politicians to win more of what they seek to win, more often, and over a longer period' they need political parties.

In short, political parties are central to the workings of democratic politics and are also a feature of the politics of many non-democratic countries. No other type of political organisation can claim to have the impact and influence that political parties have. They are simply the most important political organisation in the modern world.

However, while political parties are a feature of both democratic and undemocratic regimes this book will focus on party politics in democratic countries. 'Democratic' is obviously a highly contested term and there is no clear separation of democratic and non-democratic politics. It may at times be fairly easy to tell a clearly democratic country from a clearly autocratic one. Putting for example Sweden next to say Saudi Arabia the differences would be clear enough. However, there is a lot of grey between those two polar opposites. In essence, the focus of this book will be on parties operating in what the *Economist Intelligence Unit*'s 'Democracy index 2011' labels as either 'full democracies' or 'flawed democracies' (EIU, 2011, pp. 4–6). The EIU defines a full democracy as:

> Countries in which not only basic political freedoms and civil liberties are respected, but these will also tend to be underpinned by a political culture conducive to the flourishing of democracy. The functioning of government is satisfactory. Media are independent and diverse. There is an effective system of checks and balances. The judiciary is independent and judicial decisions are enforced. There are only limited problems in the functioning of democracies. (EIU, 2011, p. 30)

They define a flawed democracy as countries that:

> have free and fair elections and even if there are problems (such as infringements on media freedom), basic civil liberties will be respected. However, there are significant weaknesses in other aspects of democracy, including problems in governance, an underdeveloped political culture and low levels of political participation. (EIU, 2011, p. 30)

There are several reasons why this book will focus on parties in democratic countries. One is linked to how one might define a political party, which will be explored further below. Another is the close link between political parties and democracy. It was explored above how modern democracy is party-democracy. There is in the modern world an intrinsic link between political parties and democracy. We did see that some dictatorships are based around a political party. However, dictatorships do not need party politics to 'function'. Democracy does. Hence, we can understand dictatorships without necessarily paying a great deal of attention to party politics. We cannot understand democracies without understanding party politics. Considering how important democracy as a form of government has become since the end of the Cold War, the need to understand the party politics side of democracy is overwhelming.

A final reason is that a competitive party system, that is, where multiple parties are allowed to compete for power freely, unlike for example communist single-party states, is one of the defining features of modern democracy. Hence, party politics is at its most diverse and thus interesting and worthy of study in a democracy. If there is only one party in existence our task is very simple and therefore not that interesting. In a system with several parties all jockeying for position and power, the task is that much more complicated, and, therefore, also that much more worthwhile.

This chapter will next explore the definition of what a political party is. The chapter will then explore various aspects of party organisations, before looking at the main roles performed by political parties in democratic states. It will then give an overview of the idea that political parties are currently in a state of crisis. The chapter will end with an overview of the contents of this book.

Defining 'political party'

Because parties are to be found in every democratic country, and in a good few undemocratic ones, as a group they are marked by a huge variety. Parties are influenced by the environment they operate in and are as diverse as their host countries. For that reason it can often be difficult, but also endlessly fascinating, to explore them as a group. Indeed, merely defining what a party is can be problematic. Some are old well-established institutions, with long histories and strongly hierarchical structure where each member knows where they fit in the organisation and who is in charge – largely because they can read about it in the party's rules. Examples of such parties would be the British, German and French socialist parties. Others, like the Republicans and Democrats in the United States have even longer histories, but are much more loosely organised with much less in the way of a hierarchical structure or clear lines of command. Yet others, such as List Pim Fortuyn in the Netherlands and Silvio Berlusconi's Forza Italia (Forward Italy) and Il Popolo della Libertà (The People of Freedom) were set up as their founding leader's personal political projects. Some parties, usually smaller fringe parties, have a very clear political ideology were as others are more amorphous and designed to offend as few people as possible. The question is to what extent we can come up with a definition that captures all these very varied organisations. We usually know a political party when we see it, but coming up with a clear definition is not easy considering this great diversity.

Indeed, definitions of parties have varied and changed over time. In a text first published in 1770 Edmund Burke defined a party as 'a body of men [sic] united, for promoting by their joint endeavours the national interest, upon some particular principle in which they are all agreed' (Burke, 1981, p. 317). It is no doubt true that most parties would argue that what they do is in the national interest. However, this is not unique to political parties. Arguably the Church of England and other state religion organisations would claim to be doing the same. In addition, the national interest could also be said to be the focus of Political Action Committees (PAC) in the United States. A PAC will spend money in support of for example a particular candidate, but will not be running candidates itself. They do so with a view to promote a particular cause or principle, but are by their very definition not political parties. Their defined role in US legislation is to raise and spend money in the name of a cause. Any number of campaign organisations, such as Amnesty International and Greenpeace also campaign on very specific principles, but we would not regard them as political parties. In short, 'a body of men', that is, an organisation of some sort, pursuing a particular principle is not something that is unique to political parties.

Burke's definition suggests political parties are linked to political principles, something which will be explored in Chapter 4. These principles are sometimes seen as being derived from underlying conflicts in society – conflicts in which the interests of distinct groups are seen to clash. In the classic left–right view of ideology, these groups are defined as 'classes', and, according to some, parties are the organisational expression of this class conflict. So, Berntson (1974, p. 16) defines a party as an organisation that represents a social class, or an alliance of social classes, in the struggle against other social classes for control over the actions of the state. However, as with having an ideology, the defence of the interests of particular groups in society is not unique to political parties. Trade unions and numerous other interest organisations would also be covered by that definition.

However, Berntson may still have part of the answer – the part related to fighting to gain control over the actions of the state. One often cited definition of a party comes from Downs who wrote that 'in the broadest sense, a political party is a coalition of men [sic] seeking to control the governing apparatus by legal means [...] By legal means, we mean duly constituted elections or legitimate influence' (Downs, 1957, p. 24). The problem with this definition is that Downs' view of 'legal means' is sufficiently broad to also include organisations that would not normally be regarded as parties, such as trade unions. True, trade unions do not seek to gain direct control over the levers of government in the sense that the chief purpose of trade union officials is not to become members of parliament or government ministers. However part of a trade union's purpose is to achieve at least indirect control over government action through 'legitimate influence'. Hence, including 'legitimate influence' still makes Downs' definition too broad. However, if we restrict 'legitimate means' to mean 'duly constituted elections' we may be close to a definition that captures what is unique to political parties: fielding candidates in elections.

Indeed, this 'electoral' view of a political party is found elsewhere. Epstein defines a party as 'any group, however loosely organized, seeking to elect governmental office holders under a given label' (1967, p. 9). However, not all parties have government ambition, at least in the short or medium term, something which will be explored in Chapter 9. Hence, we may want to replace 'governmental office holders' with 'members of legislative assemblies'. This is the definition which Bille settles on: 'a political party is a group of people who, under a common label, field candidates to popularly elected political assemblies and who typically are capable of having candidates elected' (1997, p. 17). It would probably make most sense to exclude the last part ('and who typically are capable of having candidates elected'). Even the most electorally unsuccessful of parties is still a party if it fields candidates to legislative assemblies, because this is what makes parties unique: fielding candidates to popularly elected legislative assemblies. Yes, parties do many other things than that, but they share all of those things with many other types of organisations. What sets parties apart from other political organisations is that they field candidates for popularly elected assemblies. The definition of a political party used here will therefore be a shortened version of what Bille came up with:

> A political party is a group of people who, under a common label, fields candidates to popularly elected assemblies.

This definition, derived from several prominent scholars, also adds to the reasons for focusing on democratic countries. If the central defining feature of a political party is that it fields candidates in elections, then there needs to be such elections in place for us to talk about a party in the sense defined above. Clearly, this definition only makes sense in a democratic country. This would suggest that for example the Communist Parties of Cuba, China and North Korea are not 'true' parties. There is no currently existing definition of a party that could include 'parties' such as those in control of Cuba, China and North Korea, but exclude organisations that are usually not seen as parties, such as trade unions or other interest organisations. It could perhaps be argued that if an organisation calls itself as a party, then we should see it as a party. However, there are organisations, such as the Indian National Congress and the *Union pour un Mouvement Populaire* (Union for a Popular Movement) in France which do not have party in the title, but are usually seen as parties.

Hence, for the purpose of this book, it seems to make most sense to restrict ourselves to the definition given above, and focus on democratic countries for the reasons discussed.

The three faces of party organisations

Now that we know how to identify a party and distinguish it from other political organisations it is necessary to consider what a party looks like as an organisation. How are they organised and what elements are they made up of internally?

As noted earlier, political parties are endlessly varied. Each party will have found its own response to its political circumstances, which in turn will be different for each country and for each party within that country. However, it is still possible to make some generalisations about the structure of political parties. Very generally it is possible to argue that a party is made up of three 'faces' (Katz and Mair, 1993).

The first is what is referred to as the party in public office. This element of the party consists of its publically elected officials (e.g., parliamentarians) and members of the government (i.e., ministers). Then there is the party on the ground. This is basically the extra-parliamentary membership organisation. This part could also be expanded to include regular, but non-member, supporters. Finally, there is the party in central office. This is the party's central co-ordinating bodies. Its leading officials are traditionally elected by the mass membership and it is staffed by fulltime professionals.

The concept of three faces has a number of implications for how we analyse political parties. First, it suggests that viewing a political party as a unitary actor, akin to an individual human being, is misleading. Talking about Party X doing something does not accurately reflect what is really going on. What it actually means is that someone within Party X has taken a decision about a particular course of action – a decision which may or may not be supported by other people in the party. So, if we see a headline along the lines of 'The Moderate Party ignored its members and proposed cuts to the defence budget' this will be a massive simplification of events. A party does not 'ignore its members' – the members are part and parcel of the party. In addition, 'the members' are unlikely to be a homogenous mass with identical views on any given issue. What would be more accurate would be something along the lines of: 'Moderate Party leader Birgitte Nyborg and her allies in the party's national executive decided to propose cuts to the defence budget against the wishes of her opponents on the national executive and their supporters among the local activists'. 'The party ignored its members' is clearly much simpler, but not very accurate. A party is an organisation made up of people with different levels of influence; with more or less divergent notions about what the party should be doing; and with different levels of commitment to the party.

In addition, the three faces of a party can and often do have different priorities and short- to medium-term goals (even if they agree on long-term goals – that is, the party's basic ideological foundations). It could be argued that because the party in public office owes its existence to the electorate, this face of a party is likely to focus on satisfying short-term voter demands. The party on the ground on the other hand does not have the perks that come with public office (a salary, prestige, an office and staff) and is, therefore, less concerned with electoral expedience. This face of the party is motivated by ideological conviction and will therefore be more radical than the party in public office. The extent to which this is the case is open to debate and will be explored further in see Chapter 7. However, it does illustrate that seeing a party as a single unitary actor with a single purpose can be problematic.

Finally, the idea that different elements in the party may have divergent and potentially even contradictory goals raises the question of who decide which goals to pursue. Which of the three faces is in control of the party? The most popular idea is that the balance of power between the three faces has changed over the years. The argument is that the party in central office and the party on the ground have become subservient to the party in public office, especially in the context of policy making. This did not happen quietly or without a great deal of, to some extent ongoing, resistance from the party in central office and in particular the party on the ground, but is a point of view which is broadly accepted. This change has been particularly profound in the traditional mass-membership party (see Chapter 3). In this kind of party, the party in central office was there to organise and also represent the party on the ground. However, over time the party in central office increasingly became the tool of the party in public office, used to manage and control the party on the ground. The result is that, not only has the party in public office largely taken control of the organisation, but the party as a whole is increasingly epitomised by the party in public office. What this means is that when commentators and a great many academics write that Party X has done something or other, what they are actually saying is that the party in public office, or even just the leader(ship) of the party in public office, has taken a decision on something. In short a party is a multifaceted organisation which will act with greater or lesser degrees of unity. Hence, if we are to truly understand party behaviour we must do so keeping in mind that parties are often internally divided to a greater or lesser extent.

The structure of parties

However, the idea of the three faces of political parties only gives us a very general view of how parties are structured internally. It tells use very little about how these elements operate in practice. Saying something general about how parties operate is very difficult. The practical day-to-day running of a party is where the diversity of political parties really comes into play. Parties have found their own answers to how to organise and these answers will be affected by the history of a party, the people in it and the national context a party finds itself in.

What we can say is that parties tend to be strongly affected by a country's electoral system. At the local level most party leaders will try to ensure that there is a local branch in every electoral district to organise and mobilise members and supporters, at the very least at election time. Hence, at a very basic level, the number of branches a party has will be partly affected by how many electoral districts a country is divided into. Parties will vary greatly in the extent to which party leaders encourage members and supporters to be active in the periods between elections. Some party leaders, especially in the United States, prefer local activity to be at a minimum when there is not an election on, so as avoid local interference with the work of the party in public office. This is why parties in the United States have been referred to as 'empty vessels' (Katz and Kolodny, 1994). Traditionally in the United States only the party in public office existed continuously between elections. The two other faces would to a large extent be built up as an election came closer, and then be allowed to fade away afterwards. European parties have usually put far more emphasis on the continuous existence of all three faces in-between elections.

However, regardless of whether the local elements of a party are temporary or permanent, they will be based around the electoral districts of a country. One key exception to this pattern was the old Communist Parties from before 1989. Many Communist Parties were organised around 'cells'. Cells were not necessarily based on geography, but rather on an occupational basis. The cell 'unites all party members who work at the same place. There are factory, workshop, shop, office and administrative cells' (Duverger, 1964, p. 26). This fits with the idea that, at least in principle, Communist parties were less oriented towards the electoral arena. Their main purpose was not so much to enter parliament and potentially government, and more the complete overthrow of the existing order, through uniting the proletariat, or working class, against their oppressors in the bourgeoisie. However, the reality of working in a democratic political system caused a number of Western European communist parties to orientate themselves increasingly toward the electoral structure of the country.

How parties are structured above the local level will vary enormously from party to party, even within a single country. At the local level all the parties in a country will have to conform to the structure of the electoral system of that country, and will therefore vary less between them (but will obviously vary from country to country as each country will have different electoral systems). So for example, the number and size of electoral districts or constituencies will be decided by the national government. If the parties of a country want to be represented in all local electoral districts (which is typically the case) the number of local branches will be decided for them. However, how a party then organises itself above the local level will be decided by each party individually.

Hence, the following should be seen as a very general summary of what the trends are, and there will be a great deal of divergence from these trends. The most comprehensive study of party organisation can be found in Katz and Mair's (1992) edited book *Party Organisations: A Data Handbook*. While that book is from the early 1990s, parties are somewhat conservative organisations. This means that they tend to change slowly, and the lessons in that book remain valid today.

There are a number of constituent bodies that can be found in most political parties. Typically there will be some form of national conference where local branches are represented. These are often major events in a party's calendar and will attract sometimes 100s or 1,000s of delegates from local branches, as well as party leaders and the party's members of legislative assemblies (such as members of parliament). The exact role of this conference varies, but at least formally speaking it is often referred to as the party's highest authority. What that means in practice is frequently left unclear, and the actual powers of the conference tend to be limited. Nevertheless, the party conference will have great significance. Many parties hold up such delegates' conferences as an example of their commitment to democracy, not only nationally in their country, but internally in their organisation as well. It also tends to be the only place where representatives from all three faces of a party will come together in a single physical space. On a day-to-day basis, the people belonging to each of a party's three faces, will be spread out across the country and will not regularly come across each other. The party conference therefore has an important unifying function – it is the embodiment of the party as a single unified entity, which is part of the reason why most parties have such events, even if their actual power is limited.

The frequency of the conference varies from party to party. Often it is annual, but in some parties it can be several years apart: for example:

- The British Labour Party has its conference every year.
- The Danish Social Democrat's 'Congress' is every four years, but they then have 'themed conferences' in between.
- Both the Republicans and the Democrats in the United States have 'conventions' every four years.
- The New Patriotic Party of Ghana has an 'Annual Delegates Conference'.
- The Bharatiya Janata Party (BJP) of India has a 'Plenary Session' at least once every three years.

To deal with matters in between the main party conference, parties tend to have some form of national committee or executive. The exact powers and membership will vary, but it is often the case that the national committee is seen as the highest authority after the party conference. Membership is often made up of representatives from the different parts of the party: that is, the parliamentary party, local and/or regional branches, local and regional government politicians and sometimes other affiliated organisations such as trade unions. In some parties there will be a national committee which meets every few months, as well as a smaller executive which meets on a more regular basis. Regardless of the exact nature of the national committee, its general role is to provide leadership on a more detailed 'day-to-day', or at least 'month-to-month', level than is possible for the party conference.

In addition to the purely geographical and hierarchical structure of a party there is the party in public office. Most parties will organise their publically elected legislators into party groups locally, regionally and nationally. These groups exist alongside the geographical structure of the party, but will often have a guaranteed level of representation at the party conference, as well as national, regional and local committees.

There is certainly a huge level of variety within these general trends. However, very broadly speaking, most parties will at least have the elements outlined. It makes sense to have local branches organised according to electoral districts, and any party will need some form of national, regional and local coordinating committees. These are simply organisational necessities. Strictly speaking one could do away with the party conference, but many parties find it useful to have a relatively frequent gathering of representatives from across the organisation. This can add democratic legitimacy to the party and provide a forum for networking and sharing of good practice between regional and local officials. Ultimately, if nothing else, it is an opportunity for the leading activists in the party to get together with the national party 'celebrities' such as notable parliamentarians and ministers. This may seem trivial, but this author's own experience at the annual conference of several parties suggests that the social side is a significant part of why delegates go to these events. In the final reckoning it can be a reward for all the hard work put into running local branches and election campaigns.

However, while it is true that above the local level parties tend to vary significantly in the way they organise themselves, there are still discernible patterns. These patterns have been linked to the ideology of a party.

According to Maurice Duverger the organisation of socialist parties tend to be more formalised than conservative parties. He argues that in socialist parties, the relationships between the different elements of a party, their rights and responsibilities, are usually much more detailed and formalised, or 'articulated', than in conservative parties. Hence, a socialist party is much more likely than a conservative party to have a detailed rulebook which is adhered to relatively strictly. This has been exemplified in this author's own experience. No activist in the British Labour Party would be unfamiliar with the party rulebook. They might not know it in intimate detail, although many do, but they would certainly know of its existence and importance. By contrast, this author has come across members of the British Conservative Party, including a parliamentary candidate, who did not know the party had a rulebook. This may at first not seem to matter much: why should one care about how detailed a party's rulebook is?

Duverger argues that this is important. One key reason why it is important is that parties that are relatively informal, or weakly articulated, are inherently undemocratic. If, say, the power of the leader is left vague and informal it is difficult to accuse the leader of overstepping his or her authority. Similarly, if the rights of grassroots members are unspecified how can they demand their due influence, when that due is unclear? On the other hand, a very formalised party with a high degree of organisational articulation is not inherently democratic. A party can be articulated in a democratic or an undemocratic direction. However, because the rules are very detailed and everybody's rights and responsibilities (or the lack thereof) are clear and unambiguous it is easy to tell whether a party is democratic or not. Many communist parties, especially those with strong links to the Communist Party of the Soviet Union, tended to be very top led through a system known as 'democratic centralism'. Officially, democratic centralism meant that there would be open debate about a topic before a vote was taken. Once a decision had been made, all members were expected to stick to that decision religiously with no dissent expressed. In effect it often meant that the leadership was in control of the organisation. The leadership issues instructions and the members followed. The party's hierarchical nature was very clear from the rulebook, so everybody knew their place.

Compare this to the British Conservative Party which only acquired a formal rulebook after William Hague became leader in 1997, and even then it seems to have been largely ignored. The Conservative Party has traditionally been very top led. The members had only a very marginal influence on the work of the parliamentary party, and until the election of Ian Duncan Smith in 2001, had no influence on the selection of the party leader. Indeed, for much of the party's history the leader was not so much selected as 'emerged' out of informal deals and compromises between senior party figures. So, the Conservative Party is not very democratic, but the lack of internal democracy is achieved in a different, and informal, way compared to the highly articulated communist parties of old.

In short, the more detailed the rulebook the easier it is to tell who is in control. The vaguer it is, the more the leadership is able to assert their control through informal means and the inherent power that comes with having access to the resources associated with high office. In informal organisations, members have few tools with which to temper that power. As a general trend, left wing parties have detailed rulebooks, and right wing parties do not.

The role of parties in democratic states

Now that we know more about what parties are and what they look like, it is worth considering what they do. As was argued at the beginning of this chapter, parties are extremely important in the running of democratic states. The reason for this importance is the breadth and depth of the roles that parties fulfil.

Perhaps the most important role of political parties is that they create 'linkage' between governments and voters.

> The political party is the one agency that can claim to have as its very raison d'être the creation of an entire linkage chain, a chain of connections that runs from the voters through the candidates and the electoral process to the officials of government. (Lawson, 1988, p. 16)

Linkage is a very broad term, but Lawson is probably the writer who is most well known for having dealt with this subject in the context of political parties. Lawson argues that there are several kinds of linkage a party can engage in.

- *Participatory linkage*: is focused on giving citizens a way of participating actively in the governing of the country beyond merely voting in elections. This kind of linkage will be notable for a strong party on the ground and a high level of intra-party democracy.
- *Electoral linkage*: here the leadership keeps a tight control over the elected representatives. Elected representatives are expected to adhere to the views of the party's supporters. However, those views are independently, and more or less correctly, determined by party leaders. The role of party members is not to participate in policy making, but only to campaign at election time. Hence, the only real opportunity for supporters to express their views and participate is at election time. This has also been referred to as 'responsive' linkage (Rommele, Farrell and Ignazi, 2005, p. vii).
- *Clientelistic linkage*: this is where the focus is on 'buying' votes in exchange for favours. That is, in return for voting for a party a constituency can expect to have certain state investments made in local infrastructure.
- *Directive linkage*: in this case the party is used as a means through which those in power can control the behaviour of citizens. This can be through education (indoctrination), coercion or both.

A significant part of the debate in the context of linkage is about the extent to which parties provide each of these kinds of linkage and also which kind they *should* provide. That is, the debate is both descriptive and prescriptive. The evidence on the descriptive side is very varied and often provides evidence of all four types of linkage at various times and places. The prescriptive side, that is, what kind of linkage parties should provide often argues that parties *ought* to provide forms of linkage that foster more active and inclusive forms of democracy.

Lawson argues that depending on what kinds of linkage a party provides it may be working either for or against the development of a healthy democracy. Participatory linkage is always good for democracy. Electoral/responsive linkage may or may not contribute to democracy. It very much depends on how accurate the responsiveness is. Clientelistic linkage certainly contribute towards the maintenance of power for a party, but depending on how that power is used, may work for or against democracy. Directive linkage using education will again help a party maintain power, but that can be good or bad for democracy depending on its use. Coercion is always bad for democracy.

However, even though the idea of linkage has attracted a great deal of attention the roles that parties fulfil go beyond that. Pedersen (1989, p. 268) summarises the roles of parties as follows:

- Mobilisation and socialisation: parties mobilise citizens, not just to vote, but also to become active in politics. They identify and recruit members and show those members what being active in politics is about. That is, they socialise them into the role of political activists, which may lead to positions of responsibility in the organisation.
- Selection and training of political leaders. Through mobilising citizens and recruiting them into the party structure they also work to identify potential candidates for high office. These people will often receive training and support, both as candidates and as elected legislators. By doing so parties also act as gatekeepers to high office. It is very rare for anyone to make it very far in politics without the support of a party. Hence, parties control who gets the chance to obtain positions of power in the political structure of a country.
- Interest articulation: all parties, to greater or lesser extent, work to represent the interests of various groups in society.
- Political programme formulation: one of the key purposes of parties is to create, present, and if they get the chance, carry out a programme of political action. In doing so they prioritise between competing demands in society, and to some extent present a vision for the good society. Political programmes will often contain information about what kind of society the party would like to see built, in addition to the more day-to-day concern of allocating scarce resources.

The crisis of parties

It should be clear by now that political parties are highly complex organisations that fulfil a wide range of crucial tasks in democratic societies. However, despite how important they are, parties have never been very popular. The modern manifestation of this unpopularity is the notion that political parties are in crisis.

Parties have a long history, with the deepest roots to be found in Western Europe and the United States. For as long as parties have existed they have been viewed by many with deep suspicion, often tipping over into outright hostility. The problem is neatly encapsulated by the title of Scarrow's (2006) overview of the rise of political parties: 'the unwanted emergence of party based politics'. As early as 1835 de Tocqueville wrote that 'parties are an evil inherent in free governments' (see White, 2006, p. 7). The antipathy towards political parties has deep roots in political philosophy. One prime example of this is Rousseau's work on the 'general will'. According to Rousseau the 'general will' is what should be the guide for collective action. The general will can be reached when every individual in a society, without any kind of outside interference, considers what the right way forward is. The general will must be the collective opinion of all individuals in society, acting as individuals: 'If, when the people, being furnished with adequate information, held its deliberations, the citizens had no communication one with another, the grand total of the small differences would always give the general will, and the decision will always be good' (Rousseau, 1966, p. 23). However, it is important that every individual acts independently, and without reference to any sub-group within society. Any kind of faction will undermine the general will:

> when factions arise [...] the differences become less numerous and give a less general result [...] It is therefore essential, if the general will is to be able to express itself, that there be should be no partial society within the State, and that each citizen should think only his own thoughts. (Rousseau, 1966, p. 23)

While not often cited, the idea that parties undermine the collective will and exacerbate divisions is widely held. Hence, from the very beginning of their existence, parties were viewed as something negative, if also unavoidable.

This negative view of political parties is continued in the first comprehensive study of political parties, Ostrogorski's *Democracy and the Organization of Political Parties*, first published in English in 1902. Ostrogorski does not object to groupings of parliamentarians – that is,

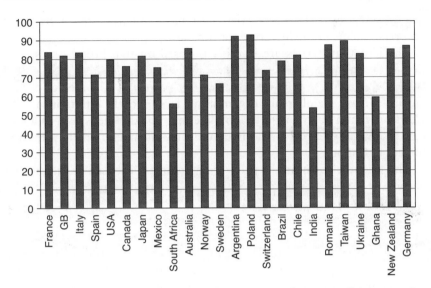

Figure 1.1 *Confidence in political parties: Not very much/None at all (percentage)*

Source: World Value survey 2005–8.

the party in public office. What he does object to is the existence of extra-parliamentary organisations – that is, the party on the ground. Their excessive control over members of parliament was alleged to undermine the smooth running of a parliamentary democracy.

This antipathy towards political parties continues today. As we can see from Figure 1.1 there is a widespread lack of confidence in political parties in all the countries for which data is presented here. There are clearly some variations from country to country; however, nowhere is lack of confidence lower than 50 per cent. In some countries the lack of confidence is almost total.

In addition to this outright hostility to political parties from both scholars and the population of the democratic world at large, doubts about the role of parties in modern politics is reflected in a growing field of study: the crisis of political parties. The idea that political parties are in crisis is not new, but it is widespread. Daalder (1992, p. 269) writes that 'we all talk about the crisis of party'. Mair (2003, p. 6) wrote: 'That political parties are in crisis, and potentially on the verge of serious decline, is now more or less accepted wisdom among commentators throughout the established democracies'. This was a theme he expanded on three years later (Mair, 2006, p. 50), but with even more glum conclusions than in the 2003 piece: 'parties may be able to fill public office, but having abandoned their representative role, they may no longer be able to justify doing so'. The party crisis idea has evidently been a regularly occurring theme in the literature for decades.

The idea that parties are in crisis is based on two broad issues. The first is that parties across the democratic world are said to have seen a significant decline in their membership organisations. The idea of parties having a mass membership organisation is so closely intertwined with views of what a party ought to look like that this decline is seen as a sign that parties are in crisis. The issue of party members will be explored further in Chapter 5.

The second element in the party crisis argument is based on claims that parties are no longer fulfilling the roles they should be fulfilling in democratic societies. This is the essence of Mair's argument. Leaders of political parties may still have a key role in governing countries in the democratic world. However, increasingly party leaders are withdrawing into the world of government institutions and away from civil society. Party leaders govern, but they no longer represent (Mair, 2006). This echoes Lawson's work on linkage. After having worked on the idea that a key function of parties it to provide linkage between rulers and the ruled she went on to argue that they are increasingly failing to do so effectively. They are losing members, their top leaders are becoming increasingly isolated from the rest of society and are failing to reflect and act on the political demands of the voters.

However, while the idea of a party crisis and party failure may be long standing and widespread, it is argued that a lot of the literature on this topic is shot through with underlying normative assumptions (Daalder, 1992). When authors talk of parties being in crisis they do so on the basis of more or less subjective assumptions about what parties ought to be doing. Early 'party crisis' ideas questioned the very legitimacy of parties (as outlined above) based on ideas about how democracy ought to function. Later there were questions over certain kinds of party – that is, a concern over the rise of fascist and communist parties. The last of the 'parties in crisis' elements is the argument that democracy has moved beyond the need for parties, that parties are now redundant.

Daalder's argument suggests that when people talk about parties being in crisis, what they really mean is that parties are no longer living up to some pre-set idea of what a democratic state should look like. Hence, if we are to fully understand the claims that parties are in crisis we would need to evaluate these underlying normative assumptions. In essence, whether one agrees with the party crisis idea is less an objective evaluation, but a normative one based on what one thinks parties ought to be doing. We will return to this theme in the conclusion to this book.

Outline of the book

The rest of the book will be divided into 10 chapters. Chapter 2 will deal with party systems. Perhaps the most important factor parties have to cope with in their political activities is other parties. The party system a party operates in is a key environmental factor in our understanding of party life. Hence, we will look first at party systems.

Chapter 3 will look at how parties have developed and, according to some, moved through different stages from one party type to another. This is a lively and expanding area of party politics, and new suggestions for party types is a regular feature of the literature.

Chapter 4 will look at the issue of ideology. One of the key ideas of what parties are is that they are vessels for an ideology. Parties are there to promote and defend a particular view of society, a view derived from underlying and long-standing divisions in society. Most of the literature on ideology focuses on Europe, and we will consider the extent to which 'traditional' views of ideology also hold outside Europe.

The focus of Chapter 5 is party members. A number of questions will be asked and answers sought, including why party leaders would want to encourage the building or maintenance of a mass membership organisation; and why anyone would want to join a party. The chapter will also look at the issue of what is happening to party membership numbers.

Chapter 6 will look at how candidates for public office are selected. One issue the chapter will pay particular attention to is whether the gender imbalance in most parliaments in the democratic world can be explained by parties not selecting enough women candidates. Selection is an important issue in party life since virtually no one gets into a legislative assembly without party endorsement. Parties therefore act as key gatekeepers to power.

In Chapter 7 the book will look at policy making. The chapter will cover issues such as: who are involved in policy making; who should, normatively, be involved; and who wants to be involved.

Following that, Chapter 8 will examine the work that parties do in election campaigning. The chapter will examine some of the arguments about the ways in which parties' campaigning activities have changed and how those changes have affected party organisations.

The focus of Chapter 9 is the struggle of parties to get into government. The chapter will look at whether all parties desire government office and what might explain the decision either way. The chapter will also look at the challenges a party faces once the decision to try to enter government has been made.

Chapter 10 will look at the internationalisation of party politics. This is a topic that has a long history, but is also an area which has delivered

less than some people would have liked. The chapter will look at the
party Internationals, at Europarties and at the internationalisations of
campaign consultancy.

Finally, Chapter 11 will consider the future of party politics and
whether parties are in crisis.

Chapter 2

Party Systems

One of the main concerns of political parties in their day-to-day activities in democratic countries is other political parties. The vast majority of a party's efforts are devoted to competing with other parties for power and influence. However, depending on the details of the political system of a country other political parties can also be potential, usually short term, partners against common opponents. In short, one of the key issues we need to understand when looking at political parties is what patterns exist in the interaction between them. The politics of a country is clearly going to be very different if there are only two parties competing, compared to there being for example a dozen roughly equal parties struggling for power. One of the main tools used to analyse how parties interact is the concept of party systems.

When we talk about the party systems we can mean one of two things. One is simply the fact that any country where parties are a key part of the political system can be said to have a party system. In short, saying a country has a party system could simply mean that parties exist. However, in a more systematic sense the study of party systems is the effort to come up with concepts that will help to structure what is in practice a very complex reality. Each and every democratic country can be said to have a party system that is unique to it. After all, there are a near infinite number of permutations when we combine the possible number of parties (from one to 100s) and their relative size. Hence, 'party system' also refers to specific categories of party systems which can be used to analyse how party politics works and changes across different countries. What these categories are will be explored later in the chapter.

The importance of understanding party systems

The idea of party systems is a key element in understanding a country's politics. One of the central elements in a party's environment, and one of the main factors determining its behaviour, is other parties in the political system – how many there are, how strong they are and what (or whom) they represent. Understanding party systems is, therefore, an important part of understanding political parties. The number and strength of competitors will affect the behaviour of a party considerably. If there are only two parties in a system there is only one 'stream of interaction' to consider. This is the case in the United States where the only two noteworthy competitors are the Republicans and the Democrats (see Figure 2.1). In a slightly simplified view of the UK party system there are three streams of interaction. If we look at the case of Denmark, which after the 2011 election had eight parties in parliament, the tactical situation faced by each party is far more complicated. Each party has to consider seven rivals when deciding on what action to take. In short, the more parties there are the more complicated is the political battlefield a party has to cope with.

The number of parties present in a parliament will also have a significant impact on government formation. In a two-party system one party will by definition get a majority of the seats. However, in a party system with more than two parties this is no-longer automatically the case. The larger the number of parties in a parliament, the bigger the chance that no party will manage to achieve an overall majority of the seats. This means that a coalition government may be necessary. This will be explored further in Chapter 9.

In addition, the extent to which seats are spread out between several parties will have an impact on how many parties will have to be involved in a coalition. Compare the situation in the United Kingdom and Denmark (Figure 2.2). In Denmark after the 2011 election no single party came anywhere near an overall majority. The two biggest parties, the Liberals and the Social Democrats, had no interest in forming a government together. Indeed, no party from either the left-of-centre or the right-of-centre 'blocks' would join in a government with parties from the other side. Collectively the parties in the left-of-centre block had a majority. However, the Red Green Alliance is regarded as being too far to the left to be a realistic government partner. The result therefore was a minority coalition of the Socialists, the Social Democrats and the Social Liberals – with the Red Green Alliance providing support from outside the government. By contrast the 2010 election in the United Kingdom was far simpler. While a very unusual result for the United Kingdom in that no party achieved an overall majority, the Conservative Party was close and only needed the support of the Liberal Democrats to be able to form a majority coalition.

This indicates another reason why party systems are important: understanding a party system will help us understand how fragmented power is in a country. In a two-party system power will be far more concentrated (in whichever party has a majority) than in a multi-party system. This will have a major impact on the nature of politics in a given country. In a country where politics is more or less dominated by two parties (such as the United States and more often than not the United

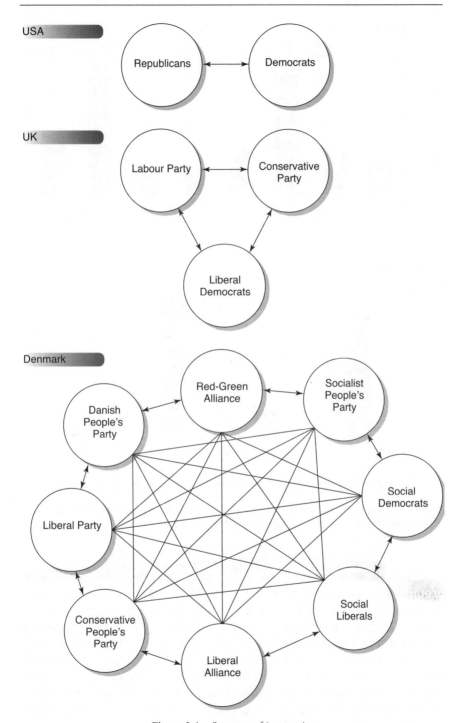

USA

UK

Denmark

Figure 2.1 *Streams of interaction*

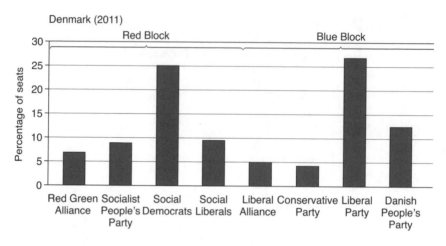

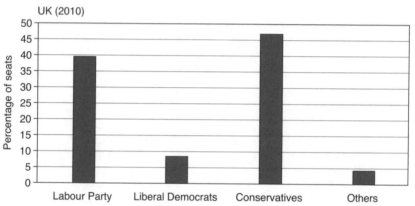

Figure 2.2   *Election results in Denmark (2011) and the UK (2010)*

Sources: Statistics Denmark (2011) www.dst.dk/da/Statistik/emner/valg/folketingsvalg.aspx BBC (2010) http://news.bbc.co.uk/1/shared/election2010/results/.

Kingdom) politics will be marked by confrontation and a lack of compromise. If a single governing party has an overall majority there is no need to compromise with any other party in the system. By contrast, in a situation where many parties have a reasonably chance of either entering government or influencing the legislative programme of a minority government, as is the case on most of the countries on the European continent, compromise and cooperation will, by necessity, be far more common. The minority government created in Denmark after 2011 clearly needs to be able to compromise in a way that a single-party majority government would not.

Finally, and as an extension of what was said above, in comparative politics the concept of party systems helps us simplify the complexities of party politics. Comparing and understanding party politics in several countries is difficult without some kind of ordering principle. Using the idea of party systems will immediately tell us something about the differences in the politics of whatever countries we are interested in. The mere fact that we can assign countries to different party system categories will help give us a starting point for understanding what the similarities and differences between these political systems are.

Early approaches to party systems

The time has now come to look at some of the most important approaches to classifying party systems.

Duverger was the first scholar to seriously attempt to classify party systems. His categorisation schema was simple and also somewhat crude. Duverger limited himself to three categories: 'the single-party, the Anglo-Saxon two-party, and the multi-party system' (Duverger, 1964, p. 203). While this is certainly a start it is also reasonably obvious that such a simple schema is inadequate for a number of reasons. The single-party system is perhaps defensible in that Duverger sees this kind of system as a non-competitive system. In other words, some form of authoritarian regime where all other parties are simply banned. It is, therefore, fairly easy to identify. The idea of a two-party system seems fairly simple on the surface. However, the exact dividing line between a two-party system and a multi-party system is not entirely clear. So, while the United States is very clearly a two-party system, the United Kingdom has often been regarded as being a two-party system, but there are several significant players in the system beyond the main two parties, a factor that became especially evident after the 2010 election when the third largest party, the Liberal Democrats, joined the Conservative Party in government. Indeed, Duverger himself acknowledged this problem.

However, perhaps the biggest problem with Duverger's schema is how he deals with the multiparty system. Duverger virtually abandons any attempt to say much about 'more-than-two' party systems. All he has to say is that they are somewhat complicated to deal with: 'The typology of the multi-party system is difficult to establish: innumerable varieties can be imagined ranging from three parties to infinity, and within each variety innumerable patterns and shades of difference are possible' (Duverger, 1964, p. 229). He is left with merely describing a number of specific examples. It therefore seems that while Duverger's approach to party systems has been called 'pioneering' (Blau, 2008, p. 169) this is mainly because he was the first to deal with the issue of party systems in a reasonably systematic way. Nevertheless, while Duverger's schema of party systems may have been somewhat underdeveloped there are still two issues in his work on this that are worth following up on: his view of the duality of politics and the impact of electoral systems on party systems.

According to Duverger, politics is usually about a duality of choices – or put differently, about a choice between two options. There may not always be a 'duality of parties', but there is always a 'duality of tendencies' (Duverger, 1964, p. 215). This means that for Duverger 'the centre does not exist in politics. The term "centre" is applied to the geometrical spot where the moderates of opposing tendencies meet: the moderates of the Right and the moderates of the Left' (Duverger, 1964, p. 215). Based on that Duverger argues that two-party systems are superior to multi-party systems since the two-party system 'seems to correspond to the nature of things' (Duverger, 1964, p. 215). However, if two-party'ism is natural and corresponds to the nature of politics, that does somewhat leave the questions of why multi-party systems exist and indeed why they are so prolific. Duverger (1964, pp. 230–3) suggests a number of reasons, but the most significant factor he proposed in the creation of multi-party systems is the nature of the electoral system. This issue will be considered later in this chapter.

Others have tried to overcome the inadequacies of Duverger's categorisation. Most notably Jean Blondel (1968) who investigates the voting pattern in 19 democratic countries and identifies six types of party systems.

1   The two-party system such as that found in the United States.
2   A two-and-a-half party system with two major parties on the left and the right of centre, and a smaller centre party.
3   A two-and-a-half party system where the smaller party is on the left.
4   A multi-party system where no single party gets more than about 25 per cent of the vote.
5   A multi-party system where a dominant left-wing party is faced by a divided right-wing.
6   A multi-party system where a dominant right-wing party is faced by a divided left-wing.

Blondel's approach is clearly much more fine grained that Duverger's. His idea of a two-and-a-half party system appears useful in dealing with the problem of countries where there are two major parties, so not a multi-party system, but where there is also a clear third 'presence'. The British Liberal Democrats is a good example of this 'half' party.

However, the problem with Blondel's is that it is based very specifically on the voting patterns of 19 countries during the period 1945–66. This is therefore not necessarily a general categorisation which can be easily applied outside of the specific context of those countries at that time.

Party system typologies

Both Duverger and Blondel are important models to mention because they provided the groundwork for what has become the most widely accepted schema for categorising party systems – that devised by Sartori. One of Sartori's key contributions was creating a system for counting 'relevant' parties.

The issue of counting may seem obvious. After all, Duverger and Blondel had already talked about one, two and multi-party systems which suggests some form of counting being used. However, according to Sartori: 'we are even incapable of deciding when one is one and when two is two' (2005, p. 106). Counting all parties that exist in a country does not make sense. Several hundred parties are registered with the UK Electoral Commission, but only three of these have been of national significance, with about half-a-dozen having some regional importance. Similarly, there are more than two parties in the United States, but only really two that 'count'. The problem then is to determine which parties 'count'.

Looking at electoral strength (which was Blondel's approach) and deciding some cut-off point is not only arbitrary, but also inadequate since electoral strength alone does not always tell us very much about the 'relevance' of the party. The British Liberal Democrats have been achieving electoral support of between 15 and 20 per cent, and the Danish Social Liberals half that. However, the Danish Social Liberals have experienced government participation, and legislative influence when out of government, beyond anything achieved by the Liberal Democrats after 1945 and before 2010. The German Free Democratic Party has had much the same experience as the Danish Social Liberals: modest electoral support, but significant government power. Between 1946 and 1992 The Italian Communist Party obtained between 22 and 34 per cent of the vote in general elections, but never achieved government power. Clearly some other criterion than electoral support is needed to understand which parties are worthwhile looking at. Sartori's solution is a twofold criterion for relevance: to be relevant, a party must have either 'coalition potential' or 'blackmail potential'.

Coalition potential is related to a party's ability to influence who is in government. A party should generally be seen as irrelevant if it remains superfluous in that it is not needed to determine any feasible government or coalition majority. On the other hand, a party, regardless of how small, must be counted if it is in a position to participate in a coalition or is the kingmaker between two competing options.

Blackmail potential is related to the fact that there are some parties which, while big enough to secure a majority for one possible government, are never asked to participate. Examples would include the Italian Communist Party which for years achieved significant electoral success, but was nevertheless excluded by the other parties. Such a party may still count as relevant if 'its existence, or appearance, affects the tactics of party competition and particularly when it alters the direction of the competition [...] of the government oriented parties' (Sartori, 2005, p. 108). In short, Party A must be seen as relevant if parties B and C, which normally compete with each other, change their behaviour to exclude Party A from power. An example of this would be the 2002 presidential elections in France. In France the president is elected over two rounds. In the first round the full list of candidates are presented to the voters. The two top candidates in the first round go through to the second round. In the second round the candidate who gets the most votes will win. In 2002 the Front National leader Le Pen managed to get into second place ahead of the Socialist Party candidate in the first round. In the second round the voters then had a choice between a far right candidate and a centre-right candidate. This meant that the normal competition between the main leftwing block and the main rightwing block was suspended in order to ensure that Le Pen was comprehensively beaten in the second round. The Front National had no members of the parliament, and thus very little real influence, but their presence changed the normal rivalry between the centre-left and the centre-right.

It should be pointed out here that Sartori insists that these two criteria for relevance or irrelevance are 'postdictive' rather than predictive (Sartori, 2005, p. 108). That is, a party is only regarded as relevant if it currently has or has recently had either coalition or blackmail potential. A party which is in a position where it may in the future have either kind of potential is not counted.

Based purely on the number of relevant parties there are seven classes of party systems (Sartori, 2005, p. 110).

1   One party
2   Hegemonic party
3   Predominant party
4   Two-party
5   Limited pluralism
6   Extreme pluralism
7   Atomised

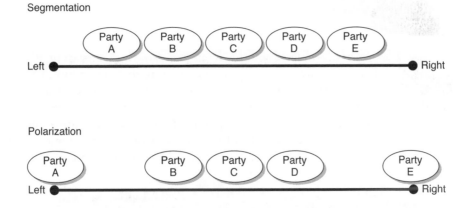

Figure 2.3 *Segmentation and polarisation*

However, focusing purely on the number of parties in a system is not enough in the case of limited and extreme pluralism. Sartori defines the border between the two as being five to six parties. This is, he admits, rather arbitrary and not necessarily very useful. What we need in addition to numbers is to include the issue of ideology. Sartori argues that ideological distance is important, in particular whether the party system is segmented or polarised (see Figure 2.3). A segmented party system is one where ideologically the parties sit next to one another like pearls on a string. Most modern democratic countries would be regarded as ideologically segmented. In contrast a polarised system is one where the parties cluster around mutually exclusive and hostile ideological positions. One key example of a polarised party system is the dying years of the German Weimar Republic. Here there were a number of moderated centrist parties, flanked on either side by Communists and National Socialists.

Based on the numerical criterion *and* the issue of ideology Sartori modifies limited and extreme pluralism. If a multi-party system is dominated by ideological segmentation it is termed moderate pluralism. If on other hand it is dominated by ideological polarisation it is termed polarised pluralism. In the final typology limited and extreme pluralism is replaced by moderate and polarised pluralism. The party systems in Sartori's scheme are then as follows:

- One party
- Hegemonic party
- Predominant party
- Two-party
- Moderate pluralism

- Polarised pluralism
- Atomised

A 'one party system' is characterised by all power being concentrated in one party. There is only one party as no other parties are allowed to exist. This matches Duverger's view of one-party systems as being identical with authoritarian regimes. Clear current examples are the Communist regimes in the People's Republic of China, North Korea and Cuba. Historical examples include all the former Communist regimes in Eastern Europe as well as Nazi Germany 1933–45 and Fascist Italy 1922–43.

The 'hegemonic party system' is similar to the one party system in that one party dominates and that this dominance is maintained through non-democratic means. However, unlike 'pure' one-partyism other parties are not banned outright. At the same time they are only allowed to exist as long as the power of the hegemonic party is not overly challenged. Examples include Zimbabwe under ZANU PF. Other parties exist, most notably the Movement for Democratic Change, but when they look like they may threaten the dominance of the ZANU PF they come under intense and often violent pressure. Arguable this pressure has lessened somewhat since the aftermath of the 2008 elections, but Zimbabwe probably still falls into this category. Another example is Singapore. The People's Action Party (PAP) has been very firmly in control of Singaporean politics since independence and although other parties are not banned, they face strong PAP pressure in the form of libel suits and censorship. The pressure the other parties face is not in the same category as that experienced in Zimbabwe, but nor is the political system sufficiently free to fall into the more democratic 'predominant' category (see next paragraph).

In a 'predominant party system' one party consistently wins an overall majority of the vote. Elections are generally free and fair, but for whatever reasons, one party dominates the electoral arena. From achieving independence in 1947 until the late 1960s the Indian political system fell squarely into this category. The Indian National Congress so dominated Indian politics that it became known as the Congress System. Since the 1960s the Congress System has steadily disappeared, to be replaced by a volatile multiparty system. For most of the post-war era until the early 1990s Japan also fell into this category with the Liberal Democratic Party dominating the political scene. Several African countries, having gone through democratisation in the early 1990s and avoided single or hegemonic party rule, have also experienced predominance by one party. One prime example of this is Botswana, one of Africa's most successful countries both economically and politically. It is also the only country to have held open, free and fair elections continuously since independence in 1966. However, despite the open and free elections the Botswana Democratic Party (BDP) has held power since independence. Finally, it could be argued that some parts of the United States have at various times fallen into this category. As an example can be mentioned the City of Baltimore which has had Democratic mayors uninterrupted since 1967 and the City Council is also dominated by the Democratic Party. Typically all 14 council members and the council president are Democrats.

According to Sartori the 'two-party system' poses 'no problem in as much as their power configuration is straightforward: Two parties compete for an absolute majority that is within reach of either' (Sartori, 2005, p. 112). The United States is a clear example of this system. The Democrats and the Republicans dominate the political system at all levels and regularly exchange power at the national level in both the legislative and executive arenas. Other parties do exist, but their impact is close to non-existent. The United Kingdom is also commonly placed in this category. Government power has since 1945 been exchanged between the Labour Party and the Conservative Party, with no other party having come close to challenging this dual domination until 2010. However, if we go beyond the national governmental level, this picture becomes significantly murkier. However, as far as government power goes, the United Kingdom was very much a two-party system from 1945 until 2010.

Both pluralism categories share the characteristics that no single party is able to achieve an absolute majority. Where they differ is in their ideological makeup. Moderate pluralism is marked by ideological segmentation with each party filling a particular ideological space, but without any parties that reject the legitimacy of the entire political system. All parties are therefore pro-systemic and work to gain influence within the system rather than change it completely. Several countries can be seen to fall into this category including all the Scandinavian countries, Germany, Spain, Israel and Ghana (one of the few relatively successful multi-party democracies in Africa). It is true that large parties dominate in for example Germany, France and Sweden, but their dominance is not usually sufficiently great that they can marshal an overall majority on their own.

The 'polarised pluralism' party system represents what one might call the down-side of multi-party systems. Eight key features characterise polarised pluralism:

1 The existence of relevant anti-system parties, that is, parties that dispute the legitimacy of the existing system of government, not just the present government, and seek to change the whole structure rather than merely take control of it.

2   Bi-lateral opposites, meaning the presence of extremist parties which oppose the existing political system and each other with uncompromising passion.
3   A triangular interaction between anti-systemic opposites at two corners and pro-systemic parties at the third corner.
4   A polarisation of ideological beliefs, which in turn leads to:
5   Centrifugal competition pulling away from the centre.
6   An increased focus on ideological grandstanding and emphasis on 'true believers' over pragmatists.
7   Irresponsible opposition, exemplified by the fact that anti-systemic parties do not have to present an alternative government programme but merely *oppose* any and all initiatives from the pro-systemic parties.
8   The politics of outbidding. Parties that have no intention of presenting a government programme that is realisable within current government structures can afford to 'over-promise' in their programmes. This in turn leads other parties to attempt to match the unrealistic promises of the anti-systemic parties.

Not all these features need be present to make a system polarised, but the more that are present the more polarised a system is. A quintessential example of polarised pluralism is Weimar Germany (1919–33). It had most of the characteristics of a polarised system, particularly the presence of strong anti-systemic parties – Communists and Nazis – which created a centrifugal pull away from the centre. The Nazis and Communists attacked both each other and the pro-Weimar parties in a triangular competition and were not concerned with obtaining control of the system, but with replacing it completely, something the Nazis were eventually successful in doing. Another example is France during the Fourth Republic (1946–58). Again there were anti-systemic parties in the form of the Communists and the Gaullists. Again one side was successful in overturning the entire government structure when the Gaullists ushered in the Fifth Republic.

It is important to note that extreme pluralism (many parties) does not necessarily mean polarised pluralism (intense ideological confrontation). The number of parties is not the distinguishing feature. For example, Denmark, Israel, the Netherlands and Switzerland all have enough parties to have 'extreme pluralism', but are not ideologically polarised and therefore remain in the 'moderate pluralism' category (Sartori, 2005, pp. 130–7). This is an important distinction to make. The number of parties can change quite quickly, certainly from one election to another. Hence, relying on the number of parties would mean that a country could shift from one category to another relatively quickly, making our analysis of the party politics of that country more complicated. By contrast, it usually takes a fair bit of time for a country to change between polarised and moderate ideological competition. Hence, using ideology in addition to numbers will create a system of categorising the party systems of countries that will remain relatively stable over time.

The final category, the 'atomised party system', is a situation where there are so many parties that counting becomes unimportant. Beyond a certain threshold the number of parties ceases to matter. Sartori describes it thus: 'The atomised party system can be defined in the same way that atomistic competition in economics, that is, as a situation where no one firm has any noticeable effect on any other firm' (Sartori, 2005, p. 111). Sartori calls this a 'residual' category, which seems to suggest that it is not a type which one will see very often in reality, but which nevertheless needs to be included in the model to complete it. One possible example of Atomised Pluralism may be India in the last few decades, that is after the decline of INC and the rise and decline of the BJP. The INC and the BJP to a certain extent dominate the political landscape. However, the most noticeable element on the Indian party system since 1989 is the explosion of small, often short-lived but constantly appearing, parties based on very local concerns. As many of these are very local affairs they often hardly notice similar localised parties in different parts of the system, which seems to fit with an atomised system.

The main innovations in this typology compared with Duverger, apart from the issue of counting and the inclusion of ideology, is that both the single-party category and the multiparty category have been split up. Compared with Duverger's typology this more detailed examination of multi-party systems is particularly valuable. Where Duverger more or less gave up saying anything sensible about multi-party systems, Sartori's typology allows for a more sophisticated approach to analysing party systems with more than two parties.

The effective number of parties

Sartori's approach is without a doubt the most widely cited way to categorise party systems. It has admittedly been subjected to a fair few criticisms, not least the fact that it can be difficult to actually judge which parties have blackmail potential.

However, another, perhaps more serious problem, is that in Sartori's scheme a party is either relevant (counts as 1) or irrelevant (counts as 0) – there is no middle ground (Blau, 2008; Lijphart, 1999). This is perhaps too black and white for the shades of grey world that is politics. Some parties will inevitable be more relevant than others. It may therefore be worthwhile to consider other ways of understanding party systems.

The most popular alternative to Sartori is to use 'the effective number of parties'. In Gallagher and Mitchell's (2008, p. 598) words 'this measure was devised [...] as an attempt to summarise the degree of fragmentation of a party system.' In other words the 'effective number of parties' is not a way of calculating exactly how many parties there are, but a way of understanding the extent to which votes and seats are concentrated in a few parties or spread out among a larger number. The effective number of parties is typically calculated for seats and votes. The details of how the effective number of parties is calculated can be found Gallagher and Marsh (2008, p. 598) and can briefly be described as follows:

- Calculate each party's proportion of the vote or seats depending on which one you are interested in.
- Square each of these values.
- Add all of these values together to get a sum of the squares.
- Divide 1 by the sum of the squares.

The background of this process can be found in Laakso and Taagepera (1979), but in essence, the higher the number is the more fragmented a party system is, either in terms of how votes are distributed or how seats are distributed. Finding the value of the effective number of parties can tell us a number of things about a country.

Figure 2.4 shows the effective number of electoral parties (ENEP – that is, based on how people have voted) and the effective number of parliamentary parties (ENPP – that is, based on how seats have been distributed) in the United Kingdom and New Zealand. In the United Kingdom we can see the effect of using an electoral system that is not designed to be proportional. The voting pattern has clearly become far more fragmented since the 1940s as can be seen in the steady increase in ENEP. However, because of the electoral system this has not been reflected in a similar rise in ENPP. Hence, when looking at how people vote, the United Kingdom has not been a two-party system for a long time. It is only the electoral system which has in the past prevented this *electoral* multi-party system from breaking through to the House of Commons.

Another interesting case is New Zealand. Until 1994 New Zealand used the same disproportional electoral system as for the UK House of Commons. In 1994 they opted for a more proportional electoral system and the effect of this is immediately clear. A slowly fragmenting system at the electoral level becomes even more fragmented. With a more proportional electoral system in place, more parties had a chance of winning

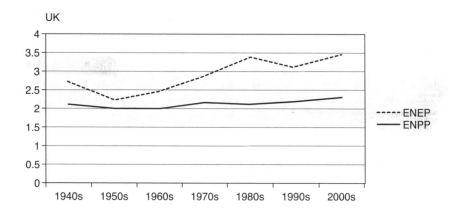

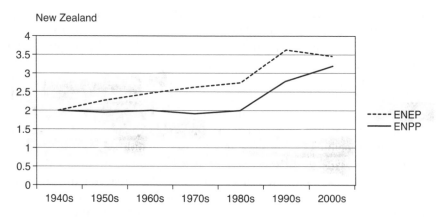

Figure 2.4 *ENEP and ENPP in the UK and New Zealand*

Source: Trinity College Dublin http://www.tcd.ie/Political_Science/staff/michael_gallagher/ElSystems/ index.php, (accessed 21 November 2013).

seats and therefore become more attractive options for voters. Before 1994 the parliamentary party system was stubbornly resistant to the increasing fragmentation at the electoral level. However, after 1994 the wider distribution of the vote was also reflected in a wider distribution of seats. So, using the idea of the effective number of parties we are able to calculate quantitatively what the impact of, for example, changing the electoral system has been.

The effective number of parties approach is not without its flaws. For example, a party which has only a very small impact on the effective number of parties score may actually be very important politically. An effective number of parties score may suggest that a country is dominated by two parties, but gloss over the fact that a small centrist party is in the position of 'king maker' and therefore wields enormous power. The effective number of parties can, therefore, not by itself tell us everything about the distribution of power in a country. However, the approach does provide useful insights into a country's party system. The fact that we have a quantifiable measure of party system fragmentation at several levels of analysis (such as electoral and parliamentary) allows us to explore changes within and across countries fairly easily.

Explaining party system variation

If we were to apply these different approaches to categorising party systems, as indeed has been done frequently, we are left with the puzzle of explaining why each country has the party system it does. This is particularly the case is we accept Duverger's idea that duality or two sides, and thus two parties, is the natural state in politics. What explains the variation in party systems across countries?

Generally speaking there have been two broad approaches to explaining the number of parties in a country. One is a sociological explanation and is based on the number of ideological conflicts in a society, what has been referred to as societal cleavages (see Chapter 4). The other is technical in nature and focuses on political institutions; in particular the type of electoral system in use. There is no doubt that the second type of explanation, concentrating on the impact of the electoral system, has been by far the most popular. Indeed. Riker (1982) argues that this is a rare example of a true 'scientific' debate taking place in social science – that is, a debate which is marked by the steady accumulation of knowledge and where new advances are based on previous advances. The investigation of the relationship between electoral systems and party systems is one of the few examples in social science where 'each one of the series of revisions is more general or more precise than its predecessor' (Riker, 1982, p. 753). It is, therefore, this area we will focus on first before moving on to ideological factors in the creation of party systems.

The concern with the impact of electoral systems is sometimes seen as having originated with Duverger (1964). He makes two statements which have since become the topic of intense and widespread debate. The first statement, what Riker (1982) and indeed many others refer to as Duverger's law, is that: 'the simple-majority single-ballot system favours the two-party system' (Duverger, 1964, p. 217). The second statement, which according to Riker (1982, p. 754) has not been elevated to a law, but merely a hypothesis, is that: 'both the simple-majority system with second ballot and proportional representation favour multi-partism'

(Duverger, 1964, p. 239). By way of explanation, the simple-majority single-ballot system, also sometimes called first past the post or single member plurality, uses single member seats, and whichever candidates gets the most votes (not necessarily more than 50 per cent) wins. This is the system used in the United Kingdom for election to the House of Commons. The simple-majority system with second ballot usually works by the two top candidates in the first round going through to a second round, and the second round of voting determines the final winner. A version of this system is used in France. Proportional representation (PR) comes in a number of forms, but basically works to ensure that there is a relatively strong relationship between the proportion of the vote a party gets and the proportion of the seats it gets.

While this general idea, that single member plurality favours two-party systems and two-round systems and proportional representation favour multi-party systems, is most often associated with Duverger, he was merely putting into formal and specific language an assumption with a very long pedigree. The earliest documented explicit mention of this effect comes from Henry Droop, the inventor of the Droop quota used in the Single Transferable Vote electoral system (used for example in Ireland), and is from 1869 – although it was also alluded to by John Stuart Mill in 1861 (Riker, 1982, p. 756). Since then the idea that the electoral system influenced the party system became increasingly commonplace. In 1901 it was part of the debate over Australia's new electoral system (Ashworth and Ashworth, 1901, pp. vii–viii; Riker, 1982, p. 756). Ramsey MacDonald, future leader of the UK Labour Party and the party's first Prime Minister, rejected proportional representation exactly because he wanted to promote a two-party system where the Labour Party would have the opportunity to form a single-party majority government (MacDonald, 1909, p. 137).

The question then is what it is about the different electoral systems that affect the party system of a given country. Broadly speaking the causal factors are said to be either mechanical or psychological (Shugart, 2008, p. 30). The mechanical effects refer to the way votes are converted into seats. In a system like the one used in the United Kingdom, larger parties tend to get a proportion of the seats that is often significantly higher than their proportion of the votes. Imagine a situation of three major parties all competing across the country. Party A and Party B usually get around 40 per cent of the vote each in every constituency. In some constituencies Party A will beat Party B by a few percentage points, and in some constituencies Party B will win. Party C gets the remaining vote – that is around 20 per cent in each constituency. Its 20 per cent of the vote will never beat the 40-ish per cent for the two other parties and thus, despite winning 20 per cent of the vote it will get no seats. Party A and B will get about 50 per cent of the seats each on 40 per cent of the vote. This is in essence what happens in the United Kingdom, except that the vote is much more unevenly distributed than in the above example which allows smaller parties to concentrate enough votes in some constituencies to still win some seats.

The psychological effects are the ways that voters and party leaders react to these mechanical effects. The idea is that if voters expect their vote to be wasted by voting for smaller parties they will be more inclined to give their vote to a larger one.

Further, within any political party there will be extremists and moderates – the 'pacific and the fire-eaters' (Duverger, 1964, p. 230). If these fail to cooperate we may see a split which creates a new party. However, the pacific and the fire eaters may *have* to work together when operating under an electoral system where smaller parties are punished. By contrast, under PR smaller parties find it easier to survive which may encourage splits within existing parties (Duverger, 1964, p. 252) as minority groups strike out on their own. In other words PR makes establishing broad umbrella parties less appealing. Groups, which may under a plurality system have joined together, will be tempted to form separate parties under PR. In a country like the United Kingdom, 5 per cent of the vote across the country is unlikely to get you any seats. In more proportional systems, such as in Sweden or Germany, 5 per cent of the vote will yield something like 5 per cent of the seats, enough to potentially make a difference in a multi-party system. This may well explain the increase in electoral fragmentation evident in New Zealand after 1994 as illustrated in Figure 2.4. With a more proportional electoral system, voters have more incentive to consider voting for smaller parties as these now have a far greater likelihood of success; which in turn makes it more tempting for political activists to strike out on their own, rather than join or remain in a larger party.

However, while the technical and psychological effects of the electoral system certainly provide reasonable and believable arguments for how different party systems came into being, there is a problem. This problem could broadly be summarised as a chicken and egg problem. In other words, what came first: the party system or the electoral system? It has been argued that 'it may be more accurate to conclude that [the electoral system is] a result rather than a cause of the party system in a given country' (Grum, 1958, p. 375). Several studies have taken up this idea. Taagepera (2003, p. 7) suggests a 'causality flowing in the reverse direction, from the number of parties towards electoral rules', which in turn echoes an earlier claim by Lipson that 'chronologically, as well as logically, the party system is prior to the electoral system' (Lipson, 1964, p. 343). In a wide ranging analysis of 219 elections in 87 countries since the nineteenth century Colomer (2005) concludes that:

Majoritarian rules induce the formation of two large parties, but two-party configurations also maintain or choose majoritarian rules. Proportional representation permits the development of multiple parties, but multi-party systems also tend to establish or confirm proportional representation rules. (p. 4, see also pp. 17–18)

The reason why it might be argued that the party system pre-dated the electoral system in a given country is that the number of parties may in fact be more easily explained by the number of societal cleavages or conflicts in society rather than the electoral system. Instead of seeing the electoral system encouraging or restricting party formation, it could be argued that the number of parties is influenced far more by underlying societal conflicts. The idea is that parties grow out of and represent groups in society sitting on opposing sides of social conflicts – such as the classic class conflict between proletariat and bourgeois, or between national and/or religious majorities and minorities. This would then suggest that both party systems and electoral systems are affected by the ways in which society is split politically in a given country. So, in a society where there is only one political conflict, for example between proletariat and bourgeois there will only be two major parties. This may then lead to the use of an electoral system that reflects and maintains this duality. Conversely, if in addition to the conflict between proletariat vs. bourgeois, there is also a conflict between say different national groups this might lead to the adoption of an electoral system that allows both of these cross-cutting conflicts to be represented in the form of political parties.

This idea is represented in Figure 2.5. This shows an example of an imaginary country with two societal cleavages. On the one hand there is disagreement over whether the government should promote national unity or autonomy for minority populations. Real life examples of such a debate would be Scotland and Wales within the United Kingdom and

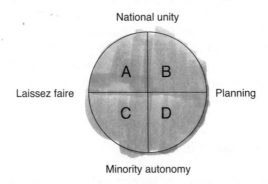

Figure 2.5 *The making of multi-party systems through overlapping political divides*

Catalonia and the Basque Country within Spain. The other disagreement is over economic laissez faire vs. planning as in the classic class cleavage found in many countries. In this example parties A and B can agree on laissez faire, but part ways on national unity vs. autonomy. They, therefore, cannot exist as one party necessitating two parties. Similarly B and D agree on the need for planning but also part ways over national unity. A and B agree on national unity, but disagree over the need for national planning and C and D agree on minority autonomy, but fall out over planning. Hence, because of over-lapping and incompatible political cleavages, this imaginary country has a multi-party system. So the underlying societal conflicts has created a multiparty system, which in turn has led to the adoption of a PR system which ensures, or at least encourages, the continuing existence of the multiparty system as illustrated. As Taagepera and Grofman (1985, p. 350) argue: 'it may be that countries with many issue dimensions do purposely pick electoral systems which enable more than two parties to survive' (see Chapter 4 for a discussion of societal conflicts and parties).

It is of course possible that an electoral system was adopted at a time when there were only two main opposing groups in society leading to the use of Single Member Plurality. However, later more conflicts started to emerge, but the two main parties created by the original conflict saw no need to change the electoral system. The traditional two-party system is therefore 'artificially' maintained by the electoral system despite not fully reflecting new political conflicts. Arguably this is what has been happening in the United Kingdom since the 1970s.

Hence, when trying to explain the variations of party systems across countries, there seems to be a complex interaction between societal cleavages, the electoral system and the number of parties in existence. Political cleavages create political parties. However, different electoral systems make it more difficult for small parties to survive, which could mean that a single large party is able to absorb several political cleavages within it. Then again, the electoral system of a country is chosen by political parties – and any party would want an electoral system that suits its situation – that is, small parties will be concerned with proportionality, larger parties less so. The electoral system chosen will, therefore, depend on how many parties exist at the time – which will to a large extent be explained by the political cleavages in a country.

Which party system is best?

Quite regardless of which party systems exist and how they are formed, there is the question of whether some systems are somehow 'better' than others. It has been argued that 'the literature on party systems is [...] replete with normative statements which extol certain party systems but damn others' (Daalder, 1992, p. 274).

Indeed, there is a long standing argument that the two-party system is better than the multi-party system. One example is Duverger and his view that dualities are natural in politics. If two opposing camps are natural in politics, so must be two-party systems. Linked to this is an idealisation of the single-party majority government. Single-party majority governments are extolled for their stability, and according to Amery's (1947, p. 19) view of 'strong and stable government first' there really is no viable alternative to the two-party system. A single party with a majority is far better able to make swift decisions, without the need for debating and reaching compromises that are said to hold back minority and coalition governments.

The strongest advocacy for the two-party system comes from the idea of 'responsible two-party government' (American Political Science Association Committee on Political Parties, 1950; Ranney, 1962). The argument here is that with two parties competing to form single-party majority governments it will be clear who is responsible for the actions of governments. Parties can thus be very easily judged on whether they have succeeded in carrying out their electoral promises.

The other side of this argument is a rejection of multi-party systems. This rejection is often based on the problems experienced in the Weimar Republic and Third Republic France before the Second World War and in Italy and Fourth Republic France after 1945. An excessive number of extreme parties made for unstable governments, and it is argued, ultimately caused the breakdown of democracy in Germany in the 1930s and the rise of Nazism. The same led to the breakdown of the Fourth Republic in France to be replaced with the Fifth Republic. Italy after the Second World War was (and arguably is) a basket case of too many parties and weak governments.

However, from the 1950s onwards there has been a re-evaluation of multi-party democracies. One moving force behind this re-evaluation was the discovery that economically and socially there was no evidence that two-party democracies did any better than multi-party democracies. Indeed, Lijphart argues that consensus style democracies, with multi-party systems at their heart, are better than majoritarian democracies and their two-party systems. According to Lijphart (1999, pp. 275–6) consensus democracies:

are more likely to be welfare states; they have a better record with regard to the protection of the environment; they put fewer people in prison and are less likely to use the death penalty; and consensus democracies in the developed world are more generous with their economic assistance to developing countries.

Ultimately, it is probably impossible to objectively say which type of party system is the 'best' one. As the above have shown there is a considerable debate about this and the final conclusion depends on one's own preferences. In essence, whether one prefers one type of party system over another depends on: a) what one thinks the consequences of each type of party system is; and b) whether one approves of those consequences or not. This is exemplified by Lijphart's argument for a multi-party consensus democracy. If one approves of, for example, welfare states, not putting people in prison, and aid to developing countries then one might well also approve of a party system that encouraged such things. However, there are many who do not approve of the things Lijphart associates with multi-party consensus democracy and who hence would probably prefer a different kind of democracy. In short, the debate over which party system is 'best' seems to be, at least partly, an ideological debate.

Conclusion

As we have seen, party systems are an important issue to consider when examining politics. Different party systems will have very different effects on the politics of a country, and may affect how well the politics of a country functions. Looking at party systems will also help us compare different countries. Knowing that the United States is dominated by two parties, whereas many countries in Europe are dominated by multi-party politics will tell us a lot about how power is distributed in each country. However, how party systems are formed and whether one is better than another is a source of considerable uncertainty. This only makes the study of party systems that much more important – we know they critically affect the politics of a country, so the more we can lean about how they emerge and change the better we can understand the changing politics of modern democracies.

Chapter 3

Theories of Party Development

Understanding the origins and early development of parties is a critical aspect of the study of party organisations. The main reason for wanting to understand the origins of political parties is that the way a party emerged has a major impact on its organisation for decades afterwards:

> a party's organisational characteristics depend more upon its history than upon any other factor. The characteristics of a party's origins are in fact capable of exerting a weight on its organizational structure even decades later. Every organization bears the mark of its formation, of the crucial political-administrative decisions made by its founders, the decisions which 'moulded' the organization. (Panebianco, 1988, p. 50)

This is not to say that parties do not change as they clearly do. The point is that once a party has become 'institutionalised', to use Panebianco's term, or set in its ways, it often takes a considerable amount of effort to change it. Parties, as with most established organisations, are 'small c conservative' in that they change only gradually and often reluctantly. To understand the current shape of parties it is, therefore, necessary to also understand how they originated and developed.

Some of the key theories of how parties emerged and evolved as organisations will be the main focus of this chapter. There are two main theories of how parties first developed. The most well known comes from Duverger. Duverger's theory is fairly simply and also the one most commonly used to understand the origins of parties and the effects those origins have on the subsequent life of parties. Panebianco starts from Duverger's theory, but critiques it and presents an alternative perspective. In the following we will first look at Duverger's theory followed by Panebianco's. After that will be a review of one of the central preoccupations of the party politics literature – the evolution of party types.

The 'internal' and 'external' origins of parties

The most popular way of analysing the origins of political parties is to distinguish between parties of 'internal' and 'external' origins. Whether a

party is of internal or external origins is said to have had profound implications for how they develop as organisations. The internal/external distinction is related to whether a party started as a group of
parliamentarians who later added an extra-parliamentary organisation
(internal origins), or as an extra-parliamentary organisation who later
succeeded in winning parliamentary seats (external origins). The relationship between the parliamentary group and the extra-parliamentary parts
of a political party is said to be permanently marked by its parliamentary
or extra-parliamentary origins.

The parties of parliamentary origins are mostly associated with early
forms of representative assemblies such as the British Parliament and the
French Constituent Assemblies of 1789 and 1848 (Duverger, 1964, pp.
xxiv–xxvi), but are still relevant in contemporary party politics. Parties of
parliamentary origins start life as groups of parliamentarians to which an
extra-parliamentary organisation is only later added. Traditionally the
impetus to add an extra-parliamentary organisation came from the extension of the franchise in many countries in the late 1800s and early 1900s.
Before that the electorate was very small and a large extra-parliamentary
organisation was simply not needed. For example, in the United Kingdom
where political parties first developed, less than 10 per cent of the male
adult population were allowed to vote before the Reform Act 1832, and
even that piece of legislation only increased it to 14 per cent. That
amounted to hundreds of thousands of voters, rather than the millions of
voters today. That meant that each constituency would have only a
couple of thousand voters. Each candidate and a few associates would be
enough to do the campaigning needed. However, as the electorate grew it
became necessary to have larger and larger numbers of volunteers to
campaign at election time. This necessitated the creation of an extra-parliamentary volunteer membership organisation. Classic examples of
parties of parliamentary origins include many European Liberal and
Conservative parties who can trace their origins back to the 1800s and
sometimes earlier (Duverger, 1964, p. 21).

The parliamentary origins of such parties have significant consequences for their organisational culture. The party on the ground is
essentially there to ensure the survival of the party in public office: 'the
winning of seats in political assemblies is the essence of the life of the
party, the very reason for its existence and the supreme purpose of it life'
(Duverger, 1964, p. xxxv). The extra-parliamentary organisation is seen
as the servant, or the 'hand maiden' as it was called in the British
Conservative Party, of the parliamentary party – there to be used as a
tool by the parliamentary party. Such parties, therefore, tend to have a
fairly oligarchic organisational ethos. The parliamentary group is the
source of power and the raison d'être of the party and the extra-parlia-

mentary party is openly and overtly controlled from parliament. Intra-party democracy is not much in evidence or even deemed particularly necessary (Duverger, 1964, p. xxxv).

In addition, parties of parliamentary origin tend to be fairly de-centralised. In their early life the party 'organisation' is little more than local election committees associated with an individual member of parliament or candidate. The external elements of the party are at this stage not really units in a formal organisation, but linked purely through the work of the parliamentarians they have helped get elected (Duverger, 1964, p. xxix). Only later is a proper national organisation created. Parties of parliamentary origins are, therefore, both highly top led, in that the parliamentary group is in control, and tend to be quite decentralised in that the main link between the different local elements of the party goes through individual parliamentarians.

In sharp contrast to parties with parliamentary origins are the parties with extra-parliamentary origins, the externally created parties. These parties started life outside parliament with little or no parliamentary presence. Their main purpose was to mobilise voters to 'break' into parliament. This party strategy is usually regarded as mainly associated with left-wing parties, particularly those based on the organised working class, that is, trade unions. The creation of these parties was very much a consequence of the extension of the franchise in several European states in the late nineteenth century. Some of the main beneficiaries of this extension were the rapidly growing urban working class of the industrial revolution. The first externally created parties were, therefore, driven by the desire to mobilise these thousands and even millions of new voters to represent their interests in parliament. The new externally created parties mobilised hundreds of thousands of voters, incorporating many of them into their membership organisations, also a new invention. A mass electorate required a mass membership organisation to campaign at election time. The candidate and a few associates were no-longer enough in the emerging mass-democracy. The issue of the mass-membership organisation will be explored later in this chapter and in Chapter 5.

The 'old' parliamentary parties, exemplified typically by conservatives and liberals, did not successfully incorporate the interests of these new voters in their programmes, leaving the field more or less open for new parties to emerge. The result was working class social democratic and socialist parties. The electoral success of these extra-parliamentary organisations with their mass-membership organisations forced the parliamentary parties of the right wing to follow suit. The idea of a membership organisation outside parliament was, therefore, a left-wing idea which spread to the right. Duverger (1964, p. xxvii) referred to this spread of mass-membership organisations as a 'contagion from the left'.

Parties of extra-parliamentary origins tend to be created around some form of nucleus – either a particular leading individual, or a pre-existing organisation – in the case of Social Democratic and Labour parties more often than not trade unions. Because the party, on the ground existed before the party in public office their formal roles tended to be the reverse of the parties of parliamentary origin. The party in public office was created through the, often hard and lengthy, work of the party on the ground and it was, therefore, expected to work to defend the interests of the party on the ground. Indeed, the parliamentary side of the party was often regarded as only one element of its work: 'the electoral and parliamentary struggle remains very important, but it is only one element in the general activity of the party, one of the means, among others, that it uses to realize its political ends' (Duverger, 1964, pp. xxxv–xxxvi). This means that the parliamentary group does not have the same central place in a party of extra-parliamentary origin. As Duverger writes: 'in such parties there is a certain more or less open mistrust of the parliamentary group, and a more or less definite desire to subject it to the authority of an independent controlling committee' (Duverger, 1964, p. xxxv). The reality of who is actually in control is often very different, but formally speaking in parties of extra-parliamentary origins the party in public office tend to be controlled by the party on the ground.

Also in contrast to the parties of parliamentary origin, the parties of extra-parliamentary origin tend to be much more centralised. This is intimately linked to how they were created. Parties of extra-parliamentary origins can often identify a founding date and just as importantly a single founding place. In the United Kingdom the Labour Representation Committee, later known as the Labour Party, had its founding conference on Tuesday 27 February to Wednesday 28 February 1900 in the Memorial Hall, Farringdon Street in London. The 'International in Denmark', later the Social Democratic Party, was founded at a meeting in number 27 Adelgade in Copenhagen on Sunday 15 October 1871. The 'General German Workers' Association', later the Social Democratic Party of Germany, was created on 23 May 1863 in Leipzig. Few if any parties with parliamentary origins can point to such founding dates and places as they evolved slowly over time. Many parties of extra-parliamentary origins therefore started on a specific date at a specific location. Often a key element of a founding conference is to agree on an organisational structure and ratify a party rule book. This is an important point to make because it gives them a very different organisational ethos and structure than parties of parliamentary origins. Because many parties of extra-parliamentary origin started from an original founding conference or meeting they were from the beginning highly centralised organisations with a single hierarchical structure. This is in contrast to the amalgamations of disparate local groups typical of parties of parliamentary origins (Duverger, 1964, pp. xxxiv–xxxv). The way a party originated can then be seen to have had a crucial part to play in the organisational structure of that party.

An alternative view of the emergence of political parties

While Duverger's view of party emergence is the most popular, it has also been criticised. Panebianco points out that it fails to explain how parties of similar origins nevertheless end up having very different structures. His claim is that we need a more complex model if we are to understand how parties develop (Panebianco, 1988, p. 50).

Panebianco develops what he calls a 'genetic model' for party emergence, which can then be applied to analyse and understand specific parties (Panebianco, 1988, p. 50). The genetic model consists of two parts. The first part focuses on how a party first emerged and the forces involved in its creation. This in turn affects how the party 'institutionalised' – that is, how the party settled into a regular pattern of organisational activity.

There are three issues we need to consider when investigating the emergence of a political party (Panebianco, 1988, pp. 50–3). The first issue is whether the party was created through territorial penetration or territorial diffusion. Territorial penetration involves a pre-existing centre controlling, stimulating or directing the creation of the 'periphery – local and regional party organisations. Territorial diffusion on the other hand is when local elites create party organisations in their locality which are then later merged into a national organisation. A combination of the two can also take place. Local parties emerge in some areas and eventually form a national organisation (diffusion). This national organisation then goes on to create local party organisation where there were none before (penetration). However, there will more often than not be a prevailing tendency in that a party is created mainly by one or the other method. Panebianco argues that liberal parties have tended to emerge through a mixture of the two. Many socialist parties and religious parties have tended to be formed through diffusion. Conservative and communist parties have typically been created through penetration.

These two forms of origins will have an effect on how the party is structured. A party created through penetration will by definition have a sufficiently strong centre to stimulate the creation of local party organisations. Such parties therefore tend to be highly centralised. By contrast parties created by diffusion will be based on the merger of many local elements with their own elites and power centres. These parties therefore tend to have a more federal character and be marked by struggles between local groups for control of the national party.

The second issue we need to consider when looking at a party's origins is whether there was an external 'sponsor' organisation (such as a trade union or a religious organisation) that created the party as its 'political arm'. This will make a difference to the legitimacy of the leadership. The leadership of a party with an external sponsor will base their power and legitimacy as leaders on the support of the external organisation. The external sponsor can, therefore, intervene in a party and shift its support from one group to another. Where there is no external sponsor the leadership base their power and legitimacy on the party itself. There is then a difference between externally legitimated parties and internally legitimated parties.

The third and final factor relates to the role of charisma in the formation of a party. Charismatic leaders more often than not have a big part to play in the formation of most parties, but the 'concern here is with parties formed by one leader who imposed himself as the undisputed founder, conceiver, and interpreter of a set of political symbols [...] which became inseparable from his person' (Panebianco, 1988, p. 52). Examples of such parties would be List Pim Fortuyn in the Netherlands, the short-lived Veritas in the United Kingdom (created by TV personality Robert Kilroy-Silk), and Berlusconi's Forza Italia. In addition to this 'pure' charisma, there is also 'situational charisma', where a particular crisis creates a leader that people are willing to follow. 'A party based on pure charisma has no existence apart from its leader [...] a party based on situational charisma is not simply the leader's creation, but is a product of many different impulses and thrusts' (Panebianco, 1988, pp. 52–3). An example of such 'situational charisma' might be the Progress Party in Denmark which was created in 1973 by Mogens Glistrup on the back of increasing reaction against raising taxes. The party was closely linked with Glistrup, but still survived his forced absence from running the party when he was convicted for refusing to pay tax.

These three key issues will combine to affect a party's 'institutionalisation'. Institutionalisation refers to: 1) the degree to which a party is able to dominate its surroundings as opposed to being dominated by them; and 2) the extent to which the various elements making up the party, such as local branches, are independent of each other or tied together into a coherent whole. A party which is highly autonomous in relation to its surroundings and where the various units are highly interdependent of each other is a party with a high degree of institutionalisation (Panebianco, 1988, pp. 55–8). If a party is to survive it has to institutionalise, but the extent of institutionalisation depends on how the party was created.

Type 1	Created through territorial penetration; strongly institutionalised; externally legitimatised.
Type 2	Created through territorial diffusion; weakly institutionalised; externally legitimised.
Type 3	Created through territorial penetration; strongly institutionalised; internally legitimised.
Type 4	Created through territorial diffusion; weakly institutionalised; internally legitimised.

Figure 3.1 *Party origins and institutionalisation*

The issue of how a party has emerged and its degree of institutionalisation can be combined to analyse and understand how a party has developed, and the importance of its origins in that development (see Figure 3.1).

The parties that most resemble Type 1 are the communist parties of the Cold War period. They were often created by territorial penetration, and although many had an external sponsor, the Communist Party of the Soviet Union, this sponsor was 'extra-national' and therefore had a somewhat indirect impact. They, therefore, tended to be highly institutionalised. Type 2 is represented by labour and social democratic parties, such as the British Labour Party and some religious parties. The fact that these parties were created by territorial diffusion and were dependent on external sponsoring organisations, in many cases trade unions, meant that they were dependent on their external sponsor and based on local semi-autonomous units. This tended to lead to low levels of institutionalisation.

Type 3 consists of parties created from a pre-existing centre, such as a parliamentary group, and with no sponsoring organisation. They are therefore highly institutionalised as they are controlled from the centre and are much less dependent on their external environment, in contrast to some social democratic parties' dependency on the trade unions that helped create them. One could mention the British Conservative Party as an example of this type of party.

Finally there are Type 4 parties. While there is no external sponsoring organisation these parties were still created by territorial diffusion. They were, therefore, federations of existing groups, which slows institutionalisation. One example is the German CDU.

This leaves the issue of charisma, which Panebianco refers to as a 'deviant case' since it does not fit into the above schema (Panebianco, 1988, p. 65). Parties based on charisma can go one of two ways. Either they simply melt away once the original leader leaves the stage – or they manage to live on after his or her departure. If the party dies then institutionalisation is not relevant. If the party continues then it will most likely end up as a highly institutionalised party. A party created by a single charismatic leader will be highly centralised as all decisions, ideology and purpose flow from that person. If the party survives the departure of the founding leader the organisation will more than likely retain that highly centralised structure.

These two different ways of looking at the origins of parties are powerful tools in understanding the current organisational state of a party. Duverger's approach has the benefit of simplicity, but is perhaps also a little lacking in detail. Panebianco gives a far more detailed tool for analysing parties, but one that is also more complicated to apply, exactly because of the extra detail. However, both approaches show the importance of taking into account a party's origins when trying to understand its current state.

Understanding party types

In addition to analysing how parties have emerged and how this affects their current situation, a lot of effort has gone into categorising different ways that parties have organised themselves internally. Indeed, one of the most active areas of party politics research is the development, operationalisation, critiquing and re-development of party types. There is not a single commonly agreed definition of what a party type is – which is a problem we will return to at the end of this section. However, the party type debate has still dominated our understanding of how parties have changed over time. Various authors have described party types as illustrations of how parties currently behave, how they used to behave and how they might behave in the future. Often the development of a new party type comes as a response to parties, or a particular group of parties, doing something in a new way. Each party type describes how parties behave, their central characteristics and motivating forces. In the following we will examine the most important party types and show how this approach to our understanding of parties has helped us to see how parties have changed over time. The following will also deal with some problems which have become apparent regarding the 'party types' approach to analysing party life.

Cadre parties to mass parties

The first two types of party organisations to be described were cadre parties and mass parties (see Duverger, 1964, p. 63). Cadre parties equated to the early parties of parliamentary origin, whereas the mass party matched the organisations of extra-parliamentary origin.

The first parties to emerge in early legislative assemblies were cadre parties (Duverger, 1964, p. 65). These parties were hardly recognisable as parties in the modern sense. They had little formal structure and tended to be based around more or less permanent agreements among parliamentarians based on short- and long-term common interests. Cadre parties existed at a time when the franchise was highly limited and there was little need for an extra-parliamentary organisation to mobilise voters, as described earlier. Cadre parties did not have card carrying and fee paying members as most modern parties do. Membership of, or perhaps rather association with, a cadre party was highly exclusive and based on a person's financial resources, personal contacts and influence or expertise. Cadre parties are primarily associated with legislative assemblies in Europe in the late eighteenth and nineteenth centuries, periods where membership of such assemblies was based on Royal favour, membership of the aristocracy or election by a small, rich and exclusive electorate based on property ownership and wealth.

The cadre parties started to face serious competition in the late nineteenth century when the franchise was extended. As described earlier, the much enlarged electorate led to extra-parliamentary organisations mobilising new voters, particularly among the working class. These new working-class parties did not rely on the significant resources of a few individual members, but the regular, albeit small, contributions of many members. In these 'mass parties' as Duverger called them, membership was not exclusive and based on recommendations from existing members, but 'wide open' to all who could support the basic goals of the party. In the mass party the main focus was the representation of a particular group or class in society, hence the phrase 'class-mass' party (Kirchheimer, 1966, p. 183). In the mass party the membership was a crucial element of the party and central to its survival: 'the members are the very substance of the party, the stuff of its activity' (Duverger, 1964, p. 63) and indeed the concept of a fee paying member has been described as a socialist mass party invention (Duverger, 1964, p. 63).

It is important to note that the main difference between a cadre party and a mass party is not one of size. Even when at their most powerful, the biggest West European communist parties, such as the French and Italian, still did not rival the main Socialist, Labour and Social Democratic parties in terms of membership numbers. However, communist parties are still to be regarded as mass parties, although of a particularly centralised and tightly run variety. In short, 'mass party' refers to a particular form of organisational principle, rather than the size of the membership organisation.

The mass parties eventually proved themselves able to challenge the old cadre parties in term of electoral success. As a result the latter started to copy the mass party model: 'cadre parties sometimes admit ordinary members in imitation of mass parties. In fact, the practice is fairly wide-spread: there are few purely cadre parties' (Duverger, 1964, p. 64). In other words, cadre parties 'after the contagious pattern of the mass party' (Duverger, 1964, p. 64) sometimes rival the largest mass parties in size. However, in the 'modernised' cadre party a 'mass membership' exists purely to ensure the survival of the parliamentary party and sometimes to add some popular democratic legitimacy to the organisation. This is in contrast to the mass party where the members are the base from which all activity of the party flows.

It is clear that mass parties emerged as a result of the enfranchisement of the working class. They were therefore '[a child] of democracy, of mass franchise, of the necessity to woo and organise the masses' (Weber, 1990, p. 35). This 'contagious organisation' (Duverger, 1964, p. 25) spread from the left to the right of the political spectrum as the success of the mass party model forced the old cadre parties to 'counter mobilise' (Lipset and Rokkan, 1967). By the 1950s the mass party model stood triumphant and seemed to be the type of party best fitted to modern mass democracy (Bille, 1997, p. 30).

Challenging the mass party model: the catch-all party

The idea that mass parties were the party type of the future, either in its 'pure' form in left-wing parties, or as imitations in cadre parties with extra-parliamentary membership organisation add-ons, was quickly challenged by Kirchheimer (1966). In an incomplete article published shortly after his death, Kirchheimer argued that the evolved cadre parties were in fact better suited to the post-war environment with its more diverse electorates and reduced class antagonism than was the traditional mass party based on class representation. The old cadre parties, having imitated some of the features of the mass party, most notably the presence of fairly large membership organisations, were becoming 'catch-all people's parties' (Kirchheimer, 1966, p. 184). As the electorate grew, the cadre parties were not able to rely for their electoral survival on the small societal elite they had previously been based on. They, therefore, needed to reach out beyond their traditional privileged audience and as a result turned more fully to the electoral area. The mass parties were based on the mobilisations of a specific, albeit large, group of voters. The evolving cadre parties based their new electoral strategy on attracting as many voters as they could from whatever groups in society they were able to tap, hence the term 'catch-all'.

As with the success of the mass party model in the late nineteenth and early twentieth centuries, so the success of the catch-all party model in the post-1945 era became a contagion which spread from the right-wing of politics to the left (Epstein, 1967, p. 257). By the 1970s the catch-all party, rather than the mass party, looked like the model of the future.

The catch-all party has a number of key characteristics, including:

- 'a drastic reduction of the party ideological baggage';
- 'further strengthening of the top leadership groups';
- 'downgrading of the traditional role of the individual party member, a role considered a historical relic which may obscure the newly built-up catch-all party image, and
- 'de-emphasis of the *classe gardée*, specific social-class or denominational clientele, in favour of recruiting voters among the population at large'. (Kirchheimer, 1966, pp. 190–1)

It is important to note that becoming a catch-all party does not mean that a party is so 'heterogeneous as to represent the whole social spectrum and whose connection with its original *classe gardée* had completely disappeared' (Panebianco, 1988, p. 263). Rather what the catch-all party is trying to do is simply to open its doors to different social groups 'whose interests do not adamantly conflict' (Kirchheimer, 1966, p. 186). A catch-all party is, therefore, not a party which has no ideological or societal connections what-so-ever. No party could survive long without any coherence or predictability to its policy preferences or legislative actions. The main difference between the mass party and the catch-all party models is that the mass party focus was primarily on the representation of the interests of one particular group, whereas the catch-all party is trying to open up to new electoral markets that do not fundamentally clash with its old position.

As we shall see later in the book, when it comes to party ideology; the role of party members; the balance of power in parties; and campaigning, Kirchheimer's description of the catch-all party seems to fit with a lot of what has been happening in modern political parties.

Organisational consequences of the catch-all party: the electoral-professional party model

The catch-all party model focused very heavily on the ideological aspects of political parties, especially the idea of not targeting one specific class, but rather casting one's net as wide as possible. Hence, one criticism of the catch-all party model was its strong focus on the ideological changes and moderation that went into becoming a catch-all party and how that affected the catch-all party's relations with other political actors such as interest groups (Panebianco, 1988, p. 263). Panebianco argued that this focus overlooked important organisational implications of the catch-all party model. The solution was the idea of the electoral-professional party.

The electoral-professional party type does not reject the idea of the catch-all model. Rather, what it does is develop the catch-all type with a focus on organisational issues and in particular the professionalization of the party. In the classic mass party 'a crucial role is played by the apparatus, the party bureaucracy: the "representative bureaucracy" [...] is used by the mass party leaders to maintain close ties with the members, and, through the members, with the *classe gardée*' (Panebianco, 1988, p. 264). By 'representative bureaucracy' is meant a system where local party members (the party on the ground as described in Chapter 1) interact with voters at the local level and thereby get an idea of the wishes and demands of the population. Party members then elect representatives and party officers to serve higher up in the party in local, regional and national executives and as delegates to the party conference (the party in central office). These party officers and delegates carry the wishes and demands from the voters to the party's parliamentarians (the party in public office) to deal with in the form of legislation. The representative bureaucracy, therefore, acts as an unbroken chain from people to parliament.

In the electoral-professional party this organising principle is replaced with an increasingly professionalized approach to running the party. The electoral-professional party makes far greater use of 'so-called experts, technicians with specialist knowledge' (Panebianco, 1988, p. 264) such as pollsters and what would now be called spin-doctors, instead of relying on members as the main source of information about what voters are demanding. Overall there are five key differences between mass parties and electoral-professional parties:

1   Where the mass party relied on party bureaucrats to run the party and foster links with the electorate, the electoral-professional party relies on experts.
2   The mass party is a membership-based party with strong vertical ties between members and leaders. The party appeals to a sense of belonging (class or group association). In the electoral-professional party the vertical link is weakened and the party appeals to the 'opinion electorate' rather than the 'electorate of belonging' – the

electoral professional party attracts voters by catering to their various and shifting individual demands rather than their interests as a group.

3   Where the mass party was dominated by leaders of the party on the ground, the electoral professional party is dominated by parliamentarians and often by the leader of the party in public office.

4   The mass party was funded by membership fees and affiliation fees from a narrow range of key interest organisations such as trade unions. The electoral-professional party is funded by donations from a range of interests groups and public funds.

5   The mass party was dominated by ideology and 'believers', whereas the electoral professional party is dominated by shifting issues, and pragmatic careerists.

It is important to note that few if any parties fit perfectly into either the mass party or the electoral-professional party categories. They are what we might call 'ideal types' which help us to analyse real-life party organisations (Panebianco, 1988, pp. 264–5). What the two types do is show that there is a tendency for parties to go from having primarily mass-party characteristics to having primarily electoral-professional characteristics.

The extent to which a party has moved from one type to another depends on several factors, relating both to the internal life of a party and its external environment. According to Kirchheimer only major parties are likely to move in a catch-all direction. Large parties are by definition parties that have managed to attract a fairly large vote share, something which would presumably be easier to achieve and maintain with a catch-all stance. Parties with a very specific and narrow focus are also by definition likely to be small and are more likely to stay away from a catch-all position. Parties not expected to reach catch-all status included organisations such as the post-War German Refugee Party, the Danish anti-tax Justice Party and the Swedish Agrarians (Kirchheimer, 1966, pp. 187–8) as their purpose is too narrow or their clientele very small. In addition even major parties in fairly small democracies, such as the Scandinavian countries, are unlikely to become catch-all parties (Kirchheimer, 1966, p. 188). Parties well entrenched in small homogeneous democracies, such as the Norwegian and Swedish Social Democrats have little incentive to move in a catch-all direction (Kirchheimer, 1966, p. 188). In addition Kirchheimer argues that 'conversion to catch-all constitutes a competitive phenomenon' (Kirchhermer, 1966, p. 188). If one party has successfully adopted a catch-all position other parties in the system are likely to follow suit, either in the hope of electoral gains or out of fear of losing to a competitor.

Two key factors are central to understanding 'the speed and intensity of transformation': the level of institutionalisation of a party and the party's environment (Panebianco, 1988, p. 265). A move from mass party to electoral-professional status is more likely to happen before a party has institutionalised, or if the level of institutionalisation is very low. A highly institutionalised party is more likely to resist pressure for organisational reform, be it from internal or external forces. In addition the argument that large parties are more like to undergo transformations than smaller ones suggests that we are more likely to see electoral-professional parties emerge in less fragmented party systems than highly fragmented ones (Panebianco, 1988, p. 265). If a political system is dominated by a few large parties 'change will take place sooner and [take] place more quickly' (Panebianco, 1988, p. 265). A political system characterised by many small parties each with a very specific electoral market is less likely to see change. It makes sense that in, for example, the United Kingdom where the electoral system punishes small parties, parties with a desire for power have an incentive to broaden their appeal as much as possible. Conversely, in countries with very proportional electoral system, such as in Scandinavia, Italy or Israel, the incentive to widen one's appeal and professionalise is much less intense. Smaller parties can and do lead very productive lives, participating in coalitions or supporting minority governments and, therefore, have less reason to professionalise.

Finally Panebianco argues that changes in two major environmental factors are important in affecting party change. The first factor is related to changes to the socioeconomic structure of a country (Panebianco, 1988, p. 265). In other words the rise of a large middle class and the simultaneous decline in working class voters will encourage party change. Electorates have 'become more socially and culturally heterogeneous' (Panebianco, 1988, p. 266) meaning that focusing on just one (possibly shrinking and certainly changing) social group is not electorally viable. This will have a major impact on parties and spur them in a catch-all/electoral professional direction.

Further, technological change will have an impact on the professionalisation of party organisations. As new ways of communicating develop, the need for experts to tap these new communication channels increases. In the context of technological change Panebianco writes about the rise of television campaigning, but in the current communication environment the rise of increasingly mobile and high-speed Internet connections is a major factor as illustrated by Barak Obama's skilled use of Internet networking in both his primary campaign and presidential victories. Clearly, to tap the full potential of such communication channels professionals are needed.

The cartel party

Where the cadre, mass, catch-all and electoral-professional party models have focused on changing ideologies and internal professionalisation, there has been a rising interest in the relationship between parties and the state on the one hand and the electorate on the other. This is where the idea of the cartel party comes in (Katz and Mair, 1995).

The cartel party model continues the move away from the grassroots organisation started by the catch-all/electoral professional party type. Having loosened their ties – in the form of the membership organisation – with civil society, modern parties have become increasingly dependent on the state.

First, as the income from membership fees has declined, so state support for parties has increased. Second, MPs have gone from focusing on their role as representatives of specific societal interests and groups to focusing on their role as legislators and members of government. This development has taken place over a number of stages. In the era of the cadre party, civil society (effectively limited to the few wealthy and privileged levels of society with the vote), political parties and the state overlapped. Indeed, civil society, parties and the state were more often than not indistinguishable from each other (Katz and Mair, 1995, p. 10). The mass party on the other hand served as a bridge between civil society – increasingly seen as all citizens limited only by age – and the state. Parties, anchored in civil society through their membership organisations, represented civil society through their MPs who also served as government ministers and therefore linked to the state. The cartel party has now more or less severed its links with civil society and is becoming increasingly merged with the state.

It is important to note that not all parties are necessarily becoming cartel parties. By definition, not all parties can become part of the cartel. The idea of the cartel party, in addition to the developments described above, is that these parties use their privileged access to state resources to exclude challengers. With the rise of the cartel party the state 'becomes a fount of resources through which these parties not only help to ensure their own survival, but through which they can also enhance their capacity to resist challengers from newly mobilized alternatives' (Katz and Mair, 1995, p. 16).

The idea of the cartel party is linked to the claim that parties are becoming increasingly separated from the people they were originally designed to represent. Becoming ever more dependent on state resources, and thus independent of civil society resources, they lose contact with the ideas, demands and lives of voters. The rise of the cartel party could therefore be seen as a negative development.

Conclusion: Beyond the cartel – beyond party types?

Since Katz and Mair's work on the cartel party in 1995, the work on party types has continued apace. Examples of party types to emerge in the literature since 1995 include the post-cartel party (Yishai, 2001) the franchise party (Carty, 2004); the media and the communitarian party types as a suggestion for two alternative paths of development (Richards, 2000); the cyber party (Margetts, 2001); the business firm party (Hopkin and Paolucci, 1999); modern cadre parties and leader-centred parties (Wolinetz, 2002); catch-all party plus (Puhle, 2002); and the grassroots party.

This plethora of supposed new party organisational forms illustrates a number of problems with the party type approach to the study of political parties. While the cadre to catch-all party evolution is more or less accepted, there seems to be no consensus on what has happened since. The competition to be Kirchheimer's successor is certainly fierce and has not necessarily served to help us get a clear picture of what the overall trends in party organisational change actually are, apart from suggesting that change is indeed happening.

The reasons for this proliferation of new types since the mid-1990s compared to the relatively straight forward cadre to catch-all development are not entirely clear. One option is that the study of parties has experienced an increase in popularity in recent decades. Hence, what we are seeing is not a sudden proliferation of new types compared to the late 1800s and early 1900s, but rather an awareness of the complexity of party organisational change. A complexity perhaps hidden by the relatively narrow field of scholars previously engaged in party organisational research, leading to an equally narrow field of theories related to how parties are changing. In other words the relatively simple cadre to catch-all theory may in fact hide a picture as complex as our current one.

On the other hand it is also possible that democracy and, therefore, party politics may have become more complicated than was previously the case, although most generations seem to view their own age as more developed or complex than the previous age. Whichever is the case, what is clear is that we are faced with a very confusing picture of party organisational development.

This would suggest that there is a need to go beyond the party types literature, important as it is, to get a clearer understanding of what the overall trends in party organisational development are. The following chapters will do just that.

Chapter 4

Ideology

One of the most important and influential ideas of what political parties are or should be is that they are the organisational embodiment of an ideology. It is a common assumption that the whole point of a party is that it has a vision of 'the good society' and its main purpose is to make that vision a reality. Indeed, a common criticism of modern political parties is that many of them, especially those that manage to get into government, have lost their ideological foundations and are interested in power and government perks not to change things, but for the personal benefits that such power brings. In other words, having an ideology is assumed to be at the core of what a party should be, and the absence of ideology is a key criticism of (some) political parties.

This chapter will deal with the issue of ideology, and what will in some places take the place of ideology as the guiding force of party action. The chapter will first explore the meaning of ideology in the context of party politics. It will then look at what drives ideology – that is political cleavages. Having done that the chapter will present the key ways in which parties are grouped when it comes to their ideological position that is into 'party families'. The chapter will then look at party ideology in Western Europe, the United States, India and Africa.

On ideology and party politics

One of the main illustrations of the importance of ideology in the lives of political parties can be found in the names that many parties have adopted. Frequently, although far from always, ideology will be at the centre of a party's name: the Conservative Party in the United Kingdom; the *Sozialdemokratische Partei Deutschlands* (German Social Democratic Party), *Partido Socialista Obrero Español* (Spanish Socialist Workers' Party), The Communist Party of India, The Liberal Party of Canada also known as *Parti libéral du Canada*, the Liberal Party of Australia, and *Partido Conservador Colombiano* (The Columbian Conservative Party) to mention but a few. It is true that the name of a political party is not always a reliable indicator of a party's ideology and frequently the name of a party is not related to an ideology in the first place. The Democratic and Republican parties of the Unites States are not named after ideologies and indeed the Democratic Party started out as the Republican Party, then became the Democratic-Republican Party and eventually The Democratic Party (Witcover, 2003). Nevertheless, the fact that so many parties name themselves after an ideology is an indication of the formal importance of ideology in the life of political parties.

The most prominent version of what party ideology is based on is the classical left–right spectrum inherited from the French Revolution. In the National Assembly created after the revolution in 1789, supporters of the monarchy would congregate on the right-hand side of the chamber. Opponents of the monarchy and the old order would congregate on the left-hand side of the chamber. This division continued through several changes and reforms of the French legislative assembly – to the point where 'left' became associated with the desire for change and opposition to the old and traditional; and 'right' became associated with tradition and maintaining existing structures. On this simple scale social demo-cratic, socialist and communist parties on the left are opposed by liberal, conservative and fascist parties on the right. Indeed, the idea of a left–right spectrum is so ingrained in discourse on political parties that Laponce (1981) referred to it as 'political esperanto', a simple and uni-versal language which helps structure a very complex world of overlap-ping policies and options. In short, the left–right spectrum helps politicians, the media and voters to understand where different parties and candidates are located both in relation to each other and in relation to the position of the observer (Freire, 2008).

It is worth noting that the 'left/right' seating of the French National Assembly of 1789 is continued in the European Parliament. The cross-national party groups in the European parliament are seated such that members of the European United Left/Nordic Green Left, commonly seen as the most radical socialist group in the European Parliament, sits on the far left of the chamber. To their right is the left-of-centre Alliance of Socialists and Democrats. Broadly in the centre is the Alliance of Liberals and Democrats and to their right the right-of-centre European People's Party which is broadly conservative and Christian democrat in character. On their right are several smaller right wing groups. Clearly, the idea of a left–right spectrum is very much alive today.

The traditional view of the left–right spectrum is based on socioeco-nomic issues principally centred on the role of the state in the operation of the free market and the extent of support offered by the state to those who have fallen on hard times. The common assumption is that 'left wing' means advocating state intervention in the free-market and gen-erous support for those unable to work, be it due to disability or lack of available work. The right wing tends to be associated with small state, free market economics and individual self-sufficiency. There is clearly much more to it than that, but this is a simplified view of the basic left-right divide.

It is also assumed that voters will be distributed across this spectrum, with the highest concentration of voters around the centre, and relatively few at the fringes. This distribution of voters is said to heavily influence the ideological position of parties. According to Downs (1957), parties will position themselves ideologically to achieve maximum voter support. Downs assumes a single left-right ideological dimension, a bell-shaped voter distribution along that dimension (see Figure 4.1a) and the existence of two parties in that system. According to Downs these two parties, if they wanted to win, would approach each other in the middle. Downs assumes that voters would choose the party closest to their own position. Voter X might not be at all happy with the position of Party A, but it is still better than Party B. The same is the case for voter Y, but preferring party B over party A. In essence each party controls everything on their flank. Under a different distribution of votes (see Figure 4.1b) the parties would position themselves to ensure maximum voter support. In the case of Party B, more votes would be available to the left of centre, but no party could make such a radical shift in their ideological position and still remain credible. In short, the ideological position of electorally minded parties will be strongly affected by voter preferences.

There are many criticisms of Downs, not least the argument that parties do not just react to voter choice. They also shape and indeed limit them (Dunleavy, 1991; Ware, 1979). Parties, especially if they are in government, can to a certain extent shape the ideological preferences of the electorate. In addition voters can only vote for the parties that exist. It is often very difficult for new parties to break into a political system to provide new voter choices. Hence, party leaders do not always have to follow voter demands. They can to a certain extent decide what they want to offer (see also Chapter 7).

Further, there is much evidence to suggest that a single left–right spectrum is not sufficient to understand the position of individual parties and their ideological relationship with other parties. Two examples may serve to illustrate this (see also Chapter 2). The first is that parties that purportedly exist on the same side of the left–right spectrum may differ quite significantly from each other. One prime example of this is liberal and conservative parties. Both are traditionally seen as being right-of-centre, but they can show quite significant variation from each other. This variation is not just about being more or less right wing – a matter of centre-right/right/far-right – but about differences which are not easily explained purely by the traditional view of a socioeconomic left-right spectrum.

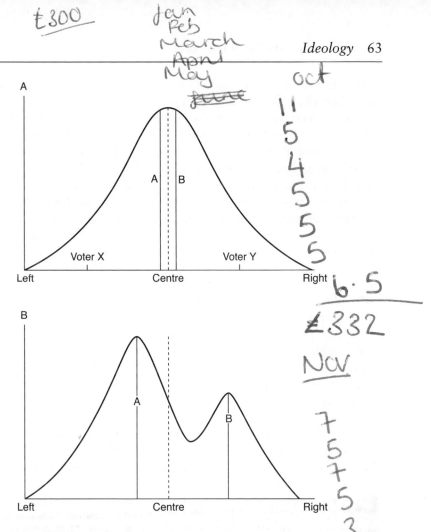

Figure 4.1 *Downs' voter distribution and party placement*

Source: Downs (1957).

Benoit and Laver (2006, p. 13) point out that while many liberals and conservatives may agree, more or less, on a fairly minimal role of the state in the economy, there can be a great difference between liberals and conservatives when it comes to the role of the individual in society. At one end we find conservative ideas of loyalty to the nation, and the need for conformity to certain cultural and social values often founded on religious beliefs. At the other end we find liberal ideas associated with the freedom of the individual to adhere to their own cultural and social values independent from what 'the nation', the state, organised religion or other institutions might think. So, while conservatives and liberals may agree on promoting a free market economy, they might well disagree strongly over issues such as abortion, gay rights and censorship. There then seems to be a second ideological dimension stretching between social-liberalism and social-conservatism.

Another example is the ideological position of the extreme right. While parties such as the British National Party, the Front National in France and the Danish People's Party might agree with their more moderate conservative neighbours on the issue of moral values, they often disagree on the role of the state. Many extreme right parties often support extensive intervention in the economy by the state and support for the less well off in society (provided these people belong to some definition of 'the nation' – in other words, are not 'foreign'). They, therefore, can have very right-wing policies on cultural norms and values, but at the same time very left-wing policies (although with a nationalistic and sometimes racist twist) on economic issues.

To add to the confusion there are issues that do not fit into either economic or social values – one main example being debates surrounding national self-determination and regional autonomy. A simple left-right scale combined with a social liberal/conservative scale would not be able to capture the full ideological stance of say the Scottish National Party, the *Partit dels Socialistes de Catalunya* (Socialists' Party of Catalonia), or the Italian *Lega Nord per l'Indipendenza della Padania* (North League for the Independence of Padania).

This has led Benoit and Laver to conclude that: 'a single "left-right dimension" [...] is not always enough to convey even the big picture' (2006, p. 13). This suggests that 'multidimensional policy spaces are [...] a reasonable assumption' (Warwick, 2002, p. 102).

It is, therefore, argued that parties are not simply expressions of left–right ideological differences but rather are to be found somewhere within more than one dimension where parties traditionally seen as opposites on the simple 'left–right' spectrum can sit side by side on some other spectrum. It is clear that to understand party ideology we need to go beyond the simple left–right ideological spectrum based on socioeconomic differences.

Political cleavages

The question then is what these other dimensions are that parties relate to. The most well known and most cited approach to dealing with this issue was developed by Lipset and Rokkan (1967). They argue that parties are driven by and are expressions of underlying conflicts and divides, or political cleavages, in society. Each party will represent the people on one side of some major political conflict. Their main argument is that the ideology of parties is shaped by two key societal revolutions:

the national and the industrial. These two revolutions have been the source of four political cleavages or conflicts.

The national revolution refers to the creation of the modern nation state. The idea of the nation state is, relatively speaking, a recent phenomenon, emerging from the treaties that ended the 30 Years War in 1648. Before this time the loyalty of an individual might be to the Pope in Rome on religious matters and to a local aristocrat on political matters, rather than to a central authority (such as a monarch). From around the middle of the seventeenth century the idea that each country would have a single political centre to which all the population owed loyalty on all matters started to emerge. In short the national revolution saw a process of unification of all power, both spiritual and political, in a single national centre. In the study of the nation state and international relations this is referred to as the rise of the Westphalian System, named after 'The Peace of Westphalia' – that is, the treaties that ended the 30 Years War. This gradual unification of power in modern states created two counter-trends which eventually led to the emergence of political organisations, including parties.

The first counter-trend was territorial and was driven by local and regional opposition to nation building, what has been referred to as the 'centre-periphery' cleavage. As modern nation states consolidated their power, 'subject peoples' or minorities within the emerging states mobilised to try to retain or regain political independence. In other words, there were those who did not want to be part of the new nation states. This problem of incomplete 'nation building' is often associated with former European colonies, especially in Africa (Clapham, 1996). When former colonies gained their independence their borders were based on the old colonial borders. These in turn were based on agreements between European powers. They thus ignored traditional tribal and national feelings that colonial populations might have. This meant that people on either side of a border between two former colonies might have more in common with each other than with people in the state they found themselves in. This then led to internal conflict as groups within a state sought independence. Sometimes the struggle for independence was done though political means (that is, a political party), but often via military means when political means failed.

However, while often associated with former colonies, this issue has also affected European states. There are numerous examples of how this 'centre vs. periphery' cleavage has affected the creation and ideological stance of political parties: The Scottish National Party, Plaid Cymru and Sinn Fein in the United Kingdom; both the Basque Country and Catalonia in Spain have left and right wing nationalist parties arguing for further autonomy or even independence; the Belgian party system is divided by language with Flanders and Wallonia spawning separate parties and Francophone parties in Quebec resist rule by Ottawa. In addition one could argue that Euro-sceptic parties such as Junibevægelsen (*June Movement*) in Denmark and the United Kingdom Independence Party are evidence of a new form of EU centre-periphery cleavage. Brussels as the 'capital' of the EU is the new political centre, and the population of (some) member states become the periphery resisting their inclusion in the EU. This has also affected more traditional parties, many of whom have taken a strong anti-integration ('anti-Brussels') stance.

The second political cleavage created by the national revolution is between church and state. As the state consolidated its power it not only acquired control over temporal matters within its territory, but also over issues which the church felt it had a stake in, such as school curriculums, the role of the church in politics, and moral issues such as abortion, pornography, and gay rights. Again, parties mobilised on religious grounds, most notable in the form of Christian Democratic parties found in, for example, Germany, but also, sometimes to a lesser extent, in much of the rest of Europe. Christian Democratic parties are also found in Chile and Mexico. It could be argued that the rise of the Christian right in the United States and its increased strength in the Republican Party is an example of this cleavage at work. The Christian right in the United States is very different from Christian Democracy in Europe but is equally driven by the debate over the role of the state and the church in political, social and moral life. Further examples of parties based on religion are the Israeli *Shas* (Sfarad's Guards of the Torah) and United Torah Judaism, both based on religious conservatism.

The industrial revolution likewise created two political cleavages. The most well know is the class cleavage which is the basis of the traditional left–right ideological spectrum. Almost every European state is dominated by the traditional socialist/social democratic/ labour party vs. liberal/conservative party struggle. A partial exception is Ireland, where reactions to independence are still a major organising factor. The two main parties find their origins in support (*Fine Gael*) and opposition (*Fianna Fail*) to the treaty that granted The Republic of Ireland (minus the six counties making up Northern Ireland or Ulster) independence from the United Kingdom. For that reason The Republic of Ireland is seen as a somewhat 'deviant case' compared to other European countries because its party system is lacking the traditional left–right class cleavage (Gallagher, 1985). Many countries outside Europe, but with strong links to Europe, are similarly affected by the class cleavage in some form, including Australia and New Zealand. There are several exceptions, including the United States and Africa, both of which we will look at later.

The second cleavage created by the industrial revolution was the struggle between urban and rural concerns. As the industrial revolution swept across Europe from the late seventeenth century onwards the agricultural sector lost much of its former predominance to the new industrial urban centres. Rural populations saw themselves sidelined and ignored as urban concerns took centre stage. As a result people mobilised, which sometimes lead to agrarian parties being formed, particularly in Scandinavia and Eastern Europe, where this aspect of political life still plays a significant role in party politics.

A final element of Lipset and Rokkan's ideas on how political cleavages have structured the ideological makeup of political parties, is that, at least when they wrote on this in the 1960s, these political cleavages were seen as being more or less permanent. Most of the cleavages and the associated parties were in place by the 1920s and very little had changed since then – the cleavage structures had frozen in place. In other words, party ideology can to a large extent be explained by the existence and overlap of these four political cleavages. Not all countries will have all, some may only have one, but in essence all parties are shaped by one or more of these cleavages. Whether this still holds early in the twenty-first century will be explored later.

Party families

The concern with ideologies has led to the development of one of the key comparative tools in party politics: the idea of party families. Party families are one of the most important ways in which parties are categorised and compared both within countries and cross-nationally. Like the idea of party types, the party family framework allows us to categorise parties and thus helps us provide structure to the often fractured and confusing party politics of democratic countries. However, a party family is different from a party type. Where a party type focuses mainly on organisational concerns, a party family is based primarily on ideology.

The party family is a way of grouping parties, principally according to their links with one or more societal conflicts or cleavages. So, most Christian Democratic parties are based on both religion and 'anti-socialist' conservatism – that is, they are shaped by both the class-cleavage and the church-state cleavage. Regional and separatist parties such as those found in Scotland and Catalonia are affected by both the centre-periphery and the class cleavages.

One of the main contributors to the party family approach is von Beyme (1985). While von Beyme does not agree entirely with Lipset and Rokkan's view of political cleavages, the idea of party ideology being shaped by societal conflict is still central to his exploration of party families (von Beyme, 1985, p. 23). Von Beyme identifies nine party families as being common to Western Europe and, according to some authors, beyond (see Mair and Mudde, 1998).

The first party family to emerge was the Liberals. Liberal Parties, in the cadre-party sense, evolved slowly over time beginning from the late seventeenth century. However, the term 'liberal' as a political label did not come into use in the English language until 1815 (von Beyme, 1985, p. 31), but many of the ideas associated with 'liberalism', such a greater individual freedom, were to be found among the so-called English 'Whigs' as far back as 1688. Liberal parties were originally dedicated to promoting the interests of the emerging middle class against aristocratic privilege and entrenched political power. They were often ranged against supporter of the monarchy, and the privileges bestowed by the monarch on loyal servants – privileges which included uncontested seats in parliament. Liberals have generally been seen as defenders of liberal democracy and individual freedom.

The next party family to emerge was the conservatives. Early conservatism is often associated with protecting royal and aristocratic privilege, and has deep historical roots. However, as political organisations Conservative parties emerged as a reaction to the rise of liberal parties. Von Beyme writes that 'Conservatism is a movement to defend positions which are threatened or – as in the French Revolution – already lost' (von Beyme, 1985, p. 46). Hence, the reason for conservative parliamentarians starting to organise in more formal structures was to defend the status quo (or Royal privilege) against liberal demands for the enfranchisement of the middle class and a reduction in the power of the monarchy and the aristocracy. Nevertheless, conservative parties tended to end up accepting most of the liberal party family's demands for democratic equality. Eventually the main struggle between these two families would not be primarily about the differences between them. Instead it became about which one of them would be the main defender of what they held in common against socialist and social democratic parties. Hence, most countries will have *either* a conservative *or* a liberal party dominating the right wing of the political spectrum. Seldom will there be both types of equal size.

The next party family to develop in opposition to both liberals and conservatives, were socialist and social democratic parties. These parties were created, often with trade union help, to defend the interests of the working class against the property owning economic elite (in other words, the interest groups behind liberal and conservative parties). In most European countries socialist and social democratic parties form the main governing alternative to liberal and conservative parties.

While these three party families emerged in rough chronological order (liberal, conservative, socialist/social democratic) the remaining party families do not necessarily follow such a straightforward line.

Christian democratic parties form a party family often based on catholic opposition to liberal secularism. Most have long since taken a non-denominational (that is, largely ignoring Protestant/Catholic divisions) route and are no-longer associated with any specific branch of Christianity, but rather based on religious conservatism. They have tended to form as an alternative to a strong conservative party in their respective country. Where there is a strong Christian democratic party there tends not to be a strong conservative party (for example Germany) and vice versa (for example the United Kingdom and Scandinavia). In short, Christian democrats and conservatives both fulfil the role as centre-right opposition to the main centre left socialist/social democratic party.

The Communist party family was created in the wake of the Russian Revolution of 1917. Their main declared purpose was to defend the working class against two main 'enemies'. The first opponent was the liberal and conservative party families – these, being as they were, often associated with property (especially factory) owners and inherited wealth and privilege. The second opponent targeted by the communists were the moderate centre-left socialist and social democratic parties. The socialist and social democratic parties were seen as having been co-opted by the right-wing parties into the state and were, therefore, no longer effective in defending the 'true' interests of the working class. Most communist parties were originally formed with support from the Communist Party of the Soviet Union (CPSU). Indeed the communist parties in many countries did not see themselves as separate parties but as 'local' branches of the 'mother party' in the Soviet Union (this will be explored further in Chapter 10). Later many broke with the CPSU and became 'Euro-communists' – still communists, but no-longer beholden to the CPSU. Key examples of this development include the Italian and French communist parties.

A further party family is made up of agrarian parties created to defend the interest of farming communities against the alleged neglect of the urban elite – as outlined in the above discussion of the rural–urban political cleavage created by the 'industrial revolution'. In a number of countries agrarian parties had a brief time of success between the First and Second World Wars, but failed to make much headway. This lack of success was driven by the fact that their concerns were either too marginal (with the decline of agriculture and rise of industry) or were co-opted by conservative parties (as happened in the United Kingdom). They have had some success in Scandinavia, although here they have often grown beyond the agrarian origins into broad centre-right parties. Very few specific agrarian parties survive, with a few exceptions in Eastern Europe.

A party family closely linked to the national revolution is made up of regional and ethnic parties based very much on Lipset and Rokkan's centre–periphery cleavage. These emerged to defend the rights of minorities against the national political centre in places such as Scotland, Wales, the Basque Country and Catalonia. These parties are to be found on both sides of the traditional left–right spectrum, albeit perhaps more often on the left than the right. Wanting to loosen the ties of one part of a country from central control, or even create a new country out of one part of an exciting one, is a serious challenge to the status quo. Such a challenge lends it self more easily to the left wing than the right wing.

One party family which has seen considerable fluctuations in support are right wing extremist parties. These rose to particular (and catastrophic) prominence in the lead up to the Second World War, especially in Germany, Italy and several East European states. This party family has seen a re-emergence since the 1970s, mainly as protest parties against the main-stream governing parties of the centre-right and centre-left. In Scandinavia some emerged as a protest against what was seen as excessively high taxes, which then morphed into protest against immigration. The anti-immigration stance is common to many organisations in the far-right party family.

Finally there is what von Beyme refers to as the ecology movement (or Green Parties). These parties mobilised in protest against the growth-oriented society, what they saw as excessive use of natural resources and the environmental damage caused by modern industrial societies. At the time when von Beyme was writing global warming and climate change were not yet on the agenda, but have since become a central concern for this party family.

Ideology in contemporary European party politics

The next big question is the extent to which the traditional views of ideology, most notable the idea of fast frozen political cleavages, are still relevant for the context, that is Europe politics, they were originally based on. Can these four ideological divides still adequately explain party ideology?

One of the key areas of debate in the context of European party ideology is whether and to what extent we are seeing the rise of a 'new', 'post-material' or 'post-industrial' politics. This has been an ongoing debate since at least 1977 when Inglehart published his *Silent Revolution:*

Changing Values and Political Styles among Western Politics. He argues that a number of key factors are changing the underlying values of voters, something which will eventually feed through to political parties and cause elites to change their ideological and policy positions. Basically people tend to worry most about the needs that are most difficult to meet due to a lack of supply in that particular area. They are much less worried about needs that are easy to satisfy. For example, if food is plentiful, but the weather arctic the need for shelter is going to be more of a concern than the need to eat. In addition, there is a hierarchy of needs. In other words, certain needs will take precedence over others. In this hierarchy physiological needs tend to come first: first we need to eat; then ensure our physical safety; then find shelter and so on. Once those basic needs have been secured people will start to turn to satisfying other needs, such as 'love, belonging and esteem' and 'intellectual and aesthetic satisfaction'. In short, the desire to live in a house with nice fittings and beautiful carpets is going to be lower down the order of priorities if one is starving to death.

In the context of modern party ideology the important thing to note is that since the Second World War, Western Europe has experienced unprecedented levels of prosperity and an absence of the wars between great powers that have been a regular occurrence in the continent's history. This is not to say that there is not poverty and sometimes hunger, but at least in Western Europe this is no longer on a mass scale. In short, basic needs are more or less taken care off. 'Old style' left wing concerns such as avoiding starvation in case of joblessness and the provision of free healthcare have been largely dealt with.

As a result, so-called 'post-materialist' issues have come to the fore, which, it is argued, are having a significant effect on the ideological stances of parties. The old ideological positions based on materialist needs no longer reflect the current demands of voters, which means that if parties want to survive electorally they need to adjust their ideological position. According to Inglehart (1977, pp. 40–50) these post-materialist issues include wanting increased influence on political decisions, better work-life balance and civil liberties such a freedom of speech.

The question now is whether, how and to what extent these changes have affected political parties. If indeed the old political cleavages were losing their power and are being replaced or at least joined by new concerns a number of things might happen. One possible symptom of new political cleavages coming for the fore would be the rise of new political parties carrying the banner of 'new politics'. This is after all how the traditional political cleavages found expression: with the rise of social democratic and labour parties representing one side of the class cleavage being the prime example. Any rise in 'new politics' parties would be matched by an equal decline in the support for parties based on traditional cleavages. We now need to consider whether this has in fact happened.

Figure 4.2 shows the combined electoral support for the main party families in 16 West European states starting in the 1950s and ending in the mid-2000s. As we can see, two of the older traditional party families, social democrats and Christian Democrats have indeed seen a decline in voter support in the post-Second World War era. This would suggest that some of the political cleavages that motivated them have declined in power draining off voters to other parties. However, having said that, despite their decline they still dominate the party systems of Western Europe. The only two party families that are new on the scene are the Greens and the New Left.

The Greens are definitely a reflection of a fairly recent concern with environmental issues and could be seen as evidence of a rise in new politics not directly related to the traditional political cleavages. The new left can also be seen as a reflection of new politics and certainly post-materialist and post-industrial concerns. Many new left parties have found their main drive in issues such as gender equality, civic liberties, anti-racism, anti-homophobia and green issues, all key post-materialist/industrial issues. However, these two groups taken together, while certainly managing to make an impact, have never come even close to challenging the parties based on traditional cleavages in a major way. There has been a rise in the far right, and as we shall see this may in fact be a reflection of a new political cleavage. However, again as with the greens and the new left, their rise has been notable, but not enough to unseat the traditional parties from their dominant position.

Hence, while there is some, albeit limited, evidence of post-material/industrial concerns finding a place in West European party politics in the form of new parties, there is also the possibility that new concerns are being absorbed into the ideological stance of traditional parties. In other words, although they were created as vessels for traditional political cleavages, the older parties are working to stay relevant by positioning themselves in relation to new political cleavages. It has been argued that the so-called new-politics of the post-war years was relatively smoothly incorporated into existing cleavage structures (Kriesi et al., 2006). According to this argument, the four traditional cleavages in Western Europe (centre–periphery; rural–urban; state–church; and class) essentially boiled down to only two: a cultural cleavage related mainly to the role of religion; and a socioeconomic one based on social class (Kriesi et al., 2006, p. 923). These two cleavages lost much of their potency with the rise in both prosperity and secularization in post-war Europe, but were revitalised by the rise of 'new politics'. New politics added concerns over social justice to the class cleavage and transformed the cultural

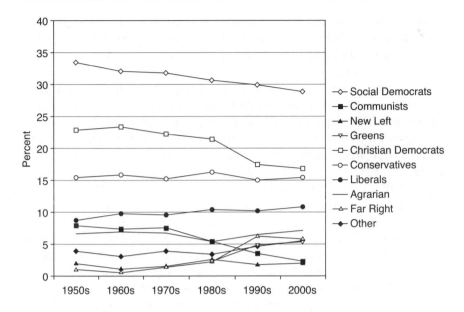

Figure 4.2 *The electoral support for party families*

Source: Gallagher, Laver and Mair (2011).

dimension's focus on religion to a broader debate between social liberalism and social conservatism generally. Hence, 'the new social movements did not add any fundamentally new dimensions to the political space, but transformed the meaning of the two already existing ones' (Kriesi et al., 2006, p. 924). What 'new politics' added to party politics was, therefore, less the rise of new parties with ideologies driven by new conflicts, but more of a transformation of existing parties and their ideologies.

Globalisation has also had an effect on the ideological stances of political parties. Globalisation has created new conflicts between what has been referred to as the winners and the losers from the globalisation process (Kriesi et al., 2006). The winners are those working in sectors that thrive from to international competition and thus welcome globalisation – banking being an obvious example. The losers are people who strongly associate themselves with traditional national values; those working in sectors traditionally protected from international competition, but increasingly forced to open up; and all unskilled workers. However, as with new politics, globalisation has been incorporated into the existing cleavages. In this context the class cleavage will now be dominated by a debate over whether to open up the national economy to international competition, or use the state to protect it from world markets. The cultural dimension will take on a distinct national and ethnic character: the protection of 'national values' against multiculturalism brought on by, among other things, immigration.

In essence, it has been argued that existing parties have a very large 'adaptive capacity' (Kriesi et al., 2006, p. 924). It is suggested that mainstream parties of both the left and the right will adopt moderate 'global integration' positions (Kriesi et al., 2006, p. 926). This also suggests that globalisation has created a powerful new demand from the 'losers' for protection against the effects of globalisation. Those parties that are able to meet that demand best will be a driving force for change in existing party systems. So, just as the demands of the 'losers' of industrialisation – the working class – created a long-standing struggle between left-wing and right-wing parties, so the 'losers' from globalisation will create a new dynamic between 'integrators' and 'demarcators' – that is, between those who want to embrace globalisation and those who want to impose limits on it. What we are seeing at the moment is that the far right has been most efficient in putting together a 'highly attractive ideological package' for the 'losers' (Kriesi et al., 2006, p. 929).

So, the new politics emerging from the 1960s onwards forced existing parties to change their ideological makeup to cope with new versions of old conflicts. Globalisation created the need to adjust ideological offerings to appeal to the 'losers' from the globalisation process. While the 'new politics' wave meant principally positioning oneself on issues of morality (gay rights, abortion and minority rights), so globalisation has meant dealing with the clash between integration and demarcation. So far the extreme right has taken the lead in a demarcation direction, forcing both the moderate left and right to take on demarcation positions to answer that challenge, often in the form of moderate anti-immigration policies.

Kriesi's idea that the mainstream centre right and centre left parties are adopting a moderate integrationist approach hints at another popular argument when it comes to the ideological development of parties, or at least the main moderate centrist parties: that of convergence on a neoliberal free market agenda. Some suggest that the traditional cleavages have not just thawed from their previously frozen state to be replaced by new conflicts, but that by and large we have seen 'the successful resolution of the societal conflicts which had been embodied in the traditional cleavages' (Kriesi, 1998, p. 165). That is, the old conflicts have been solved, or perhaps rather won by the supporters of the free market, and now all that is left is a disagreement over who is best able to manage the day-to-day running of the state. This is also reflected in the idea of the 'third way' taken by some social democratic parties, most notably 'New'

Labour under Tony Blair and Gordon Brown, and to a lesser extent the SDP under Gerhard Schroder (Giddens, 1998, 2000; Gould, 1998). The third way is seen by its supporters as achieving traditional social democratic ends, but to a greater or lesser extent using the free market to do so – and by its critics simply as selling out to the neoliberal dogma. At the heart of this view of convergence is the popular refrain that 'they are all the same now.'

While this point of view is popular there are many who argue that the convergence theory is in fact somewhat exaggerated. Some (for example, Haupt, 2010) argue that the main parties of the centre left and the centre right are in fact not converging but are keeping in tandem and maintaining their ideological distance – if one party moves to the middle it is usually because the other has vacated that political space. Others, such as Kriesi (et al., 2006, see above; Kriesi, 1998) have argued that while the societal conflicts that spawned parties may have been modified by succeeding waves of societal change, they are still more or less intact, if in somewhat changed forms. Finally, there are those who argue that the level of working class socialism on the centre-left has long been exaggerated and that the 'third way' is in fact not so radically different from traditional social democratic positions (see, for example, Hinnfors, 2006).

A final possibility when it comes to how parties have reacted to societal change is that they have to a large extent ignored it. Williams (2009) in her study of the catch-all phenomenon in France found that while the main parties had indeed taken up a catch-all position, including moderating their ideology as expected from the catch-all approach (see Chapter 3) this had not in fact been driven by ideological changes in society. Rather, the institutional structure of French politics has pushed parties in a catch-all direction. The main parties need to attract a wide range of voters to win a presidential election and gain enough seats to control a majority in the National Assembly. This is driven by a very disproportional electoral system and has forced the main parties to develop a political stance designed to be as inoffensive as possible. The name of the game is to avoid scaring anyone away – which means avoiding strong ideological positions. This does not mean that voters do not want ideologically committed parties, but for parties to win they have to attract people from a wide range of ideological positions. To do that, parties need to adopt moderate ideological positions. One of Williams' conclusions is, therefore, that in France 'One implication of these findings may be that for France ideology exists rather independently of the party system. The importance placed on parties by Kirchheimer as the vessels and perpetuators of ideology may have been misplaced in the French case' (Williams, 2009, p. 610). In other words, at least in the case of France, the ideological position of parties seems not to be related to 'demand side' factors – what the voters want – but to the structure of the political system. The demands of the electorate are, therefore, less of a deciding factor in the ideological position of parties than might otherwise have been expected.

That this may indeed be the case in a wider context beyond France has been suggested before. Ware (1979) has argued that partly due to the lack of internal democracy in most political parties (see Chapter 7) and the fact that new parties find it difficult to survive, the leaders of older more established parties are able to ignore new political divisions and keep to tried and tested ideological positions. The problem is that these positions 'by their very nature hark back to a vision of political reality that is probably obsolete' (Ware, 1979, p. 51). Because demands from the electorate are not filtered through to the party leaderships, and because new parties are unable to effectively challenge old parties, leaders of established parties are able to keep to ideological positions which may no longer reflect the underlying tensions and conflicts in society. Party leaders are able to both ignore internal demands for change and exclude most challenger parties from competing effectively. The result may be that parties and the electorate are drifting further and further apart, leading to dissatisfaction with the political system.

Party ideology beyond Europe

A lot of the discussion of ideology presented above is heavily based on European party politics. There is an open question whether the existing debates about party ideology, based on the European context, is relevant outside Europe. To consider that issue the following will look at three important geographical areas: the United States as the most powerful democracy in the world; India as the largest democracy in the world; and Africa containing some of the youngest democracies in the world.

United States

First, we will look at the United States. The United States is one of the oldest democracies in the world and is also the home to some of the oldest continuously existing parties. However, the United States is in many ways different from the traditional European heartland of party politics, not least so when it comes to the matter of ideology. The first thing to note is that the two parties, Democrats and Republicans tend to be seen, at least from the European perspective, as remarkably similar. In his analysis of party families across a range of countries Ware (1996, p.

25) put both parties in the liberal party family. It is however, worth remembering that 'liberal' has different connotations in the United States than it does in most of the rest of the world. In the context of US politics liberal is commonly seen as indicating left of centre. Very few Republicans would identify themselves as 'liberal'. Indeed, 'liberal' is regarded by some parts of the political right in the United States as a term of abuse.

Looking at the United States in the early post-war years Hofstadter (1948, p. xxxvii) expressed a commonly held view when he wrote that 'the fierceness of the political struggle has often been misleading for the range of vision embraced has always been bounded by the horizons of property and enterprise.' This very much supports the idea that both the Republicans and Democrats are in essence liberal parties. While Gerring (1998) has argued that the Republicans are sometimes seen as conservative and the Democrats liberal, he also points out that it is not entirely clear what this means in European terms. Ware flatly states that the Republican Party simply cannot be seen as a conservative party. The problem according to Ware is that the terms liberal and conservative have taken on different meanings in the American context (Ware, 1996, p. 26). He argues that Roosevelt 'hi-jacked' the term liberal as a label for his 'New Deal' which was in essence a massive intervention by the state in the market to deal with the problems of the Great Depression in the 1930s. As a result of this usurpation of a term usually associated with small state politics, those opposed to state intervention was left without a label. Hence in the 1960s 'conservative' eventually became to be associated with the anti-state position taken by the Republican Party. In the European context 'conservative' is most associated with an adherence to traditional values. A small state position may also be found in many conservative parties, especially since Thatcher added a strong element of neo-liberal *laissez faire* to the conservative position. However, traditionally in Europe 'conservatism' is not synonymous with 'small-state' or unfettered free market (see, for example, Gray, 1997).

In short, ideological terms do not have the same associations in the American context as they do in the European. The ideological differences between the Republicans and the Democrats are not as easy to understand as is the case when looking at the traditional divide between socialist/social democrats and conservatives/liberals in the European party politics context. However, that is not to say that there are no differences between the two parties. There clearly are. In his comprehensive overview of ideology in the American context Gerring (1998) argues that the two parties have been based on long-standing differences and two relatively continuous standpoints, even if those standpoints have been expressed in very different ways over time.

According to Gerring the essence of the Republican ideological position is one of national (if not always individual) prosperity, social order and patriotism. While this position has been present throughout Republican Party's history it has meant different things in terms of policy at different times (Gerring, 1998, pp. 14–19). In the period 1828–1924 the Republican position was highly statist. They took a mercantilist (that is protecting domestic industries from international competition) position to national prosperity and saw the state as having an important role to play in protecting the prosperity of the nation from foreign competition. In addition, the state was seen as having an important role in maintaining good social order. Gerring argues that while national prosperity, social order and patriotism remained the main Republican bedrock, by 1928 the means to their realisation had changed. From 1928 and to the present day the Republicans have come to view the state with suspicion. Increasingly the Republicans came to see the free market as the best route to national prosperity. In addition civil society, rather than the state, was the main source of social order. Hence the state should be kept out of the affairs of individuals as far as possible. The exception, as Ware points out, is when certain practices, seen as threatening traditional social values, such as abortion and homosexuality, have to be banned or at least limited. Hence the modern Republican position is one of economic free market liberalism and social conservatism, the main role of the state being to occasionally help out with maintaining the latter and largely staying out of the former.

The Democrats by contrast have had a long standing concern with equality (Gerring, 1998, pp. 19–20) and have gone through three different phases in terms of how equality was interpreted and promoted. In the period 1828–92 equality was about personal liberty free from state intervention, with the role of the state being limited to protecting property rights. Liberty was in much of this period limited to the white population – meaning it excluded African-American slaves.

The second phase was dominated by what might be called populism: a defence of 'the people' against special interests, particular 'big business' and monopolies, and in support of some limited redistribution of wealth by the state. Hence, the state was now seen as a means by which 'the people' could be protected from special interests and to improve demand-led economic growth through state spending on, for example, big infrastructure projects. This is most clearly exemplified by the New Deal.

The final phase, starting from 1945 onwards, focused on the extension of civil rights to previously excluded groups. Hence the appeal was less one of class (the people against big business) but rather one of marginalised groups against unjust exclusion from social and economic rights. In addition progressive social policies were to be achieved less through the state and more through an active civil society.

Hence, the Democrats have according to Gerring had as their core principle the protection of individual liberty, sometimes from the threat of the state, sometimes from exploitation by privileged groups, and sometimes from racial and other forms of discrimination. The Republicans have traditionally seen national prosperity, social order and patriotism as their main and enduring focus. At various times the state has been an enabler of or a hindrance to these principles, but the principles have remained largely stable. The differences between the Republicans and Democrats have therefore been real and enduring, but are not easily translated into traditional categories of 'liberal' and 'conservative' as understood in Europe. The two parties may both exist within a common economic liberal framework of 'the virtues of capitalist culture' (Hofstadter, 1948, p. xxxvii) but there has been and remains a wide scope for disagreement within that framework.

India

The second party system outside of Europe we will look at is India. India is in many ways a remarkable case and is notable for, among many other things, being the world's largest democracy. That alone makes it worthy of attention. However, it is also worthy of attention because, unlike so many other post-colonial countries, it has managed to maintain a relatively well functioning democracy – no mean feat considering its sheer size and diversity. The question is then how the European notions of ideology fit within the Indian party political system – and the answer is, as with the United States, not all that well.

As mentioned in Chapter 2, for a considerable time after it gained its independence in 1947, India was dominated by the Indian National Congress (INC) in a predominant party system. The INC won elections by massive majorities and controlled both national and local government until the 1960s. To understand the role of ideology in the INC it is necessary to keep in mind this dominance. No party achieves such dominance in a democratic system, relatively free of fraud and corruption, without sacrificing a good deal of ideological coherence. As Krishna (1967, p. 29) writes, the INC engaged in 'promiscuous accommodation of divergent elements' in order to maintain its dominance.

This means that thinking in terms of ideology does not necessarily make much sense when looking at the INC as a whole. It is true that the INC did adopt socialism as its official ideology in 1955 (Hardgrave and Kochanek, 2008, p. 271). However, this was, at most, the official line of the national leadership and certainly a very poor reflection of the party's actual stance, especially the further towards local politics one got. The INC was for a significant length of time successful at politicising and integrating large sections of the electorate which had previously not had a great involvement in politics. However, while these newly politicised elements of society might have been integrated into the party organisation, their integration into the party's official stance of socialism, economic development and democracy was less successful. Often, newly integrated segments of the electorate were 'caste conscious and parochial in orientation' (Hardgrave and Kochanek, 2008, p. 273). In short, as the electorate was politicised by the INC, so the INC was traditionalised by the electorate (Brass, 1966, p. 2; Hardgrave and Kochanek, 2008, p. 273).

As the INC's dominance started to fade in the 1960s so new parties emerged – often based on issues not directly related to the traditional left–right spectrum. Especially religious and regional concerns started to dominate rather than traditional socioeconomic positions in the traditional European sense. According to Verney (2004) there are five types of parties in the Indian party system each with different approaches to ideology (taken in a very broad sense).

One group is made up of various communist parties. While these parties are not based on caste or religion, their support tends to be concentrated in a few regions, especially West Bengal. After the end of the Cold War these parties have suffered from the general decline in support and ideological confusion common to many communist parties throughout the world. Most of them have moved away from revolutionary rhetoric in a more reformist direction.

Another group is the so-called transitional parties which rarely survive from one election to the next. They tend to be focused on a very specific and often local issues or the personal appeal of an individual politician.

Then there are parties that are based on fairly narrow religious, caste or tribe appeal. These parties tend to be geographically concentrated, neither able nor willing to expand their appeal beyond a fairly specific group.

The fourth group is similar to the third, but instead of religious, caste, or tribal foundations they are based on ethnic and regional identities such as the Tamil population in the south east.

The final group is made up of parties which try to be or actually are 'national' parties. In other words, they approach the catch-all model by trying to have a presence throughout the country and attract a wide range of voters. The only two parties to really achieve this position are the INC and the BJP. The BJP is very much based on Hindu nationalism and as described above the INC has been increasingly taken over by a plethora of local caste, religious and tribal concerns.

In short, while the INC formally adopted a socialist position shortly after independence, ideology has increasingly been driven out of the Indian party system by group identities based on religion, caste, locality and tribe. To understand the position of Indian parties, European party families appear to be of little use.

Africa

The final area we will look at is Africa. It is probably fair to say that successful, stable multiparty democracies have not been a regular feature of post-colonial African politics. Early attempts at multi-party democracy in the years immediately after independence very quickly descended into single-party-ism or military dictatorship. However, the 1990s, in what has been called the 'third wave of democratisation', saw a 'dramatic' move away from single-party and military rule (Manning, 2005, p. 715).

Although party-based democracies are now becoming more common on the African continent, the party systems in the new democracies have tended not to be based on socioeconomic cleavages – in contrast to European party politics (Burnell, 2001, p. 251; Manning, 2005, p. 715). The key socioeconomic cleavages in Europe, in particular the class cleavage, have been based on how the proceeds of economic growth, especially growth created by the industrial revolution, should be distributed. This also implied that there were a range of social and economic policies to choose from – that is, whether and to what extent the state should be involved in the management of the economy and the extent of the freedom of the market. As Manning (2005, p. 720) argues:

> the presumption in the comparative party literature is that by pursuing certain sets of economic policies rather than others, parties in advanced industrial democracies will redistribute national income to their constituents. Economic policies determine the degree to which growth benefits labour [workers] relative to capital [owners], or the upper income groups relative to the 'working poor', for example.

In Africa, parties have had a much narrower range of policies to choose from, largely due to chronic economic crisis and consequent aid dependence (Manning, 2005, pp. 716, 720). Many African states rely heavily on foreign aid, which often comes with ties attached as to how it should be spent. The government in question, therefore, does not have much flexibility to choose one economic policy over another. Whitfield (2009) shows that in the case of Ghana the two main parties, the National Democratic Congress (NDC) and New Patriotic Party (NPP) self-identify as social democratic and right of centre respectively. However, when it comes to policies actually pursued while in government, the parties have very little scope for divergence due to the country's dependency on foreign conditional aid (Manning, 2005, pp. 715–16). In other words, donor countries are to a significant extent able to determine the economic policies pursued – whichever party is in power. The differences between African parties are, therefore, not based to any significant degree on socioeconomic mobilisation since such mobilisation would require divergent economic policies.

One traditional view of African party politics is that rather than being based on socioeconomic mobilisation parties rely on politicising tribal and ethnic cleavages. However, while tribal and ethnic ties do play a role they should not be exaggerated (Basedau and Stroh, 2009; Burnell, 2001, p. 250; Norris and Mattes, 2003). Several studies have found that personal ties, often based on the region a politician is from, are far more important than ethnicity (see, for example, Basedau and Stroh, 2009). So, while there may be an overlap between tribal and regional origins, they are not identical and regional ties outweigh tribal ties. These regional ties tend to be based on so-called neopatrimonal and clientilistic relationships (Basedau and Stroh, 2009, p. 20; Burnell, 2001, p. 253; Manning, 2005, p. 715). In essence, politicians gain the loyalty of voters by ensuring that voters gain some direct, perhaps even monetary, benefit in return for their vote.

The main difference between parties and politicians are, therefore, not based on disagreements over socioeconomic policies, but based on who should benefit from access to the resources of the state. A politician's primary goal is not to implement certain policies but to gain access to state resources which can feed personal networks in their respective regions. African party politics, therefore, seem to be based on a personal 'scramble for the spoils of office' (Burnell, 2001, p. 253) rather than on ideological differences. This is well illustrated by the fact that in Zambian politics, prominent politicians frequently change their party allegiance, taking with them significant numbers of members and supporters. People are literally following the money when they join a politician in moving from one party to another (Burnell, 2001, p. 251). Again, as with the United States and India, the ideological battles identified in European party politics seem a poor guide to understanding what drives competition between parties in African democracies.

Conclusion

Based on the above, it seems that many of the common assumptions about ideology only really apply in the European context where they emerged in the first place. Here it still makes sense to talk about traditional ideologies even if they have changed considerable from their early origins. However, as soon as we move outside the European party systems, ideology based on socioeconomic cleavages decreases significantly as the basis for policy choices in political parties.

In short, it seems that party politics in the European context can still be understood in ideological and party family terms. This is significantly less the case in the other three cases we have looked at. In the United States terms such as 'conservative' and 'liberal' certainly have real meaning, but a meaning very different from the European context. In India, tribal, religious and ethnic ties have been rapidly replacing ideology as a mobilising force. In many African democracies personal ties ensuring access to the resources of the state are more important than either ideology or ethnicity in explaining party allegiance and mobilisation. Hence, when considering the issue of party 'ideology' in a given region is seems advisable to focus on local issues, rather than using preexisting models and assumptions derived from different contexts. Indeed, in many cases, such as India and African democracies, the very idea of ideology is difficult to apply as other concerns are of greater importance in determining party action.

Chapter 5

Party Members, Activists and Supporters

The mass party as described by Duverger is often seen as the standard of what a political party *should* be: an organisation based on a mass-membership organisation, open to anyone who is willing to support the goals of the party. In the mass-party model, party members are the life and soul of the party – not only campaigning on the streets to get their candidates elected, but also keeping those candidates in touch with the views and demands of the voters once elected. Clearly, from this perspective party members are an important element of party politics and, therefore, something requiring our attention.

As we saw in Chapter 3 the existence of party members is historically speaking a relatively new phenomenon – created, according to Duverger, by the mass parties of the late 1800s. This chapter will consider a number of crucial issues related to party members. The chapter will first consider what is meant by terms such as party member, activist and supporter. The second section will examine the development in membership numbers in European political parties. The focus will be on Europe as this is where membership numbers are easiest to come by, especially for Western European parties. Parties in the new Democracies in Eastern Europe have only recently started to settle down after a period of very rapid change, with parties emerging and disappearing again in short order. Parties in the United States 'do not have any kind of formal membership' (Ware, 1996, p. 90) and cannot, therefore, be analysed in those terms. Having looked at changes in party membership numbers the chapter will then consider at length why people might want to join a political party and what reasons party leaders may have to either encourage or discourage membership recruitment. The chapter will then explore some of the reasons behind the changes in membership numbers and concludes by considering the consequences for democracy of the apparent decline in party membership organisations.

Defining party member, activist and supporter

Broadly speaking, 'party members', 'activists' and 'supporters' make up the 'party on the ground'. However, what each category actually involves is far from clear.

Defining exactly what is meant by 'party member' is not straightforward. Different parties have different ideas of what is behind the term, and different ways of registering who they regard as party members. The easily identifiable 'type' of party member is the card-carrying and dues-paying member. This type of member will literally have a membership card and will pay a regular and specific amount of money as a membership fee. Being a card-carrying member will entitle the individual to certain privileges, such as being able to stand and vote for positions in the party. These positions will include being on local, regional and national committees or being the party's candidate for publically elected assemblies (such as local government councils or national parliaments). However, the difficulty is that some parties afford such privileges to those who have merely expressed some form of support for the party, but are not dues-paying members holding a membership card. A key example is the United States where the two main parties do not have formal card carrying members, but registered supporters.

A further noticeable element of the US system is that in some US states, voters do not register as supporters with the party. Instead, when a citizen registers to vote many states allow citizens to also register their support for one or another of the main parties. In other words, they declare their alliance for a party with the state and not the party. This is clearly different from being a paid up card-carrying member, but in many states will still give the same kinds of privileges in terms of standing and voting for internal posts.

The card-carrying dues-paying party member is often found in the most well established parties in longstanding European democracies. This type of membership tends to be associated with parties that adhere most closely to the 'mass party' organisational model. However, a plethora of more recent parties have far less formal membership structures, where some loose form of registration is enough to count – but also grants very little in the way of privileges. For example, when what is now the Liberal Alliance in Denmark was first founded, members were simply those people who had registered an interest in the party on their website. The Italian Forza Italia was based on a network of very informal 'clubs' set up through the sales force of Berlusconi's commercial company Fininvest (Hopkin and Paolucci, 1999).

Further, even within the more formal membership arrangements there are different ways in which one can belong to a party. Heidar (2006, pp.

303–3) argues that there are three ways in which one can be a formal member of a party: individual; auxiliary and collective. The individual member is the person who has paid a membership fee directly to the party, and may well have been issued with a membership card (although not all parties issue them anymore). Auxiliary membership is gained through organisations attached to the party, such as its youth organisation. A party's youth organisation may formally speaking be a semi-independent organisation and, therefore, be separate from the national party. So, being a member of the youth organisation makes you an auxiliary member, but not automatically a direct member of the party. However, someone who is a member of, for example, the party's youth organization might also at the same time be an 'individual' member – that is, be paying a membership fee to both the youth organisation and the national party. This somewhat blurs the boundary between the two. Finally, collective membership is through an organisation, such as a trade union, which is formally associated with the party in question. The trade union's members are at the same time collectively members of the party. As with auxiliary members, a fees-paying member of an affiliated trade union may also be a direct member of the national party.

The most notable example of such 'multiple memberships' is the British Labour Party. A person can be a direct fees paying member of the national party; a member of, say, UNISON, a trade union affiliated to the party; of Young Labour – the party's youth organisation; of the Fabian society – a think tank affiliated to the party; and of the Co-operative Party – an organisation which is affiliated to the Labour Party and supports candidates for public office. This way one would be a member of the party five times, but in slightly different ways. It would also give such a person five votes in electing the party's leader.

The exact definitional boundary between 'member' and 'supporter' is, therefore, far from clear, and there is a considerable grey area between the two categories. It also makes calculating the membership strength of political parties very difficult, something which will be considered further later.

As mentioned earlier, being a member gives certain privileges. However, depending on the party's culture, becoming a member may demand meeting certain requirements. Especially in the early to mid-twentieth century some socialist parties had very stringent membership requirements. So, the Argentinean Socialist Party in the 1930s required a new member to formally and in writing declare his or her support for the party's goals, rules and methods. In addition, the applicant needed the support of two existing members with at least six months membership (Heidar, 2006, p. 302). Up until the middle of the twentieth century it was not unusual for British political parties to tell applicants that their local branch was 'full' and that they would have to wait until a place became available. In addition, many parties have requirements for how long a person has to be a member before acquiring the full privileges of membership, that is the right to stand and vote in internal elections. It is probably fair to say that as many parties (although not all) have seen a serious decline in their membership numbers the requirements for joining and the time it would take to acquire the full privileges of membership have declined significantly (Heidar, 2006, p. 301).

There are also considerable differences in the level of loyalty that parties try to instil in their members. There was a longstanding tradition, especially among some major European social democratic and socialist parties, to encourage very strong links between party members and the party organisation. This connection was so strong in some parties that they were referred to as 'cradle-to-grave' parties, a term sometimes particularly associated with Austria. However, the idea is also to be found elsewhere. In the context of Denmark, Pedersen (1989) describes how membership of the Social Democrats could be an all-embracing experience. A party member might have his or her money with the Workers' Bank; buy the workers' co-operative's beer, bread and milk and 'when one had popped one's (workers' co-operatives') clogs, and could not be resuscitated by the workers' Samaritans, then the Workers' Burial Association would deal with the final arrangements' (Pedersen, 1989, pp. 56–7). For some, the party was almost literally from cradle to grave. This though is no longer the reality of membership for the vast majority of members. For most members of contemporary parties, membership means little more than paying their membership fee.

However, regardless of whether one is a member or a supporter, one may or may not also be an activist. As with 'member' and 'supporter' how to define an 'activist' is not clear. Clearly, an activist is someone who is active in the party. There is though no clear definition of how active one has to be to be regarded as an activist. Some people spend a significant proportion of their free time doing voluntary work for their party – campaigning on the doorstep, sitting on committees, and attending conferences. Others limit themselves to displaying a poster for the party in their window at election time. However, regardless of how formal a person's attachment is to a party, it is very clear that many modern parties are very keen on encouraging their members and supporters to also be activists. As we shall see in Chapter 8 local volunteer activist-based campaigning plays an important part in election campaigning.

What should be clear by now is that a very significant element of a political party, the so called party on the ground, is a very amorphous entity. The party on the ground is, in some form, a key element in the vast majority of parties and carries out very important tasks. However, it is clearly not an easy entity to define in precise terms. The changes that the party on the ground is undergoing and the consequences of these changes will be considered next.

The rise (and fall?) of party members

One of the key pillars of the argument that parties are in crisis is that party membership is in decline. This then assumes that a mass-membership organisation is something a party ought to have. Clearly political parties have not always had membership organisations.

Duverger claimed that the mass-membership organisation was invented by socialist and social democratic parties in the mid-to late 1800s. There is some evidence that this may not be entirely accurate. For example, in the United Kingdom both the Conservative Party and the Liberal Party had already started organising their supporters well before the time the Labour Party was set up in 1900 (Scarrow, 1996, p. 5). Also, some religious parties had mass-membership organisations by the time the left wing and trade union-based mass parties described by Duverger emerged (Ware, 1996, p. 66). Whatever is the case, the main argument in much of the literature is that the idea of mass-membership organisations emerged in the late 1800s and by the mid-1950s had become the standard way of organising political parties. Indeed, as was described in Chapter 3, the mass-membership party was briefly regarded as the party of the future and was seen as a new step on the party evolutionary ladder, superior to its predecessors (Scarrow, 1996, p. 5). However, this view did not last long and was soon replaced by arguments surrounding the probable and even inevitable decline of membership organisations.

In considering the accuracy of the claim that party membership organisations are declining we are faced with several problems. As we saw earlier, the nature of the party on the ground is somewhat amorphous, which makes it difficult to establish how many members a party has. First, and as we saw earlier, it is not always clear what counts as a 'party member'. It is usual to separate a 'member' from a mere 'supporter' – that is, someone who votes for the party on a regular basis, and may even sometimes volunteer during elections, although the distinction is not always very clear (Duverger, 1964, p. 62). Perhaps, the easiest way to distinguish between a member and a supporter is that a member has signed a membership form and agreed to pay regular fees for their membership (Duverger, 1964, p. 71). However, particularly in the United States, this kind of fees-paying, card-carrying member is not the norm. By Duverger's definition US parties are largely made up of supporters rather than members in this sense.

To complicate the picture further, there is also the concept of indirect member mentioned above. This is particularly important in the case of parties set up by trade unions and has been a distinguishing feature of the British Labour Party. The British Labour Party was originally set up by a group of trade unions and socialist societies, such as the Fabian Society. For the first 18 years of its existence it did not have any direct individual members. Its membership consisted exclusively of people who were members of the trade unions and societies who had affiliated to the Labour Party. The members of the affiliated organisations where then also 'indirect' members of the Labour Party. Only in 1918 was it possible to join the Labour Party directly. This means that while the Labour Party has typically had a direct membership numbering in the hundreds of thousands, it has had an indirect membership numbering in the millions (Laybourn, 2001, p. 177). So, when the Labour Party's membership organisation reached a peak of 1,014,524 direct individual members in 1952 its indirect membership was 3,071,935 – that is, more than three times as large.

Second, even once we have decided how to define 'party member', getting hold of membership numbers is notoriously difficult. Some parties are reluctant to share that kind of information with outsiders. This may be because a particular party is generally secretive about their internal life – a feature of many parties on the ideological fringes. Some parties may be reluctant to share membership numbers because they fear that it will make them look weak compared with other parties in the country.

However, it is just as likely that a party may simply not know how many members it has. It may sound strange that a party is unaware of its own membership strength, but looking at the work of Duverger and Panebianco (outlined in Chapter 3) it actually makes sense. The problem arises because some parties are highly decentralised. If a party is very decentralised, the centre may have little knowledge of, or indeed interest in, what happens at the local level. Hence, each local branch may know its own membership strength, but this information is not passed on to the centre. In the case of such a party anyone wanting to establish the total number of members would have to contact each local branch, of which there may be several hundred.

The difficulty in examining the development in membership numbers is illustrated by two important journal articles on the issue (van Biezen, Mair and Poguntke, 2011; and Whiteley, 2011). While, as we shall see, both articles reach the same overall conclusion as to the movement in membership numbers, there are some considerable discrepancies in the data for individual countries. Van Biezen et al. rely on data gathered from country specialists. Whiteley uses data from the *World Value Surveys*. In addition to using different sources the two papers use slightly different ways of presenting the data. This makes direct comparison difficult.

However, some issues still stand out. Van Biezen et al.'s data shows that party membership has fallen dramatically in Slovakia in the period 2000–7. Whiteley's data shows a slight increase in 1989–99 to 1999–2004 which are the periods during which the surveys he uses were carried out. In France van Biezen et al. see an increase in membership in the same period as above. Whiteley's data shows a decline. Van Biezen et al. (2011, p. 28) note that Austria is a country with continuing high levels of party membership. Whiteley points to Austria as a West European country with a high level of decline (2011, p. 25). There are several similar discrepancies between the data in the two papers. This is not to criticise either of the papers, but to illustrate the difficulties in analysing party membership numbers.

However, both papers agree that party membership is generally in decline. Looking at 23 European countries (East and West), van Biezen et al. (2011, p. 32) find that in all but six of them, membership numbers had declined, sometimes quite dramatically. They note that several former Communist countries have seen very dramatic declines which they ascribe to Communist Parties losing their dominant position in society. Whiteley (2011, p. 25) makes a similar observation. Both articles also note that several West European countries have seen major declines including the United Kingdom, Germany, and Finland – something that can clearly not be ascribed to the sudden change in the political system as in the case of former Communist Eastern Europe. Whiteley also finds that membership numbers have declined outside Europe. His data shows decline in Chile, South Korea, Mexico and Canada. He does find a small increase in Japan (Whiteley, 2011, p. 26). The overall conclusions are fairly clear: Whiteley (2011, p. 36) writes that 'party activism and membership have been declining across most of the democratic world.' Van Biezen et al. (2011, p. 42) likewise conclude that 'while political parties continue to play a major role in the elections and institutions of modern European democracies, it seems that they have all but abandoned any pretensions to being mass organisations.'

The argument that party membership organisations are in decline raises the question of what they are declining from. Presumably, there was a time when they were in a better condition than now, and it is from this former state that they are declining. There is sometimes a suggestion that there was some form of a 'golden age' of mass membership organisations – and that this golden age was located sometime in the middle of the twentieth century. The golden-age argument is closely tied with the mass-party model and the idea that parties *ought* to match that model of party organisation – that is, large membership organisations that help politicians stay in touch with the electorate via local branches as part of a healthy democracy of politically active citizens. In other words, the mass-membership organisation is not only what parties *used* to look like, but also what they *ought* to look like.

However, the mass-membership 'golden age' may be more imagined than real. Scarrow (2002, pp. 92–5) suggests that mass-membership organisations have in fact never been the norm in democratic states. She argues that the 1950s and 1960s constituted a fairly brief period of wide-spread mass-membership mobilisation: 'Before and after this period, parties exhibited an uneven pattern of commitment to, and success in, enlisting supporters in permanent organizations' (Scarrow, 2002, p. 94). This would suggest that parties based on mass membership should not necessarily be seen as the default party organisational form. It would also suggest that talking about 'decline' may not be entirely accurate. The talk of decline suggests that parties used to be stable mass-membership organ-isations, and what we are seeing is a change away from this norm. Scarrow suggests that the high membership numbers in *some* parties in the 1950s and 1960s were in fact somewhat unusual, rather than the norm (Scarrow, 2002, p. 94). The changes we are seeing in party mem-bership numbers should perhaps, therefore, not be seen as a change away from a pre-existing 'normal' state of affairs. Rather, parties are ever changing organisations that are in a process of continuous adaptation to the dynamic political environment in which they operate. Hence, when we analyse changes in political parties we should do so from the perspec-tive that change itself is normal, and any pre-existing state of affairs that parties are moving away from was itself inherently temporary. It could, therefore, be argued that mass-membership parties were an organisa-tional form that fitted with a fairly brief moment in the development of modern democracies.

Why members?

Having considered the problems of defining exactly who make up the party on the ground, and looked at what may be happening to it; there is one key question that has not yet been addressed: why have a party on the ground in the first place?

We have seen earlier that one of the key reasons for the rise of mem-bership-based parties was the extension of the franchise from a small propertied elite to the vast majority of the population. As the franchise was extended it became necessary for political parties to build, often large, membership organisations to mobilise enough voters to survive. However, while this might explain why the leaders of existing parties and the founders of new parties might want to add membership organisations to 'their' parties or create parties with membership organisations, this does not explain why citizens would want to become members of these organisations. The following will explore two of the main attempts to explain the existence of membership organisations: the concepts of supply and demand.

Party membership incentives: supply

Considering the apparent decline in membership number it may be worthwhile to consider why anyone would want to be a member of a political party. Several different theories have been proposed to answer this question. In Downs' model of democracy he assumes that party members act solely to attain power (Downs, 1957, p. 28). Consequently, members are power-seeking individuals and presumably any party that succeeds in obtaining power should see its membership rise. However, as is evident from the declining membership of many parties, even those with long histories of being in power such as the Scandinavian Social Democrats, this does not seem to be an adequate explanation.

It is true that Downs makes his assumptions about the behaviour of individuals primarily to create an elegant model and that '[t]heroretical models should be tested primarily by the accuracy of their predictions rather than the reality of their assumptions' (Downs, 1957, p. 210). However, as some government parties are losing members, the pursuit of power does not seem to predict changes in membership numbers. There must, therefore, be more to it than that. Nevertheless we should not reject Downs entirely as there are good reasons to believe that some degree of self-interest is involved and that for a party to survive it must be able to satisfy the personal needs of the members (Eldersveld, 1964, p. 272).

As outlined above, at least some parties were created to represent the interests of their members in parliament. For example, mass parties started out as working-class parties devoted to the protection of working-class interests. In that light it would seem sensible for people whose interests are being promoted to assist the party by joining it.

However, there is evidence to suggest that this commonsense conclusion is wrong. The problem is that any general benefits that a party will provide, say a minimum wage, employment laws and unemployment benefits, will be enjoyed by members and non-members alike. These benefits are collective and it would be difficult to somehow limit them to party members – at least in a democratic society. Rational thinking people, therefore, whilst having an interest in acquiring these common goods, have an equal interest in avoiding paying for them through party membership (Olson, 1965, p. 21). Consequently, in order to explain party membership we need some reward or incentive that is available only through membership of a political party.

Clark and Wilson (1961) identify three groups of selective incentives – that is, incentives that are available only to members. The first is material incentives – tangible incentives of monetary value, or things that can easily be translated into monetary value (Clark and Wilson, 1961, p. 134). In this category they include 'the improvement in property values for a neighbourhood redevelopment association or the increase in wages and other tangible "fringe" benefits obtained by a labor [sic] union' (Clark and Wilson, 1961, p. 134).

Their second group of incentives they call soldiery incentives. These include the enjoyment derived from socialising with likeminded people, and from being part of a group (Clark and Wilson, 1961, p. 134) as well as any feelings of loyalty to the organisation itself (Clark and Wilson, 1961, p. 136 n8).

Finally there are purposive incentives. These are incentives that are tied to the stated purposes of the organisation itself (Clark and Wilson, 1961, pp. 135–6). That is, people are drawn to a party because they believe in its goals.

Clarke and Wilson's selective incentives as a solution to the problem of free riding identified by Olsen has been generally accepted as a reasonable explanation of party membership (Ware, 1996, pp. 67–8). However, there are problems with their model, most notably in their view of material incentives. Their examples of material rewards include, for example, wage rises secured by a trade union and property value increases from neighbourhood redevelopment. These examples are exactly the kind of benefits that are subject to free-rider problems – a wage increase would be enjoyed by all workers whether unionised or not. It, therefore, seems necessary to develop Clark and Wilson's model a little, which is exactly what Seyd and Whiteley have done. Seyd and Whiteley explain party membership through their general incentives model (Seyd and Whiteley, 2002, pp. 89–93). They argue that five issues influence the decision to join a party:

1 Collective incentives, that is individuals want to promote certain goals, such as defending a national health service or employment rights, through the party.
2 Selective incentives which involve personal advancement through the party, such as using the party to get elected to a legislative assembly.
3 Group incentives – that is the belief that the party as a group can and is making a difference to the country.

4   Expressive incentives, by which they mean affection and loyalty towards the party.
5   Social norms, the meaning of which seems a bit vague, but seem to refer to the idea that people will be more likely to be active in a party (and not leave) if they were asked to join by a 'significant other', especially a family member.

These, or a combination of these, incentives will explain why people join political parties. Conversely, the deterioration of the same incentives may explain why some parties lose members, something which will be explored below.

Leadership incentives: demand

The other side of the coin is the extent to which party leaders want to encourage people to join. This will depend on whether they see party members as an asset or a liability.

There are a number of reasons why a large membership might be regarded as an asset. First, having a large membership can be seen to add legitimacy to the party. If a lot of people want to join, the party will appear popular and well anchored in the community, with party members acting as 'ambassadors' for the party spreading its message (Seyd and Whiteley, 2004, p. 361). Further, if a party is able to claim that it has a large membership that is actively involved in deliberation and debate about the big issues facing society, the party will have a certain level of democratic legitimacy (Scarrow, 1996, p. 42).

There will also be a direct electoral benefit from having party members. While party members make up a fairly small, and shrinking, part of the electorate they can usually be relied on to turn out to vote for the party whatever the circumstances (Scarrow, 1996, p. 43). This could potentially 'provide a crucial margin of victory' especially if turnout is low or the race tight (Scarrow, 1996, p. 43). However, while party members turning out to vote could help clinch victory for the party they also perform an important role following defeats. In bad times having a solid membership organisation can be essential for a party's survival and eventual recovery (Seyd and Whiteley, 2004, pp. 360–1).

In addition to being able to rely on party members to turn out on election day, the leadership also gain important benefits from party members as local campaigners. There is a tendency to see party members and labour intensive campaigning at the local level as somewhat old fashioned and less effective than modern high-tech capital intensive campaigning. This is one of the central aspects in the rise of the electoral professional party. However, there is extensive evidence to suggest that local campaigning is in fact crucial for a party's electoral success (this will be explored further in Chapter 8). It would, therefore, be very unwise for party leaders to discount the contribution that local campaigning by party members makes to the electoral success of a party.

There is also more to the local work of parties than campaigning. Having a strong local membership will help the party communicate with voters in a personal way that cannot be replicated through mass media communication or opinion polling. As Seyd and Whiteley write: 'members can be political communicators, both upwards and downwards. Upwards, they are *one among many* means of informing the party of voters' opinions [...] Downwards, members are one of the means by which parties can communicate their ideas and policies to a wider group of people' (Seyd and Whiteley, 2004, p. 362). Voters may get a great deal of their political information from the media and party campaigns, but it has also been argued that voters, through conversations with family and friends, will validate and confirm what they hear (Popkin, 1991; Seyd and Whiteley, 2004, p. 362). If the party has a large membership organisation it will improve the chances that the party's stance is validated when party members interact with their social circles.

This indeed is a crucial element in Lawson's concept of linkage. By assisting the two-way process of communication between politicians and voters, party members strengthen the link between rulers and the ruled.

Having a strong membership organisation also increases the pool of talent the party is able to recruit from, both for internal office holders, such as organisers, agents and managers, and candidates for public office. Membership organisations have been called 'greenhouses for new political talent' (Scarrow, 1996, p. 45). It is true that party leaders could look outside the party for potential candidates, but there are advantages to being able to recruit internally. Recruiting candidates for public office from within the party is more likely to ensure a high level of loyalty to the party, its policies and its leadership than people who are brought in from outside. As Cowley points out, by the time many politicians reach public office they have invested a considerable amount of time and energy in the party:

> By the time someone becomes an MP they will have been a member of their party for years, usually decades. And not just a sitting-on-their-arse-in-front-of-the-telly-having-paid-their-membership-fee-by-direct-debit type of member either. Those who become MPs will have been amongst the most active members of their party. By the time they reach Westminster, they'll have put in hours, days, weeks of unpaid work on behalf of their party. They will have canvassed, donated

money, delivered leaflets, and attended meeting after godforsaken meeting. (Cowley, 2005, p. 25)

Cowley argues that people like the ones described in this quote are much less likely to rebel against the leadership than some fair weather friend brought in from outside the party who has not proven their commitment to the organisation. Indeed, as was mentioned above, many parties require both candidates for internal positions and would be candidates for public office to have been a paid up member of the party for a certain length of time before they are allowed to put their name forward. In short, having a substantial membership organisation allows parties to 'reproduce' themselves (Seyd and Whiteley, 2004, p. 361) at all levels including in parliament. A party with few members may find that difficult, especially in bad times when outsiders with little commitment to the party will be less willing to be recruited and more likely to withdraw their support.

A final reason why party leaders might want a membership organisation is the funding it provides. As mentioned above, the typical definition of a party member is someone who has signed a membership form which includes paying a regular fee to the party. Indeed, as Duverger points out this was one of the main reasons why mass parties emerged in the first place:

> Instead of appealing to a few big private donors, industrialists, or important merchants, for funds to meet campaign expenses – which makes the candidates (and the person elected) dependent on them – the party spreads the burden over the largest possible number of members, each of whom contributes a modest sum. (Duverger, 1964, p. 63)

This lesson still holds today. Seyd and Whiteley (2004, p. 361) point out that membership funding is 'less tied to the whims, pressures and particular policy preferences of large financial donors'. Big private donations also cause problems for parties in that questions will be raised about what donors are getting in return for their money: 'accusations that a party is selling influence are much harder to make when its funds come from a wide variety of voluntary actors, rather than from a small number of rich supporters' (Seyd and Whiteley, 2004, p. 361). An additional problem with reliance on a few large donors is that the party and its candidates run the risk of losing touch with the daily concerns of the people they are there to represent. Addressing the issue of the need for large funds to run election campaigns Obama wrote:

> The path of least resistance – of fund-raisers organized by special interest groups, the corporate PACs [political action committee], and

the top lobbying shops – starts to look awfully tempting, and if the opinions of these insiders don't quite jibe with those you once held, you learn to rationalise the change as a matter of realism, of compromise, of learning the ropes. The problems of ordinary people, the voices of the Rust Belt town of the dwindling heartland, become a distant echo rather than a palpable reality, abstractions to be managed rather than battles to be fought. (Obama, 2006, p. 115)

It is true that large donations do hold a very big place in the life of modern politics and it seems the lessons of Duverger have been forgotten or abandoned under the pressure of running capital hungry election campaigns. However, for parties with mass memberships, membership fees still play a large role. For example in 2011 out of a total budget of just over £31 million the British Labour Party got over £5 million from membership fees. While other sources of funding were clearly very important, membership fees still accounted for about 17 per cent of the Labour Party's resources – money it would have to find elsewhere in the absence of a membership organisation.

The costs of a membership organisation

There are clearly many reasons why a membership organisation is a good thing to have for a political party. These reasons also explain why there is such worry about the decline of membership organisations (something which will be examined further later. However, there are also a number of costs associated with building and maintaining a membership organisation.

It was argued above that having large membership organisations might enable the party to engage in a dialogue with voters through the members. However, involving members in the policy making of a party in this way might equally limit the room for manoeuvre of party leaders. As we saw in Chapter 3 one of the factors that caused the rise of the catch-all party was the decline in class-based voting and the subsequent rise in electoral volatility. The result was a need for increased leadership control in order to be able to react quickly to changes in the ever more volatile and unpredictable electoral market. Having a large membership organisation might limit the ability of leaders to react swiftly to such changes since involving significant numbers of people in consultation on policy takes time.

However, even if it was possible to overcome the practical problems of involving the members in the policy-making process, there are arguments for why it may be better to avoid this. One argument is that internal party democracy is incompatible with parliamentary democracy, because it undermines the independence of parliamentary representatives. There is also a strong and long-standing view that party members, and especially activists – the people most likely to be involved in intra-party activities such as policy making – are more extreme than a party's likely voters. Even though this may not actually be true, the mere impression that they are may be enough for an electorally driven leadership to worry about the image that party members give the party. Hence, justified or not, leaders may be motivated to avoid the troubles believed to be associated with large membership organisations. Both of these arguments will be explored further in Chapter 7 when the details of policy making will be explored.

One solution to the problems of involving members may simply be to ignore them and just use their services when needed at campaign time. However, even this carries problems as not all members are likely to accept being ignored by the party leadership. Surveys of party members in Canada, Norway, Denmark and in the British Labour Party have shown that influence on policy is important to a great many party members (Pettitt, 2007, pp. 231–2). They are, therefore, not likely to take kindly to being excluded from influence and may protest in very public ways. This raises the problem that signs of internal disagreement are seen as being damaging to a party's electoral prospects. Internal debate tends to be framed by the media as being damaging to a party's electoral prospects and testimony to its inability to govern (Stanyer, 2001, p. 85). Hence membership rebellions are regarded as damaging to the party's electoral chances. In short, considering that both excluding party members from influence and incorporating them may be damaging to a party's image, electoral prospects and indeed parliamentary democracy as such, it could be argued that it is perhaps best to not recruit too many of these troublesome people.

A final reason why party leaders may want to avoid having too many members attached to the party is that membership organisations are expensive and time consuming things to run – time and money party leaders may decide could be better invested elsewhere. This is especially the case if party members are seen as a source of trouble. In Scarrow's (1996, p. 41) words membership organisations carry 'opportunity costs' which the leadership may simply not be willing to pay.

There are then several reasons why new party founders may avoid trying to build a party organisation in the first place; or why leaders of existing parties may be happy to let the membership organisation whither and perhaps ultimately die.

Explaining and reversing decline

Despite the arguments against building or maintain a membership organisation it is still generally seen as 'the done thing' for a party to have some form of 'party on the ground'. As will be explored at the end of the chapter, there are strong normative arguments supporting the position that healthy party-membership organisations are good for democracy. The question then is how we explain and reverse the apparent decline in membership numbers.

As we have seen the trends in membership development vary quite significantly between different countries. However, we have also seen that there are many countries which have seen quite dramatic declines in membership numbers. The question then is if this trend can be reversed in the countries where membership numbers *have* declined.

According to Seyd and Whiteley (2004, p. 357) the answer to this question depends on why the decline has happened in the first place. There are two main suggested explanations for membership decline.

One is that the decline is due to structural factors – major socioeconomic changes in society. Traditionally, parties attracted voters based on key issues such as religion and class. However, as such social and cultural identities have become weaker, people's attachment to parties based on group identities has also weakened. If voting and party support is now based on short-term cost-benefit analysis – that is, deciding at each election which party will give me the best 'deal' – then making a semi-permanent commitment to a party by joining it makes little sense.

In addition, Seyd and Whiteley (2004, pp. 357–8) suggest that a related structural reason for membership decline may be that the political market place has become much more competitive than before. Social and technological changes have provided a plethora of new ways of being politically active. Citizens no-longer define themselves politically primarily according to their employment, religion or place of birth. Instead, a multitude of factors come together to create someone's political standpoint, aided by the ease of access to information and social groups via the Internet. This has led to a rise of ad-hoc forms of political participation such as demonstrations, consumer boycotts, blogging and petitions and of single-issue pressure groups. These have provided alternative and, one might argue, less demanding ways of being engaged in politics than party membership.

If these major changes in society do explain the decline in party membership numbers, then this decline, or indeed any potential future increase, in membership numbers is basically beyond the scope of political parties to change. The rise and fall in membership numbers follow societal trends and parties simply have to cope as best they can.

The second possible explanation is that changes in membership numbers are based on the incentives provided by the parties for membership. In other words if parties provide more of the incentives for membership outlined previously in this chapter they could attract more members should they want to.

Based on extensive questionnaire survey evidence, Whiteley and Seyd (2002) argue that incentives-based explanations for changes in party membership numbers are more convincing than structural explanations, although structural factors still matter. In other words 'decline of membership can be turned around with the right incentives' (Seyd and Whiteley, 2004, p. 357). Indeed, there are several examples of how an increase in membership incentives has reversed a decline in members. The Labour Party saw an (albeit short lived) increase in members in the mid-1990s because the leadership decided it was worth growing the membership organisation. The leadership invested extensive resources in the recruitment and retention of party members. However, in the years after 1997 when the party entered government, the leadership became increasingly divorced from membership concerns, leading to a major decline in membership numbers. The Danish Socialist People's Party, the Danish Social Democrats, the British Labour Party and the French Socialist Party all saw an increase in membership numbers in connection with leadership elections in the first decade of the 2000s – elections which gave members the power to choose the leader, which provided a significant incentive to join. This would then suggest that membership decline is not inevitable, but can be reversed should the leaders want it. Whether they do or not depends on how they weight the costs and benefits of members outlined above.

The effects of membership decline

The final question this chapter will deal with is whether there are any wider reasons why parties should be encouraged to have members. As we saw above, whether party leaders want members or not seems to depend on a cost–benefit analysis based on what priorities the leaders have. However, there are more fundamental reasons why parties ought to have members.

Seyd and Whiteley (2004, p. 364) argue very strongly that a general decline in membership organisations would have the effect of undermining democracy. Without members parties cease to be linked to civil society. This is a theme also found in the cartel party model (see Chapter 3). Further, it is view backed up by Mair who argues that what we have seen in recent years is a mutual withdrawal by both citizens and politicians into separate spheres of activity:

Citizens retreat into private life or more specialized and often ad hoc forms of representation, while party leaderships retreat into institutions, drawing their terms of reference ever more readily from their roles as governors or public-office holders. The traditional world of party democracy – as a zone of engagement in which citizens interacted with their political leaders – is being evacuated. (Mair, 2006, p. 33)

This is a key element of Lawson's (1988) claim that parties are failing in one of their chief roles – to provide 'linkage' between voters and politicians. Indeed, this failure of parties to fulfil their representative function makes Mair question the sustainability of our current conception of democracy as involving some form of mass participation. Mair sees a worrying trend in the arguments about democracy where the popular (that is, voter-based) element is being stripped away, thereby ending up with a democracy without a demos (Mair, 2006, p. 29). This does not necessarily mean the end of democracy, but perhaps the rise of a much less meaningful version of it where the role of voters is radically reduced.

However, as we have seen, while Seyd and Whiteley (2004, pp. 364–5) acknowledge that recruitment has become more difficult it is far from impossible provided the right incentives are offered. Indeed, it has been suggested that there is an increasing desire among the public to participate in decision making (Kittilson and Scarrow, 2003, p. 63) – hence part of the reason why citizens are withdrawing from parties into alternative methods of engagement may be because many, if not all, parties do not provide adequate opportunities for engagement. As Russell (2005, pp. 47, 48) writes:

If political parties are to be seen as worth joining by those who are passionate about political issues, they must provide a real site of negotiation with political leaders [...] Thus a key part of ending the disappointment [with politics] is a re-engagement not only between the voters and the politicians, but between the politicians and the parties that sustain them [...] The potential prize – a better engagement between the parties and the voters – is great.

This theme will be picked up again in Chapter 7 where the issue of policy making and in particular membership influence on this process will be addressed.

Conclusion

It should by now be clear that party members are a central, but also much debated part of party political life. Despite disagreement and uncertainty regarding who exactly count as party members, supporters or activists; how many of them there are; and whether they are a good thing or not, there are few if any parties that have managed to survive and thrive without some form of party organisation outside of parliament. Party members provide legitimacy, crucial links with voters, and funds and personnel for campaigning. Many party leaders may view party members as a source of trouble as much as an asset, but the decline in their numbers has led many to worry about the health of modern democracies. It would then be fair to say that despite any doubts, party members continue to be a crucial element in the life and thus academic study of political parties.

Chapter 6

Candidate Selection

The last few weeks before an election usually receive inordinate levels of attention from the media. However, in many respects this part of the electoral process is to some extent the least important in terms of deciding who gets to run the country. It is widely recognised that the 'long campaign' – basically, the period of time from the morning after an election until the next one – is what decides elections, not the last few weeks that make up the 'short campaign'. The problem is that even the long campaign is only half the story when it comes to deciding which specific individuals get to run the country. The other half is the process of selecting the candidates for election.

When compared to the excitement of an election campaign or the passion of ideological debate, the importance of candidate selection is often under appreciated. Candidate selection is indeed something often carried out by small groups of dedicated party activists, behind closed doors, out of view of the general public. It is often a private process carried out more or less in secret. This is problematic because selecting candidates for public office is arguably one of the most important elements of a party's life. If the definition of a party is an organisation fielding candidates for public office (see Chapter 1), then the selection of those candidates clearly lies at the very heart of what a political party is.

Hence, the first part of this chapter will explore the wider importance of candidate selection before moving on to examining key elements in the selection process itself. The chapter will look at the impact that different processes have on those finally selected; it will explore two key areas of variation between parties in the selection process: territorial (de-)centralisation and the in/exclusiveness of the selectorate; it will finish by looking at two explanations for the under-representation of women in parliaments: the supply of and demand for candidates.

The importance of candidate selection

Regular, free and fair elections are seen as one of the foundations of a functioning democracy and are, rightly, given an enormous amount of attention in political debate and study. However, when it comes to determining and understanding exactly who ends up in elected assemblies, elections are only the last step in a long and complex process. What happens before the election – the selection of candidates by parties – is arguably even more important to the social, ethnic and gendered composition of parliaments: 'a party's candidates will help define its characteristics – demographically, geographically and ideologically – more than its organization or even its manifesto' (Hazan and Rahat, 2010, p. 6).

It has also long been recognised that control over candidate selection is a key factor in the balance of power between different actors in a political party. At the beginning of the twentieth century Ostrogorski wrote that while the day-to-day business of the local 'caucus', or branch, would be left to 'the small fry' the 'bigwigs' took control when it came to the selection of candidates. He further argued that control of the selection of the candidate showed who 'the real masters of the Organisation' were (Ostrogorski, 1902, p. 345). This is still seen to be the case today (Hazan and Rahat, 2010, p. 6). Those who control the selection of candidates will have a key influence on the ideological make up of the party's parliamentary group, which in turn will help determine the policy direction of the party. Because of that, it could be argued that the struggle over candidate selection will be far more intense than the struggle over the content of election manifestos (Gallagher, 1988). Members, it is argued, find it almost impossible to influence policy making directly and, therefore, direct their energies towards selecting candidates sympathetic to their particular ideological standpoint.

In addition, in many democratic systems, especially parliamentarian democracies, becoming a candidate for a legislative assembly is the first step on the career ladder that potentially leads to the highest political office in a country. A Prime Minister will often have served in other ministerial offices previously; becoming a minister frequently requires also being a member of parliament; to have any chance of becoming a member of parliament, one must first have been selected as a candidate.

Further, understanding the process of selecting candidates is important since across the globe, democratically elected assemblies are typically highly un-representative of the general electorate. This is especially so when it comes to gender. Only about 19 per cent of parliamentarians globally are women despite women making up more than 50 per cent of the population. By and large this under-representation of women is not because voters reject female candidates, but because parties fail to select them as candidates in the first place. To understand why that is the case one has to look at how candidates are selected.

Therefore, candidate selection is a key concern when trying to understand the composition of parliament in terms of ideology, gender and social characteristics, as well as when examining intra-party power struggles and cohesion.

Selecting candidates

The key point to understand about candidate selection is that it is a filtering mechanism (Norris, 1997, p. 3). The candidate selection process eliminates 99.96 per cent of those who are eligible to stand (Gallagher, 1988, p. 2). It can be seen as a multi-stage funnel where more and more people are eliminated at each stage (Krook, 2010a, p. 709; see Figure 6.1). The rest of this chapter is about how we go from often millions of eligible people via the vastly fewer who aspire to stand to a few thousand actual selected as candidates.

When considering candidate selection we need to consider both formal and informal factors that influence who gets through the funnel. Formal factors include national legislation on who are eligible to stand, usually involving limitations based on citizenship and age. They also include party rules determining both who are eligible to stand and how the process is run. It is also important to understand the impact of the political system of a country – such as whether it is federal or unitary and which electoral system is in use. On the informal side we have the impact of career paths (some types of jobs are perceived as being more conducive to learning the skill necessary for a successful political career); overt and covert discrimination by those who select candidates; and the ambitions and resources of would be candidates. These factors will have to be considered in the context of selection processes that are both enormously varied and also very often hidden from public view. Norris (1997, pp. 1, 2) boils all of these issues down to four key areas of particular concern:

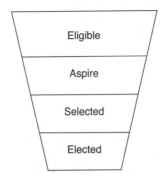

Figure 6.1 *Funnel of candidate selection*

Source: Norris and Lovenduski (1993).

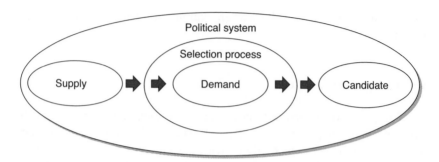

Figure 6.2   *The candidate selection context*

Source: Norris (1997).

the political system; the formal recruitment process; the supply of candidates (those who aspire for office) and the demands of the people with the power to select candidates (see Figure 6.2). The rest of the chapter will examine each of these areas in turn.

The political system

That a country's political system will have an impact on candidate recruitment should hardly be surprising. Countries such as the United Kingdom, the United States, India, Canada and France hold elections for their national legislative assemblies using single seat constituencies. Each party will need to select only one candidate for each seat. By contrast countries such as Spain, all of Scandinavia and Israel use List Proportional Representation. The process used for selecting a single person per constituency clearly has to be different from selecting and rank ordering candidates on a list. It will make a difference whether the lists in List Proportional Representation systems are open (voters can vote for individuals within each party's list) or closed (voters merely vote for the whole list and the party decides who is at the top of the list and, therefore, more likely to get elected). In short, each electoral system will need a different selection process – and electoral systems are nearly as varied as are political parties.

In addition the attractiveness of a seat in a particular assembly – be it national, regional or local – will differ depending on factors such as: the extent to which power is centralised in the national capital or devolved downward to local and regional government; whether a particular legislative assembly is unicameral or bicameral; and the party system (Norris, 1997, pp. 11–12). The issue of (de-)centralisation is particularly important. In federations such as Germany and the United States, regional and local legislative assemblies have far more power than in more centralised countries such as the United Kingdom. Hence getting a seat in a sub-national assembly will be more attractive, and therefore more highly sought after, in the United States and Germany than in the United Kingdom.

It is also argued that the political system of a given country will affect how centralised the selection process of a party is likely to be. First, the electoral system may affect the degree of centralisation in the candidate selection process. In essence, the argument runs that local *election* means local *selection*. Hence, in systems with relatively small, single member constituencies, candidate selection is more likely to be decentralised than in a List Proportional Representation system with much larger multi-member constituencies (Gallagher, 1988, p. 9; Lundell, 2004, p. 26).

Second, it has been argued out that a party's organization tends to mirror the political structure of the country it is operating in (Epstein, 1980). In other words, in a country where most political decisions are taken at the centre, parties are also more likely to be highly centralised. Duverger (1964, p. 398) did argue that the effect is the other way around in that the 'internal structure of parties [...] exercises a fundamental influence on the degree of separation or concentration of powers' in a country. However, most writers see the effect running from wider polit-ical structure to party structure (Gallagher, 1988, p. 8). So, the argument is that candidate selection in federal countries tends to be de-centralised, where as in unitary countries it is more centralised (Lundell, 2004, p. 26).

However, the empirical evidence for the connection between the polit-ical system in a country and the internal selection processes of a party is mixed. It has been suggested that a more important issue is whether a party cares that much about elections, or is more focused on ideological purity. In radical parties focused on ideology rather than electoral success, candidate selection is more likely to be centralised than in elec-tion-oriented parties (Duverger 1964, p. 60). In highly ideological parties, the leadership will want to ensure that all candidates meet a strict measure of ideological purity. At the same time, if no-one in the party is particularly interested in winning elections then there will be less resist-ance to the leadership controlling candidate selections. On the other hand if elections are seen as important – and winning seats a route to power and influence – then there will be many in the party with an interest in influencing the process. As a result, local elements of the party will want to have a say.

Further, in his study of West European countries Lundell (2004) finds no statistical connection between the degree of centralisation in candidate selection processes and either the electoral system of a given country or whether the country is federal or unitary. Interestingly, what he does find is a regional effect: the candidate selection processes in Scandinavian parties tend to be more decentralised than parties in Southern Europe. This is consistent with Gallagher's (1988, p. 10) suggestion that 'political culture [...] could help explain the form that selection takes.' He further argues that 'political culture [...] is naturally influenced strongly by historical experience' (Gallagher, 1988, p. 10). This is the line that Lundell (2004, pp. 39–40) takes when trying to explain the regional variation that he finds in his data. He argues that the Scandinavian countries are strongly influenced by their long histories of parliamentary democracy. There is a long tradition of popular participation in politics and strong local government. By contrast, Southern Europe has had a much more tortuous route to democracy. Italy did not become democratic until after 1945, and Greece, Portugal and Spain had to wait until the 1970s. As a consequence 'politics in Southern Europe is characterized by strong and charismatic leadership, centralization and authority' (Lundell, 2004, p. 40), which is reflected in the more centralised candidate selection processes of Southern European parties. It could, therefore, be argued that when trying to explain variation between parties in how centralised their candidate selection procedures are, looking at the political structure of the country they operate in may not be very fruitful. Instead we may be better off looking at the characteristics of each party (Lundell, 2004, p. 41). It, therefore, seems that while 'macro-political' factors (the political system of a country) may have an impact on the selection process – the selection of individual candidates for single member seats will be different from constructing lists in List Proportional Representation – it matters just as much how individual parties respond to these macro factors. To understand how parties respond we may, therefore, need to look inside each party. Making generalisations about how parties select their candidates is, therefore, not as easy as simply looking at the political system of a country.

National legislation

Much more indisputable is the impact that national legislation has on the selection of candidates. It is true that candidate selection is generally speaking relatively unencumbered by national legislation (Hazan and Rahat, 2010, pp. 3–4, 7). Parties are by and large left to do their own thing when it comes to selecting candidates for public office. Nevertheless, it would be wrong to ignore national legislation completely. Particularly in the United States, state level legislation has a huge impact. For the vast majority of legislative bodies, that is, the Senate, House of

Representatives, governorships and state legislatures, state law determines how candidates are to be selected, not party rules (Hazan and Rahat, 2010, p. 19; Ware, 1996, p. 259). That this can have a significant impact on who wins the selection is exemplified by Plouffe's (2009) description of the 2007 Democratic Primaries. States allocate delegates for the Convention that selects the presidential candidate using very different methods. Some are proportional to the candidate's vote; others use a 'winner takes all' approach. Plouffe argues that by understanding these differences better than the Clinton campaign, the Obama campaign was able to allocate their resources better, which helped them secure victory (Plouffe, 2009, pp. 167–73).

However, even outside the United States, national legislation affecting candidate selection still exists. Often legislation is less about how candidates are to be selected and more about who are eligible to stand for election (see Table 6.1 for legal requirements in selected democratic countries around the world). As can seen from Table 6.1 age and citizenship are pretty much universal requirements for would-be candidates for the lower chamber in these examples. Indeed, if we were to look at all the 208 countries and territories in the world – regardless of their actual level of democracy – 93.2 per cent have age requirements and 94.7 per cent have citizen requirements (see the ACE Electoral Knowledge Network website http://aceproject.org). In addition, in many countries would-be candidates have to register with the authorities and a number of countries require candidates to be resident in the electoral district they are targeting (which presumably would prevent a candidate from standing for more than one constituency at the same level of representation). None of this is likely to be very controversial or exclude very many people (in the case of the age requirement the criteria would be met automatically in due course).

However, a number of countries have more stringent requirements. Some demand that candidates must have been born in the country in question, which would permanently exclude some people (although perhaps not that many except in countries with large numbers of recent immigrants). There are though some requirements which would be a serious hindrance for potentially large parts of the population. This includes the demands for a minimum level of literacy and education, something particularly prevalent in African countries. In poor countries, such as much of Sub-Sahara Africa, which lack universal education of a certain length and quality this does have the potential to exclude significant sections of the population from even seeking to become candidates. It is largely the countries with low levels of literacy and education that have such requirements. In short, in a number of countries, national legislation is preventing a notable proportion of the population from the pos-

Table 6.1   *Illustration of registration requirements for candidates for the lower chamber*

Country	Age	Citizenship	Country of birth	Residence	Minimum level of education	Minimum level of literacy	Registration	Other
Europe								
Austria	•	•						•
Denmark	•	•						
Estonia	•	•						
France	•	•						
Germany	•	•		•				
Greece	•	•					•	•
Hungary	•	•						
Italy	•	•						
Poland	•	•						
Romania	•	•		•				
Spain	•	•						
Americas								
Argentina	•	•	•	•				•
Brazil	•	•	•	•		•	•	•
Canada	•	•		•				
Chile	•	•		•	•	•	•	
Ecuador	•	•	•	•			•	
Mexico	•	•		•			•	•
Paraguay	•	•					•	•
Suriname	•	•		•				
Uruguay	•	•						•
USA	•	•		•				

Country	Age	Citizenship	Country of birth	Residence	Minimum level of education	Minimum level of literacy	Registration	Other
Africa								
Botswana	•	•		•		•	•	
Cameroon	•	•				•	•	
Chad	•	•		•		•	•	
Ghana	•	•						
Kenya	•	•				•	•	•
Madagascar	•	•	•				•	
Mozambique	•	•					•	
Nigeria	•	•			•		•	
Tanzania	•	•			•	•		•
South Africa	•	•					•	
Asia and Oceania								
Australia	•	•						
Bangladesh	•	•						
India	•	•		•				
Indonesia	•	•		•		•		
Japan	•	•						
Korea, Republic of	•	•					•	
Malaysia	•	•		•				•
Nepal	•	•		•				
New Zealand	•	•		•				•
Thailand	•	•	•	•	•			

sibility of even trying to obtain positions of political power. This shows the importance of considering the issue of candidate selection. In most democratic countries there is a lack of representatives from the poorer sections of the population. However, when there are such stringent requirements to even become a candidate, such under-representation will only be exacerbated.

In addition to the legal requirements that must be met, the imposition of quotas for certain types of candidates can have a major impact on who is selected. The most common quota is for gender, specifically for female candidates, which makes sense since women are the most notable example of under-representation across the world. According to Murray (2010) at least 100 countries around the world use some form of gender quota, with France being the first to bring in a parity quota (50 : 50). Quotas come in many forms, but have the common purpose of alleviating the massive under-representation of women in parliaments. The extent to which parties actually stick to these quotas varies (Murray, 2010), but they still have a significant impact on candidate selection procedures.

The candidate selection process: impact of different methods

In most countries the actual process of candidate selection in a given party is rarely if ever known to the general public. Indeed, a ground-breaking study of candidate selection was entitled 'the secret garden of politics' (Gallagher and Marsh, 1988). The obvious exception is the United States where the process tends to be specified in state legislation. However, the rules, regulations and informal byways of this area of party life are vitally important for understanding who gets the chance of representing their party in parliament. It has been argued that rules on who are involved in selecting a party's candidates (commonly referred to as the 'selectorate') will have major consequences for the balance of power in a party. It will also have an impact on how easy it is for the leadership to control MPs (Norris, 1997, p. 7).

To illustrate the impact that different selection methods can have on MPs' loyalty to the leadership, Hazan and Rahat (2010, pp. 1–3) explore the behaviour of a particular (unnamed) candidate, based on real-life experiences in Israel. This candidate is selected by a membership-wide ballot, rather than a smaller committee as had been the case before. Once selected by the mass membership and later elected to parliament the new MP saw his loyalty as lying with the grassroots and not with the leadership. He was, therefore, difficult to bring into line with the wishes of the leadership – until, that is, the process was re-centralised under leadership control and the MP went from rebel to loyalist. As Hazan and Rahat point out this is not a one off example.

The British Conservative Party has been experiencing similar problems after the 2010 election. In the aftermath of a major political scandal that broke out in the United Kingdom in 2009 involving dozens of MPs from all the major parties, the Conservative Party under David Cameron attempted to show they wanted a new politics. One way of doing that was by inviting people not associated with traditional political career paths to apply to become candidates, and have them selected through new methods, including open primaries. This certainly created a new kind of MP – one not loyal to the party leadership, but to their constituency and/or personal causes.

The problem of independently minded legislators is taken to the extreme in the United States, where the party leadership have far less control than in many other countries. Even the rules are not determined by the parties themselves. This can be seen as part of the reason for the notoriously undisciplined politicians of American parties. In short, candidate selection processes may often be hidden away from the general public, but they are of vital importance to how political parties, and therefore politics in general, function.

Territorial (de-)centralisation and in/exclusiveness of the selectorate

What should be clear by now is that the variations in the way that candidates are selected have important consequences for politics. It would, therefore, be worth looking at some of the key ways in which selection processes vary. The following will focus on two crucial areas where variations can occur: territorial (de-)centralisation and in/exclusiveness of the selectorate.

Territorial (de-)centralisation is concerned with where the selection is done. For example, is it the party's national head office that is responsible, or a regional head quarters, or local branches? In/exclusiveness is concerned with how many people are involved. Is it a small group of people in the party's top leadership, or the wider membership? Arguably there is a link between the two issues. There is tendency to see decentralisation as also involving increased inclusivity – that is, if candidate selection is done locally it will involve more people than if it is done centrally: 'Generally the more decentralized candidate selection is, the greater the possibility for individual party members to play a role' (Hazan and Rahat, 2010, p. 55). However, it has also been pointed out that 'this is an inclination, not a rule' (Hazan and Rahat, 2010, p. 55). If all candidates

were selected at a single big national conference made up of several delegates from each constituency, that would be a very centralised way of
doing it. If selection was done by the chairperson of each local constituency party, that would certainly be very decentralised, but also less
inclusive than the central national conference. So, there *is* a relationship
between the two factors, but it is not simply a matter of decentralisation
being equal to greater inclusiveness.

Figure 6.3 summarises the relationship between the two factors. Some
of the positions in Figure 6.3 face quite severe practical problems and
should perhaps be seen as illustrations of what is theoretically or logically
possible rather than an indication of what actually goes on in political
parties. For example, in all but the smallest of democratic countries the
top right and top left positions would be very difficult indeed from a
purely practical perspective. Even in unitary states it would be difficult
for a single leader to select all candidates. As an example, the French
National Assembly has 577 seats. For the leader of a major party to have
to select that number of candidates would be a huge task. Likewise, con-
ducting a ballot of the tens of millions of voters for 577 seats would be
both hugely expensive – and no voter is likely to want to make that many
choices. Even in smaller countries (for example Denmark 179 seats; New
Zealand 122 seats; Singapore 94 seats) the task would be considerable.
Hazan and Rahat (2010, p. 47) do give examples of where a single party
leader selects all candidates, although this does seem to be fairly rare.

Indeed, these practical considerations seem to have had the consequence that candidate selection, as a rule, tends towards being fairly
decentralised. Even through the sheer diversity of candidate selection
processes makes generalisations difficult, Ranney, (1981, pp. 82–3; see
also Hazan and Rahat, 2010, p. 58) argues that in most parties selection
tends to take placed at the constituency level, although often with
national level supervision. In terms of whether there have been any
general changes Bille (2001) concludes in his study of West European
party rule books that the overall trend between 1960 and 1990 is
towards greater decentralisation.

However, the issue of national level supervision suggests that Figure
6.3 does not give the full picture. One of the things that serve to muddy
the waters is that often selection takes place in several stages, each stage
with different levels of centralisation and inclusiveness. As we can see
from Table 6.2 the national leadership often has some level of veto of
constituency decisions, or puts together a national 'pool' of aspirants
from which the constituencies have to choose. It would be fair to say that
being able to control access to a pre-approved pool of potential candidates will give the leadership more control than having to reject local
choices. Limiting the number of available choices tends to cause fewer

| | Organisational exclusiveness | | | | |
| | Most inclusive | | | | Most exclusive |
Territorial centralisation	Voters	Party members	Party delegates	Party elite	Leader
National (Most centralised)	All the party's candidates selected by all voters.	All the party's candidates selected by all members.	All the party's candidates selected by a national delegate conference	All the party's candidates selected by party executive.	All the party's candidates selected by the party leader.
Regional	The party's candidates in each region selected by all voters in that region.	The party's candidates in each region selected by all members in that region.	The party's candidates in each region selected by a regional delegate conference.	The party's candidates in each region selected by the regional party executive.	The party's candidates in each region selected by the regional party leader.
Local (Most decentralised)	The party's candidates in each constituency selected by all voters in that constituency.	The party's candidates in each constituency selected by all members in that constituency.	The party's candidates in each constituency selected by a constituency delegate conference.	The party's candidates in each constituency selected by the constituency party executive.	The party's candidates in each constituency selected by the constituency party leader.

Figure 6.3 *Territorial (de-)centralisation and in/exclusiveness of the selectorate*

Source: Hazan and Rahat (2010).

Table 6.2   *Illustrations of candidate selection procedures*

Party	National electoral system	Brief overview of process
Parti Socialiste (France)	Two-round single member seats	A call is issued for members to put themselves forward as candidates. In a small number of cases a prominent personality may be asked to stand in a particular constituency. Members then vote on all aspirants within a constituency. National committee must validate choice and can reject a candidate. Due to constitutional parity law some seats are designated as all-women shortlists.
Union pour un Mouvement Populaire (France)	Two-round single member seats	Party members select candidates within their constituency. Chosen candidates are scrutinised and validated by a national selection committee. The national selection committee then reports to the Political Bureau for final approval, although the latter body is seen as too large and unwieldy, and meeting too infrequently to have significant input.
African National Congress (South Africa)	Closed list PR, two tiers, national and by province	Local branches make nominations and select delegates for Provincial List Conference. Candidate nominations submitted to provincial level. Provincial List Committee, appointed by Provincial Executive Committee, screen nominations and draft consolidated list. To be on consolidated list candidates most have been nominated by at least five branches. Provincial List Conference votes on consolidated list and select delegates to National List Conference. National List Committee drafts national list based on candidate popularity. National List Committee vote on draft national and provincial lists. Provincial lists opened up for appeal, decided on by an Appeals Committee. Nation List Committee finalizes lists.
The Conservative Party (UK)	Single Member Plurality	National party creates approved list (includes training of applicants for national list). National list regularly replenished and contains more candidates than there are seats. Local branch members select candidate from national lists. Some recent experiments to increase number of ethnic minority and women candidate by requiring some constituencies to select candidate from 'A-list' containing higher proportion of desired candidates. Also some experiments with open primaries.

Party	National electoral system	Brief overview of process
The Labour Party (UK)	Single Member Plurality	Would be candidates fill in application form for National Parliamentary Panel (NPP) of preapproved aspirants (encouraged but optional). Regional Assessment teams interview candidates for NPP. Constituency Parties advertise vacancies and potential candidate contact the constituency parties to declare an interest. Local branches and affiliated organisations (e.g., trade union branches) within constituency nominate individuals for constituency short list. Membership wide vote selects candidate from short list. Selected candidate submitted to National Executive Committee (NEC) for endorsement. Candidate not on the NPP must attend NEC endorsement interview. Some constituencies designated as all-women shortlists.
The New Patriotic Party (Ghana)	Single Member Plurality	National Executive Committee (NEC) instructs constituency executive committee to invite applications from aspirants. National level officials vet applicants and NEC approves list of candidates for next stage. Constituency delegate conference convened consisting of constituency executive and chair of each polling district within constituency (typically about 100 delegates) and selects candidate from list by secret ballot.

Source: Murray (2010), Conservative Party (2012), Labour Party (2013), African National Congress (2012); New Patriotic Party (2009).

problems than rejecting decisions by constituencies once they are made. As Norris (2006, pp. 93–4) points out, when analysing 'who nominates' one should also, and ideally first, consider 'what choices are available'. Excluding certain people from becoming candidates by ensuring they are not available for selection, what Bacharatz and Baratz (1963) call a 'non-decision', is much more efficient and less problematic than vetoing selections once made. Indeed, party leaders have sometimes used the promotion of gender equality to make unwanted (for whatever reason) male candidates unavailable for selection (see for example Cutts, Childs and Fieldhouse (2005) for an example from the United Kingdom – in this case it went horribly wrong as the unwanted aspirant stood as an independent and won the seat). Hazan and Rahat (2010, p. 37) point out that based on the experience of a number of countries when the national leadership has a veto it is rarely exercised, which further supports the idea that filtering out unwanted aspirants before selection bestows more effective control that a post-selection veto.

Another issue worth mentioning is the degree of democratic control exercised by the membership, and the extent to which there have been any changes in this area – that is, how inclusive the process is. As is so often the case, the evidence is contradictory (Bille, 2001; Hopkin, 2001; LeDuc, 2001). However, overall it appears that two conclusions can be drawn: the first is that party members have acquired greater power to choose candidates; the second is that pre-selection has increased, or put differently the choice available to members has been restricted (Norris, 2006, p. 106). This again confirms that when analysing who controls candidate selection one has to consider not only who selects, but also who has the power to decide the range of choices. Clearly, being aware of the impact that multi-stage selection processes have is important to get the full picture. A highly decentralised and inclusive selection may be preceded by a centralised and exclusive long-listing stage, potentially undermining the democratic element of the second stage. Hence, candidate selection processes may often be done away from the public eye, but appreciating their intricate details is central to understanding who wins the chance to become a member of a legislative assembly with all the consequences for democratic representation that follows from that.

Supply and demand

The last issue this chapter will deal with is 'supply' and 'demand'. In this context supply is about who are willing to put themselves forward as potential candidates. Demand is about is what the selectorate is looking for in would-be candidates. The study of supply and demand springs from trying to understand one of the most notable features of modern elected 'representative' bodies: the massive under-representation of women. Despite making up over 50 per cent of the population in the democratic world, women still account for less than 20 per cent of parliamentarians, with a high of just over 40 per cent in the Nordic countries and a low of 12.5 per cent among Arab states (see the Inter-Parliamentary Union website – IPU.org). If we go back to Norris' 'funnel' (see above) this means that women make up more than half of those eligible to stand, but somewhere along the line get filtered out and end up amounting to less than 20 per cent of those elected. Most studies in this field have found no evidence that voters generally discriminate against female candidates (Krook, 2010b, p. 157; Murray, Krook and Opello, 2012; Norris, Vallence and Lovenduski, 1992; Studlar and McAllister, 1991). Hence, if the voters tend not to discriminate between male and female candidates in their voting choices, the explanation for the lack of women legislators must be found in those parts of the filtering process that take place within political parties before the election.

Supply

One of the reasons given by party leaders for why there are so few female candidates, and therefore MPs, is that women simply do not put themselves forward for political office – an idea reflected in several publications on women's under-representation (for example 'If only more candidates came forward' (Norris and Lovenduski, 1993) and 'Men kvinderne vil jo ikke selv' ('But, the women themselves don't want to') (Dahlerup, 2001)). In short, parties would like to select more women candidates, but there is simply a lack of aspiring women putting themselves forward.

There are two key factors that influence supply: ambition and resources. When it comes to ambition several studies have found that education is a key predictor of political activism. Education increases 'political knowledge, interest, confidence and skills' (Norris and Lovenduski, 1993, p. 388). This may not affect women unduly in much of the Western world where women's educational attainment often matches and sometimes outdoes that of men. However, it is a factor in many parts of the world, especially developing countries, where boys' education is given priority over that of girls'.

In addition, research has found that gender itself has a major impact on ambition, quite apart from any differences in educational attainment (Lawless and Fox, 2005; 2010). According to Krook (2010b, p. 158) this can be explained by 'long-standing patterns of traditional socialisation which associate men with the public realm and women with private'. Put slightly bluntly, men are raised to be ambitious and encouraged to build careers for themselves, whereas women are encouraged to think of themselves primarily as wives and mothers. This may not be overt and deliberate but is displayed in simple things such as buying girls a cookery set and boys a home chemistry set.

This difference is also found in survey studies. Lawless and Fox (2005) found that women were twice as likely as men to believe themselves not to be qualified for public office. In addition they also routinely underplay their chances of winning compared to men. Hence, this argument suggests that ambition and confidence is about gendered socialisation which drives women to underestimate their skills and chances and men to overestimate theirs, regardless of their *actual* skills and chances. As one senior female business women said about the private sector 'I believe that we will only have true equality when we have as many incompetent women in positions of power as incompetent men' (http://www.bbc.co.uk/news/business-12518277) a sentiment which could equally well be applied to politics.

In addition to ambition, resources also play a role. Simply being unable to pay to be a candidate can prevent people from standing. Even where campaigns are not as capital intensive as for example in the United States it can be expensive to even attempt to be selected as a candidate (Norris and Lovenduski, 1993). With a high proportion of women being concentrated in low paid and part time jobs compared to men, the lack of financial resources is likely to affect women more than men. In many countries once an aspirant has been selected as a candidate, the party will step in and support their election campaign. However, there is rarely any outside financial support available for becoming a candidate. This early cost has to be borne by the aspirants themselves. Indeed, in the United States the issue of financial barriers to women candidates has led to the creation of several groups aimed at supporting and encouraging women to put themselves forward as would be candidates (Krook, 2010b, p. 158). Two examples of this are the National Women's Political Caucus (www.nwpc.org) and The Wish List (www.thewishlist.org). In addition to raising funding these organisations also provide training and encouragement for women to enter politics.

Another resource issue is time. Becoming a candidate is a time consuming business and can take up a lot of free time as well as require working time flexibility. Such flexibility is not available in many jobs. The issue of job types is important beyond finding enough time to become a candidate. Jacobs (1962) argues that what he calls 'brokerage occupations', such barristers, teachers, trade-union officials, journalists, and political researchers, often provide not only the necessary time and flexibility, including the option of career breaks, to run for political office, but also lead to politically oriented networks and useful skills and expertise. In the case of the United Kingdom Norris and Loveduski (1993, p. 386) write that the brokerage explanation:

> helps illuminate not just the class disparity, but also why women and ethnic minorities are under-represented in Parliament since they are often concentrated in low-paying skilled and semi-skilled occupations, or in family businesses, with inflexible schedules and long hours, in sectors which do not provide traditional routes to political life.

Hence, parties may have a point when they say that they would like to select more female (and other under-represented) candidates, but the supply is just not great enough.

Demand

When it comes to demand there is both a formal and an informal side. Many parties will stipulate some basic and more or less stringent qualities that any aspirant must have if they are to have any hope of becoming a candidate. These frequently involve a minimum length of party membership, donations, party activism, commitment to the party's goals, and experience and expertise useful for being a candidate. According to Hazan and Rahat (2010, p. 21) catch-all parties that are primarily concerned with electoral success are likely to have fairly minimal formal requirements. This is in order to have greater flexibility to select candidates which are seen as being able to attract voters, even if they are not long standing party 'soldiers'. By contrast more ideologically focused parties are likely to have far more stringing requirements in order to ensure the ideological purity of the parliamentary group. Gallagher (1988, p. 247) argues that variations in how stringent the requirements are also affected by left/right positioning, with left-wing parties being more demanding than right-wing parties. This fits with the discussion in Chapter 2, which suggested that the catch-all party model first appeared on the right of the political spectrum. By definition, a catch-all party is more concerned with electoral success than ideological purity.

However, while formal requirements will have some impact on who are able to get selected it is possible to argue that informal demands can be as, or even more important. Sometimes the lack of supply of female candidates is the function of subtly gendered demands – the criteria for what counts as a 'suitable' candidate is more likely to be found in a man than in a woman. This has been referred to as the 'unconscious valorisation of masculine or male-dominated qualities' (Murray, 2010, p. 58). One example of this was the very stringent requirements of the Belgian Socialist Party which includes 'have his wife and children enrolled in the appropriate women's and youth organisation' (Obler, 1974, p. 80). This requirement does not state that a candidate has to be a man, but clearly the reference to having *his wife* enrolled in the Women's Section suggests that men are regarded as the standard. Hence the unspoken assumption is that anyone wanting to stand as a candidate for the party is a married man.

The criteria for what counts as a good candidate may not be quiet so blatantly gendered as in the above example, but rather the overall profile of a candidate is one more likely to be found in man than a women (Murray, 2010, p. 46). Hence discrimination by the selectors against women may not be overt. Indeed, in their study of selectors in the British Labour Party, Bochel and Denver (1983) did not find gender to be something selectors mention in either positive or negative terms. Further, selectors may honestly believe that they are selecting on the basis of merit. However, since few selectors actually know all the aspirants personally, certain background characteristics, such as gender, race, education and occupation, step in as proxies for merit. In short, electors are looking for 'the right sort' of candidate (Norris and Lovenduski, 1993, pp. 378–9). In this context the 'out-group effect' (Niven, 1998) makes an impact. Selectors will look for characteristics that are associated with successful or at least 'typical' candidates in the past, one key characteristic being that they are overwhelmingly male. The typical member of the political elite is male and few women make it to the top. So, when looking for a candidate that is likely to make it to the top, based on the status quo, the choice will be a man (Krook, 2010a, p. 709).

However, while these subtle, hidden and often unconscious elements of the discrimination against women will take their toll, there are also many case studies that find overt gender discrimination and sexism. In her study of women and politics in Chile, Franceschet (2005) found frequent examples of patronising attitudes towards women at party meetings. Even in the UK Liberal Democrats, which prides itself on its equality agenda, Evans (2008, pp. 598–600) found many examples of female aspirants having experienced overt sexism from selectors.

So, while there may be issues of supply when it comes to the underrepresentation of women, there also seems to be a problem of demand, even if it is sometimes covert and even unconscious, rather than overt and deliberate. Indeed, problems with demand can have an effect on supply. Norris (2006, p. 93) argues that evident lack of demand for certain types of candidates, such as women, may lead to some aspirants being discouraged from even putting themselves forward. Further, when female aspirants, or aspirants from other under-represented groups, do come forward they do not fit the requirements for being the 'right sort'. Hence, those aspirants that do come forward are seen as lacking in merit because they belong to 'out-groups' that do not match what a 'typical' candidate 'ought' to look like.

Conclusion

Candidate selection may not appear to have the same importance as ideology or campaigning. However, as the above has illustrated it is a key battle ground in intra-party power struggles, and has a critical role to play in who gets the opportunity to run the country. Hence, candidate selection processes have a major impact on how parties operate and who make it to parliament. If elected assemblies do not look like the populations they are elected to represent, the most likely explanations are to be found within parties. In short, if we are to understand who gets to represent us in modern democracies we need to understand candidate selection processes.

Chapter 7

Policy Making

Ideology is often seen as sitting at the heart of what a party is, or at least *should* be – that is, a body of people united by the pursuit of a common vision of the ideal society. As we saw in Chapter 1, this was Edmund Burke's definition of a political party. Chapter 4 also illustrated that ideology is not necessarily the prime motivating force behind a political party. However, regardless of what drives the people behind a political party – an ideology, ethnic or religious loyalties or the desire to control the resources of the state for the benefit of themselves and their followers – this driving force will have to be turned into practical action. In a democratic society such practical action will usually take the form of policy proposals. Policy making is therefore an important part of what a party does – it is the process through which the driving force of a party is turned into practical real life action.

This chapter will explore four key issues related to policy making. The first is related to the question of who *should* be involved in the making of party policy. The chapter will consider both the normative and pragmatic arguments for and against inclusive and even democratic policy making processes. The chapter will then look at some of the practical obstacles to open and inclusive policy making processes. Having looked at the background to this debate, the chapter will consider the extent to which there is a demand to be involved from the party on the ground – that is, from party members and supporters. Finally, the chapter will look at who are *actually* involved in the making of party policy.

Who should be involved?

The issue of whether party members should be closely involved in the making of party policy has been the subject of intense debate – in essence, a debate over the desirability of intra-party democracy. This debate can be split into two broad areas: a normative debate; and a pragmatic one. The normative debate deals mainly with whether or not internally democratic parties are a help or a hindrance for democracy at the national level. The pragmatic argument deals with whether, irrespective of the normative pros- and cons, a party leader would want to include party

124

members in the policy-making process. In short, whether or not one thinks intra-party democracy is 'A Good/Bad Thing', what are the costs and benefits for the party leadership of including/excluding party members from the policy making process? The following will deal with both sides of each of these debates.

The normative argument against intra-party democracy

The normative argument against intra-party democracy has a long history, and, it could be argued, is somewhat old fashioned. There are nevertheless several distinguished scholars who have argued against intra-party democracy and their arguments should be noted. The main thrust of the argument against intra-party democracy is that representative democracy as practiced in the modern world is about citizens choosing their leaders, rather than themselves taking a very active role in public affairs. Democracy is limited to citizens taking decisions on only very broad national issues through electing representatives, rather than making decisions on the details of the issues facing the country. In democracy 'the deciding of issues by the electorate [is] secondary to the election of men [sic] who are to do the deciding' (Schumpeter, 1976, p. 269). Hence, democracy is a system 'in which the people have a choice among the alternatives created by competing political organizations and leaders' (Schattschneider, 1960, p. 141). According to this view democracy consists purely of the ability of voters to choose between competing teams of elites. Indeed according to McKenzie 'intra-*party* democracy [...] is incompatible with democratic government' (McKenzie, 1982, p. 195).

The reason for McKenzie making this stark assertion is that party leaders, when making decisions on policy, have to act as leaders of the entire political community and not just as leaders of a single party. The wishes of the party can only be one of many sources that party leaders take into account when making decisions (McKenzie, 1982, p. 195). If the extra-parliamentary party did have the ability to control the parliamentary party

> then these party organs would supplant the legislature and the executive as the ultimate decision-making bodies of the polity. The organs of party would transcend in importance the organs of government, as is usually the case in totalitarian regimes. (McKenzie, 1982, p. 196)

This is echoed by Schattschneider (1960, p. 141) who argued that the role of the extra-parliamentary party is to sustain competing teams of parliamentary leaders that the electorate will be given the periodic opportunity to choose between by casting their vote in elections.

Common to all of these views is that the role of the people is not to do the deciding themselves, but rather to chose those who are to do the deciding. Parliamentary leaders need not be *responsive* to public opinion in between elections, as long as they remain *responsible* to the electorate by giving the voters the opportunity to pass judgement of their record in regular elections (McKenzie, 1982, p. 200). It is though argued that this system will most likely have the result that parliamentary leaders will indeed be responsive to the voters in order to attract their vote (McKenzie, 1982, p. 200).

A further central element of this view of democracy is that those chosen to lead must be given time and independence to enact their programme for the country:

> democratic government based, in principle, at least, on delegation from below can, no doubt, be made to work. But in order to do so, the government, however chosen, must enjoy a real measure of independence and for a reasonably long period. (Amery, 1964, p. 19)

In the context of the United Kingdom, Amery further argued that: '[the British] system is one of democracy, but of democracy by consent and not by delegation, of government of the people, for the people, with, but not by, the people' (Amery, 1964, pp. 20–1). This is what has been defined as 'Tory democracy' (Beer, 1965, p. 91). The key concern of this approach to democracy is:

> to put those who are best able to identify and pursue the national interest into office with sufficient independence to do so. The system is democratic because the authority of the government rests on the consent of the people, but it is not government by the people. (Katz, 1997, p. 30).

Once the best people to lead the country have been identified, they should be left in peace to get on with doing their job until the next election. Clearly, intra-party democracy would disrupt the work of the great and the good we have selected to lead us.

The normative argument for intra-party democracy

There are a number of counter arguments to these objections to intra-party democracy. For example, if the most important aspect of a democracy is that parliamentary leaders open themselves up to the judgement of the people through regular elections, then the power of the extra-parliamentary organisation over the parliamentary party ought not to be a problem. In essence, from a democratic perspective it should not matter whether it is the parliamentary party or the extra-parliamentary party that makes the decisions, as long as those decisions are open to be judged by the voters in elections.

In addition, there is no particular reason to believe that intra-party democracy will produce policies that do not take into account inputs from a wide range of sources, as McKenzie correctly asserts is necessary. In other words, why would decisions taken by a small group of party leaders be more likely to take account of wider societal interests than decisions made by a much larger number of party members through party organs?

Further, it has been argued that elections are not good enough at communicating the wishes of the 'people' to the governors of a polity (Gutmann and Thompson, 1996, p. 130). This is the essence of Ware's (1979) defence of intra-party democracy. Ware argues that 'by itself, the electoral mechanism does not provide the autonomy of citizens' choice that is necessary for the existence of a liberal society' (Ware, 1979, p. 32). The 'electoral competition' model of democracy, as represented by Schumpeter and McKenzie, draws on an erroneous analogy with competition in free markets (Ware, 1979, p. 36). In other words, the argument against intra-party democracy sees parties as companies working in a market, engaged in a competition for votes. The party that fails to satisfy voter demands will not gain enough votes to stay in business – acquiring government power, or just staying in parliament. If at election time voters are unhappy with the work done by a particular party they will simply shift their votes to another party.

However, the analogy is erroneous because the party political market is not perfectly competitive the way the electoral competition model of democracy implicitly assumes (Ware, 1979, pp. 38, 40). Rather than being perfectly competitive, party political markets are in fact often highly oligopolistic, that is, controlled by a few players (Ware, 1979, p. 38). This has serious consequences for the view of democracy as competition between elites. In an oligopoly, parties have little interest in redefining the political reality in which they operate (Ware, 1979, p. 51). In other words, parties may compete on providing policies that will attract voters, but only within a fairly limited range of issues which party leaders deem to be relevant to contemporary society and which these leaders feel comfortable competing on. Demands for policies that go beyond the 'norm' are rejected by party leaders. Even if these new issues are what voters want to hear about, they are still often excluded since only the leaders of big parties can set the parameters for political competition and it is in their interest to stick to tried and tested issues.

Hence, even if the actual wants and needs of voters change, they cannot articulate those wants and needs through the ballot box since parties define which issues they compete on. In other words, if none of the main parties presents policies reflecting new wants and needs then voters are not able to express a desire for such policies since their only choice is voting for existing policies. Because of the oligopolistic nature of the electoral market, new parties with policies outside the accepted parameter of normal politics find it difficult to successfully challenge the existing parties. Indeed, if we are to believe Katz and Mair's (1995) cartel party thesis as explored in Chapter 3, this is an increasing problem as existing parties actively cooperate to exclude challengers. This means that if voters want a new set of policies to challenge 'normal' politics, they will struggle to make that clear if their only option is the ballot box. When parties lack internal democracy, the agenda is controlled by the leadership, who more often than not prefer to compete on long-established issues they are comfortable with, but which 'by their very nature [...] hark back to a vision of political reality that is probably obsolete' (Ware, 1979, p. 51).

Ware's solution is intra-party democracy: 'the argument being presented here is that parties that provided for real control over policy goals by their activists would come to have a leadership that took account of new conflicts' (Ware, 1979, p. 78). By having intra-party democracy, parties will provide voters with a direct influence on policy to supplement the often ineffective option of merely voting for another party. This will deal with the problem that 'the pressure to search for a new conception of political reality [...] is most easily rejected when the party organisation is least open to mass movements' (Ware, 1979, p. 51). In parties with intra-party democracy members will be able to bring onto the agenda issues that the leadership might not otherwise have wanted to deal with.

Echoes of this argument are found elsewhere as well. John Stuart Mill wrote that 'a democratic constitution, not supported by democratic institutions in detail, but confined to the central government, not only is not political freedom, but often creates a spirit precisely the reverse' (Mill, 1994, p. 334). Sartori (2005, p. 28) argues that while parties have many functions, their most important is that of 'expression'. Expression involves 'the party as the agency which typically communicates the demands of the society to the state, as the basic link or connector between a society and its government' and the 'expressive function is a continuous flow which outlasts electoral intervals' (Sartori, 2005, p. 24). Hence parties ought to work as conduits between citizens and governments not just at election time, but continuously. This is clearly linked to

Lawson's idea of linkage. Arguably, in order for them to perform that function best, membership influence on policy is necessary. This is seconded by Miliband who writes:

> Members of Parliament cannot nowadays realistically claim Burkian independence nor is it in the least evident that democracy would be better served if they could. To suggest that they should be free from commitment on the great issues of the day until they have heard those issues debated in Parliament is to take a purely mythical view of the working of the political process. (Miliband, 1958, p. 173)

This argument also finds support from the 'deliberative' view of democracy (Teorell, 1999). It has been argued that the view of democracy as a competitive marketplace where voters 'buy' a party product, erroneously assumes that voters have a set of well-established preferences. Instead, it is better to think of voters as having an 'empirical' and a 'hypothetical' standpoint. The empirical standpoint is what they would come up with if they were stopped on the street and asked to give an instant response to an issue. The hypothetical standpoint is what people would come up with if they had had time to consider all the facts and to deliberate with others. The argument is that the hypothetical standpoint is a more constructive one than the empirical one, and that intra-party democracy is a good way of getting to the 'hypothetical popular will'.

The desirability of membership influence is further strengthened by the concern over the breakdown of the representative function of parties. As was outlined in Chapter 5, there is a strong argument that parties are being separated from their voters because membership organisations are shrinking. Bringing party members in to policymaking could help rebuild those membership organisations because this increase in influence would provide greater incentive for membership. In addition, strengthening the role of members would help rebuild party linkage. As was argued by Miliband 'whatever contributes to the growth of [the non-professional politically interested individual's] significance also contributes to the vitality of democratic politics' (Miliband, 1958, p. 172).

In many ways, the pro intra-party democracy camp can be seen as having won the argument – at least when it comes to the official position taken by many parties and widely held views of with what counts as 'good practice' in terms of how to run a party organisation. Mill's view of the need for 'democratic institutions in detail' has been taken up by projects dealing with advising emerging democracies on the best way to build good democratic structures. So, The Netherlands Institute for Multiparty Democracy (NIMD, 2004) writes that there are a number of 'institutional guarantees' parties need to meet in order to be able to play their proper role in democratic societies – one of which is internal democracy. In other words if parties are to be constructive players in democratic societies they must practice internally what they preach externally (Scarrow, 2005, p. 3). This was echoed by the conclusion drawn by a group of Catholic bishops in Eastern Africa: 'Our conviction is that it is within the political party that democracy starts; it is also here that it starts to fail' (Svåsand, 2008, p. 6). Hence, while the academic literature is fairly evenly split on the issue, although most recent works are pro, the 'official good practice' view seems to be fairly firmly in the pro-camp.

Pragmatic arguments against intra-party democracy

However, even if there are good normative arguments why members should be involved in policy making, there may also be equally good pragmatic reasons for excluding them. One of the main pragmatic arguments against involving party members in the making of policy is that they are not the kind of people sensible vote-oriented party leaders would want to decide the party's platform. Party members, and especially activists – those most likely to want to be involved in the making of policy – have long been regarded as ideological extremists. Sidney Webb said of members of the British Labour Party that they were 'frequently unrepresentative groups of nonentities dominated by fanatics, cranks and extremists' (see Seyd, 1987, p. 202 n1). The situation was hardly better in the Conservative Party where local branches were described by the Conservative politician Hugh Cecil as 'knots of vehement, uncompromising and unbalanced men' (Cecil, 1912, p. 238; also May, 1973, p. 140). Indeed, the idea that activists hold extreme views can be traced back to the very first study of party organisations:

> It is an almost general fact that the Association is more Radical than the mass of the party [...] It follows in the first place that the Caucus is incapable of supplying a correct estimate of public opinion, of giving a more or less accurate idea of its tendencies and aspirations. It has proven this incapacity more than once. (Ostrogorski, 1902, p. 596)

This view rests on the idea that these 'assiduous attenders of branch and constituency meetings' (Seyd, 1999, p. 388) are active not because of the trappings of public office, but because of their commitment to a particular view of society often based on strong ideological foundations. They are, therefore, more extreme than both the broad electorate and the electorally conscious party elite.

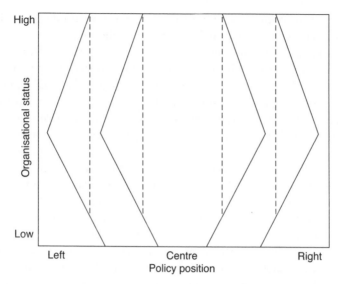

Figure 7.1   *Curvilinear disparity*

Source: May (1973, p. 139).

This argument has found its most popular and elegant expression in May's so called 'law of curvilinear disparity' (May, 1973; see Figure 7.1).

The idea is that parties are stratified, with an upper, middle and a lower layer (May, 1973, pp. 135–6). The main components of the upper layer are a party's members of publically elected assemblies and members of executive bodies (ministers). The middle layer consists of a party's membership base: active and inactive members and those who express strong loyalty for a party without necessarily being members. This also includes US style registered supporters. The lower layer is made up of lukewarm and occasional supporters – 'ordinary' voters with only a low level of party political attachment (or indeed political interest). It is argued that while each layer will be very diverse in its opinions, there will still be an overall trend (May, 1973, p. 136). That trend will vary markedly between the three layers. The most important variation is that the middle layer will be relatively more extreme in their political stance than the other two layers. The bottom layer will tend to be moderates, and the top layer will be somewhere between the two (as indicated by the vertical dashed lines in Figure 7.1), although closer to the lower layer than the middle layer. Hence, there is a curvilinear disparity between the ideological trends of the three groups.

This disparity is caused to a large extent by the different patterns of recruitment to the three layers. Activists without leadership ambitions are not required to follow anything other than their own ideological fervour, which is likely to be strong. Indeed, the tangible rewards for party membership and activism are few and far between (May, 1973, p. 149). Hence, the only reason why someone would want to be active in a party is the fire of their own convictions. If as an activist you want to get elected to internal positions in the party you will have to appeal to fellow activists and their strong ideological views. In short, people in the middle layer tend to be driven by strong ideological views, or required to appeal to such views.

People in the top layer on the other hand do get substantial tangible rewards for their position in the form of a salary and all the trappings of power that come with reaching high political office. At the same time, people in the top layer of a party are highly dependent on the bottom layer (or voters) to remain in their position. Hence 'legislators whose opinions deviate from those of many of their constituents stand to gain from discarding such opinions' (May, 1973, p. 149). Even if politicians have radical opinions that deviate from the ideological centre of gravity of their voters, they are more likely to succeed if they moderate those opinions.

All told this means that when it comes to determining a party's policy position, the top layer of the party is better off ignoring the middle layer as much as possible.

Pragmatic argument for intra-party democracy

However, while this view of party member extremism has a long tradition, there is good evidence to suggest that things may not be as simple as May's model makes it look.

The first issue is that May's law has been subjected to extensive testing, and the results have been weakly supportive of the law at best, outright against it at worst. One key criticism is that each layer in a party is far too heterogeneous in terms of motivations and ideological positions to make general statements about them Kitschelt (1989, p. 403). Others have found general trends, but as opposed to May concluded that in fact the top layer is more radical than the middle layer (Norris, 1995). Some have found limited support for May's law, but only under very specific circumstances (Kennedy, Lyons and Fitzgerald, 2006, p. 802). In other words, the law was not necessarily generally applicable.

Hence, while May's law seems plausible and has the strength of simplicity on its side, there is little evidence to show that it is actually an accurate reflection of the opinion structure of political parties. Indeed, it would seem that there is little in the way of structure in the opinions of each layer due to the heterogeneous nature of political parties. Different people become active in political parties and strive for high office for a plethora of different reasons, and to say that one part of a party is generally driven by one or another concern appears not to be backed up by the evidence.

Finally, in the context of declining membership numbers (see Chapter 5) it been found that despite the fact that party members seem to be an ever-shrinking minority there is no evidence that they are becoming minorities in terms of other characteristics (Scarrow and Gezgor, 2010). On a range of measures – income, union membership, religiosity, and perhaps most importantly, ideology – the smaller membership organisations are becoming more, not less like society around them. It has, therefore, been suggested that modern membership organizations 'still have the potential to help link their parties to a wider electoral base' (Scarrow and Gezgor, 2010, p. 823).

Indeed, there is good evidence to suggest that letting party members participate in policy making is not a danger in electoral terms, and may also be a positive benefit. Local activist-based doorstep campaigning is becoming increasingly important for the electoral success of parties, something which will be explored further in Chapter 8. However, in order for party supporters and members to be willing to invest time and effort in campaigning they need to be motivated to do so. It has been argued that one of the most effective and long-term sustainable means of doing so is to involve party member in the making of the 'product' (policies) they are asked to go out and 'sell' on the doorstep (Pettitt, 2012a). If party members feel a sense of ownership of the policies they are campaigning for, they are more likely to invest the time and effort in campaigning and to do so with conviction.

Who can be involved in policy making?

However, even if a party is committed to an internal policy making process that is democratic, there may be practical obstacles to involving very many people in this process. In order to survive, political parties have to act like fighting machines and as such must 'conform to the laws of tactics' (Michels, 1915, p. 41). By 'laws of tactics' is meant that widespread consultation takes time, and in the day-to-day struggle of politics, swift decisions have to be made: 'democracy is utterly incompatible with strategic promptness, and the forces of democracy do not lend themselves to the rapid opening of a campaign' (Michels, 1915, p. 42). So, for a party to be able to react with sufficient speed to events and moves by other parties 'a certain degree of cæsarism' is required (Michels, 1915,

p. 42) and hence in political parties, 'democracy is not for home consumption' (Michels, 1915, p. 42). In other words, to be effective fighting machines, parties have to be organised along oligarchic rather than democratic lines. In making this argument Michels is supported by Duverger: 'Democratic principles demand that leadership at all levels be elective, that it be frequently renewed, collective in character, weak in authority. Organized in this fashion, a party is not well armed for the struggles of politics' (Duverger, 1964, p. 134).

Michels and Duverger are not the only ones to make this assertion. Explaining some of the reasons for the oligarchic nature of parties Bille writes that:

> a problem is presented in the morning and a solution is expected to have been found by the evening or at the latest by the next day. The demand for efficiency and authoritative action is great. That does not leave much space for continuous consultation with very many people. Centralisation is strengthened. The top must lead. (Bille, 1997, p. 229, translated from Danish)

There are however reasons to believe that the 'laws of tactics' would not be such a problem when it comes to the making of some aspect of a party's policy platform. While it may be true that politicians are often required to take policy decisions very quickly – sometimes, as Bille argues, in a matter of hours – this is not necessarily the case on all issues. When talking about policy it is important to keep in mind that the policy concerns of a party exist on several levels in terms of details and timeframes. Party policies obviously have to cover a vast range of issues over the full spectrum of government, from international to national to local. Party policy also has to be dealt with in temporal terms, from grand long-term ideological foundations of a party, to day-to-day issues. It is this latter consideration that will be the topic of the following discussion. Temporally it is possible to divide party policy into four levels (see Table 7.1):

1 The general and fundamental principles of a party; that is a party's basic ideology. This level tends to be very broad and unspecific in nature and also tends to remain unchanged for long stretches of time.
2 The party's plans and goals for each parliament/electoral period, that is from election to election. These policies are what tend to be found in election manifestos. By the nature of this category, the frequency of change depends on how often elections are held.
3 A party's plans for each parliamentary year.
4 The day-to-day work of a party negotiating with other parties in committees, whipping errant MPs and the other work that goes into

Table 7.1   *Levels of policy and potential for consultation*

Policy Level	Consists of...:	Potential for wide consultation
1: Long term	Basic principles, statements on ideology	High
2: Medium term	Electoral period, election manifestos	High
3: Short term	Annual, parliamentary year	High
3: Day-to-day	Daily negotiations internally and externally, crisis management	Very low

steering legislation through parliament. It also involves responding to short-term issues and crises.

The question, then, is if the laws of tactics are equally relevant at all levels. The problems of involving the wider party membership in the day-to-day struggle of politics are obvious, as exemplified by the quote from Bille above. However, when it comes to deciding on the party's basic ideological foundations, the contents of the election manifesto and even the plans for a parliamentary year it is a lot less obvious why a need for speed should automatically exclude widespread consultation. Especially in countries with fixed-term parliaments there really should be little problem in organising a process of consultation over broad themes for the election and even more specific drafts of a manifestos.

It is true that there may be other costs than loss of speed associated with a democratic policy making process. It has been argued that 'a united party is more likely to do well at the ballot box' (Katz, 1986, p. 63) and while the connection between party unity and electoral success is not entirely straightforward, party unity is certainly perceived to be of importance by party leaders (Dominguez, 2005). This is supported by Laffin, Shaw and Taylor (2005, p. 3) who write that 'the assumption among the party leadership is that a party must present an image of unity to succeed electorally'. This is a problem when it comes to policy making. Policy making is often seen as a very 'messy' process and one which is better not done in public. As Spirer and Spirer (1991, p. 347) write: 'Bismarck, the 19th century German chancellor, is supposed to have said that there are two things you don't want to watch being made, sausages and policy'. Hence one of the reasons intra-party democracy is problematic for party leaders is that it is associated with (seemingly electorally damaging) disunity (Hoffman, 1961, p. 233).

However, as was argued above, there are also benefits in terms of the incentives for activism generated through the sharing of ownership of the policy-making process. Hence, party leaders will have to weigh up the costs–benefits of apparent unity at the cost of lowered activism, or increased activism at the cost of apparent unity. There not necessarily a single right or wrong answer to this dilemma.

Who wants to be involved in policy making?

Even if intra-party democracy is regarded as something to be encouraged and there are no insurmountable practical obstacles, there is still the issue of whether or not anyone lower down the hierarchy actually wants to be involved in the making of party policy. There is a long-standing opinion that most party members are not that interested in policy making and are generally quite happy to let the leadership get on with it. Michels argued that the politically active part of the population, or those who have 'a lively interest in public affairs', is very small (Michels, 1915, p. 49). The same pattern is observable in a political party: 'In the life of modern democratic parties we may observe signs of similar indifference. It is only a minority which participates in party decisions, and sometimes that minority is ludicrously small' (Michels, 1915, p. 50). Further, not only are party members generally quite inactive, they are positively grateful to those who are willing to take on the reins of power: 'Though it grumbles occasionally, the majority is really delighted to find persons who will take the trouble to look after its affairs' (Michels, 1915, p. 53; see also pp. 60–8). On this issue Duverger is in agreement with Michels:

> leaders tend naturally to retain power and to increase it, because their members scarcely hinder this tendency and on the contrary even strengthen it by hero-worshipping the leaders: on all these points the analysis of Roberto Michels continues to hold true. (Duverger, 1964, p. 134)

However, there is evidence to suggest that members are not as acquiescent as Michels and Duverger claim. Surveys of party members in Canada, Denmark and Norway show strong evidence that policy making is of great importance to most. The notion that the leadership should listen more to the voters than to the members was opposed by a majority of members in 11 of the 16 parties in the Scandinavian surveys (Hansen and Pedersen, 2003, p. 110; Heidar and Saglie, 2002, p. 195). In a survey of Canadian Party members, very similar sentiments were found. When asked about their opinions of the influence of various groups within the party, the members identified 'the perceived over-influence of pollsters' and 'under-influence of ordinary party members' as the 'greatest source of discontent' (Young and Cross, 2002, p. 682). The survey also documented strong support for the idea that members should have a greater say in the making of the national policy platform. Similarly, in Norway a majority in five of the seven parties in the survey felt that the party on the ground should have the power to make the parliamentary group take a specific standpoint on issues not dealt with in the election manifesto or in congress resolutions (Heidar and Saglie, 2002, p. 236). Finally, in Denmark there was little support for the suggestion that politics could be too complicated for the members to understand (Pedersen and Hansen, 2003, p. 121).

Further, The German Greens have long been marked by membership rebellions against the leadership's move to the right and eventually into government (O'Neill, 2000; Poguntke, 2001; Wolf, 2003). Also in Germany both the Social Democrats and the Communist successor party *Die Linke* have had problems with membership rebellions (Hough, Koß and Olsen, 2007). Further, the former Israeli Prime Minister Ariel Sharon suffered several defeats at the hands of Likud party members on the issue of the government's policies towards the occupied territories. Finally, the Republican National Convention in 2012 saw repeated protests by delegates objecting to what they saw as the leadership's attempts at undermining their influence.

So, Michels' and Duverger's claims about the willingness of party members to let their leaders take a lead in staking out the direction of the policy of the party may be true in some cases, but certainly not all. There are, therefore, good reasons to believe that not all party members are happy merely to follow the leadership's line.

Who are involved in policy making?

When it comes to who actually makes party policy one view has a very wide following: some parties, especially the mass parties of the left used to be internally democratic, but with the rise of the catch-all, electoral professional and cartel party models, policy making is now firmly concentrated in the hands of the leadership. The changes wrought by the catch-all party engendered conflict between the party in public office and the party on the ground. In the mass party, the membership organisation existed before the party in public office and therefore felt a sense of ownership of the party in public office. With the catch-all party came an 'increased assertiveness of the party in public office' which brought it into conflict with the party on the ground and the traditional view of membership supremacy (Katz and Mair, 2002, p. 121). A similar conflict occurred in the old cadre parties. Here the membership organisation was created to maintain the party in public office. However,

> once recruited, party members start to make demands, abetted by the principle first articulated as part of the ideology of the mass party that the party in public office should be responsible to the party's members. The result is that, although the party in public office may be the dominant face of the party, its dominance is constantly under challenge. (Katz and Mair, 2002, p. 121)

However, it is argued that this period of conflict has come to an end and we have witnessed the 'victory' of the party in public office over the party on the ground:

> In contemporary party organisations, however, these conflicts seem to have been settled, in that what we now appear to witness is the ascendancy of the party in public office, which assumes a more or less undisputed position of privilege within the party organization. In other words, we suggest that the development of party organizations in Europe has gone beyond the catch all period and has entered a new phase, in which parties become increasingly dominated by, as well as most clearly epitomized by, the party in public office. (Katz and Mair, 2002, p. 122)

There is, then, a widely accepted view that party members have gone from having a significant level of influence on the organisation, to being virtually completely side-lined. As Carty (2004, p.13) writes, most modern theories on party organisations 'appear to agree that the imperatives of modern electoral competition have worked to consolidate control of [decision-making on policy and programmatic issues] in the hands of the party in public office, and often the party leadership more narrowly defined'. So, it is widely believed that party members have seen a decline in influence.

However, there is an alternative view – that members have never had, nor can they ever have, influence on policy. This is because organisations are inherently oligarchic:

> It is indisputable that the oligarchical and bureaucratic tendencies of party organisation is a matter of technical and practical necessity. It is the inevitable product of the very principle of organisation. (Michels, 1915, p. 35)

Hence, rather than having seen a decline in intra-party democracy and an exclusion of members from policy making, parties, and indeed all organisations, have always been and will always remain oligarchies. Still, in both views the result is the same: policy making is concentrated in the hands of the leadership.

The extent to which this view of policy making is accurate is difficult to ascertain with certainty. Policy making in political parties, and especially the issue of membership influence is not a very well researched area. Research to date has served only to expose how little is known about the role of party democracy in the making of policy (Scarrow, Webb and Farrell, 2002, p. 144). Studies of membership influence have not gone much beyond candidate and leadership selection. There is no separate investigation of policy making in Bille's study of Danish parties' organisations, only a reference to the 'regrettable lacuna' in our knowledge of the field (Bille, 1997, p. 45). Scarrow et al. (2002) do deal with the role of the members in policy making but are forced to rely heavily on feedback from subject specialists rather than 'hard data' (Scarrow et al., 2002, p. 144). The issue is not central to Katz and Mair's data set based on party rule books (Katz and Mair, 1992; Scarrow et al., 2002: 144), nor to the 1993 collection of essays based on those data (Katz and Mair, 1993). The one place where such rule book data have been used to explore membership influence is as part of a study by Widfeldt of parties as instruments of linkage (Widfeldt, 1997, pp. 41–51). Even here it only merits a subsection of one chapter. This lack of attention to policy making may be explained by the fact that it is generally assumed to be absent.

There are however some exceptions and also some evidence that policy making is becoming more widely studied. McKenzie's (1963) work on the Labour Party and the Conservatives in the United Kingdom is an exception to the traditional silence on policy making. He finds that regardless of the very big differences in official rhetoric on the matter, Labour claiming loudly and proudly to be more internally democratic than the Conservatives (Attlee, 1937) both parties were in fact very similar in being highly oligarchic.

In a study of the Swedish Social Democrats, a party that fits neatly with the 'mass party evolving into catch-all party' idea, it was found that membership influence on policy had not declined (Loxbo, 2013). Rather, compared to the 1950s and 1960s membership influence had in fact increased. This would then very much be a deviation from the decline idea. Further, in a study of the rule books of Danish parties it was found that, as opposed to what might have been expected from the decline argument, Danish party organisations had in fact seen very little change (Pedersen, 2010). There was certainly no sign that they were moving towards an oligarchic convergence. Further it was found that Danish parties afforded their members with very different levels of influence –

from firm oligarchies to much more open and even democratic organisa-tions. This would then go against both the decline argument and Michels' view of permanent and unavoidable oligarchy.

One the other hand, in a study of Malawian parties, it was found that all were more or less firm oligarchies (Svåsand, 2008). There was some variation, but only in the severity of the oligarchic practices. On the other hand, considering the limits put on the policy options of many African governments (see Chapter 4) having internally democratic policy making processes, even in a governing or potentially governing party, may to a certain extent be of limited use.

Whilt the idea of 'party member' is somewhat more complicated in the United States than elsewhere, and the idea of intra-party democracy, therefore, somewhat difficult to apply, researchers there have still found variations in how open the processes are. Reinhardt and Victor's (2008) study of the making of the Democratic platform for the 2004 election found a process which involved hearings in several cities and written and well as oral submissions from both individuals and groups. By contrast, Weinberg (1977) found the Republican process in 1976 to be very much more secretive and limited to a relatively small elite.

This suggests that rather than general decline or longstanding oli-gopoly, membership influence in facts varies from party to party depending on a number of factors (Pettitt 2012b). It has been argued that left-wing parties tend to have more rebellious members than parties of the right. There is, therefore, more likely to be a demand for intra-party democracy on the left. Further, the challenges of getting into and staying in government may make it less likely for intra-party democracy to flourish. Government-seeking parties have to be more internally disci-plined than those without government ambition. This is what is suggested by Michels' idea of the 'laws of tactics'. Finally, it has been suggested that intra-party democracy has a greater chance of survival in consensus-style democracies than majoritarian-style democracies. Consensus-style democ-racies have a greater tradition of negotiation and compromise, and even when a party is not in government it can often still have influence on leg-islation. By contrast majoritarian democracies are dominated by con-frontation, and any party which is not in government has very little, if any, influence. This means that parties operating in a consensus democ-racy can more easily afford to pay the costs of a democratic decision-making process (it being slower and will potentially make the party look divided). This is a lot less so in majoritarian democracies where the margin between victory and defeat is tiny and both victory and defeat tends to be total. Anything that impairs efficiency is less easily accepted in majoritarian than consensus democracies. In short, the ability of members to influence policy may not be in terminal decline or perpetually absent. Rather, it will vary depending on the context that each party finds itself in.

Conclusion

The making of policy in political parties is clearly an important issue. Indeed, it seems to have a certain times been seen as an issue of such importance that it is better kept out of the hands of the masses. There does seem to have been a change in that view towards a greater awareness of the desirability of intra-party democracy in the area of policy making. However, as we have seen there are also obstacles to democratic forms of policy making and many, indeed most, parties tend towards the less democratic end of things in this area. However, these obstacles are not insurmountable and some parties do appear to have managed to build reasonably democratic organisations.

Chapter 8

Campaigning

As we have seen throughout this book, political parties are multifaceted organisations. They contain a wide range of internal actors – leaders, activists, inactive members, casual supporters, indirect members, and affiliated organisations such as trade unions. These actors will have an equally wide range of goals. Hence, parties can be geared towards anything from the realisation of abstract goals to the cynical pursuit of power and personal aggrandisement. However, the winning of seats in parliament must be seen as one of the central activities of any serious party organisation. Indeed, going by the definition of a party used in this book (as discussed in Chapter 1), the act of fielding candidates for publicly elected office is what distinguishes parties from other political organisations. This definition of a political party has led Farrell and Webb (2002, p. 102) to conclude that: 'Given this symbiotic relationship between parties and elections, it is important to have a clear idea of how parties operate in elections and elections affect parties.'

This chapter will look at a number of issues connected to the relationship between election campaigning and parties. It will first examine the ways in which campaigning is said to have changed and some critiques/modifications to that view. It will then look at how this change has impacted on party organisations. Finally, the chapter will look at the issue of party financing, a key element in modern capital-intensive election campaigns.

How campaigning has changed

Election campaigning is seen by many as having gone through three eras so far (summarised in Table 8.1). Different people take slightly different views on the details of each era and use different names for each. So, Farrell (1996) refers to the 'premodern', 'television revolution', and 'telecommunications revolution' eras; Norris (2002) calls them the 'premodern', 'modern' and 'postmodern'. Somewhat simpler Blumler and Kavanagh (1999) talk of three 'ages' and Farrell and Webb (2002) talk of three 'stages'. In this chapter we will use three 'eras', partly because this is simpler than Norris and Farrell's versions, but also because it will

Table 8.1   *Eras of campaigning*

Eras	*'Style' of campaigning*	*Personnel*	*Voter feedback*	*Voter segmentation*	*Communication channels*
			Characteristics		
First	'Propaganda' approach; rallying the 'masses' behind a pre-existing product.	De-centralised local campaigning by volunteer activists.	Local canvassing returns. Impressions and 'gut instincts'.	Heavy emphasis of specific class (class-mass party).	Party press, posters, billboards, pamphlets, word of mouth via volunteers. Little if any focus on press management.
Second	'Selling' approach; research to find out which voters might be interested in pre-existing product and explore which elements of the product might resonate with the potential voters at a given time.	Highly centralised campaign organised by internal media and polling experts; heavy focus on a leadership driven national media campaign.	Extensive nationwide polling.	Catch-all approach; attempting to attract voters from across society irrespective of social background.	Heavy focus on national media, especially television. Decreased emphasis on local channels. Rise of media management; building relationship with journalists.
Third	'Marketing' approach; less about attracting voters to a pre-existing product and more about discovering voter needs and designing a product accordingly.	Highly centralised campaign making increased use of external campaign professionals contracted in on an ad-hoc basis. Return of the local campaign relying on volunteer activists to sell the product door to door, but local campaign co-ordinated from the centre.	Increasingly advanced polling and use of focus groups.	Continued use of catch-all approach; also increased use of detailed voter segmentation according to array of social and demographic factors.	Targeted direct mail to carefully selected sectors of the electorate; return of volunteer driven word of mouth; increasingly intense media management 'spinning' the message.

Sources: Farrell (1996); Norris (1995); Blumer and Kavanagh (1999); and Farrell and Webb (2002). Table amended from Pettitt (2012a).

inevitably one day be necessary to add a fourth era, and rather than having to find a name for whatever is beyond the 'postmodern' stage, being able to call it the 'fourth era' is considerably more straightforward. Despite the differences in terminology, there is a great deal of overlap between the different views of campaigning eras and the following will seek to summarise the overall view of each era based on Farrell (1996), Norris (2002), Blumler and Kavanagh (1999) and Farrell and Webb (2002). One feature of many of these explorations of 'eras of campaigning' is that they are not always very well defined temporally – or put differently, it is not always very clear when each stage is supposed to have started and finished. Nevertheless, this approach does help give some structure to changes in campaigning. The following will look at the general features of each era.

First era

The first era of campaigning was dominated by short-term campaigning. A party's election campaigning efforts would be focused on the so-called 'short campaign'. By 'short campaign' is meant the period of time from when the election is called to election day. There would be little prior preparation for the campaign. The campaign would be overwhelmingly local, based around the activities of the local party machine and local party activists, with very little national coordination. Campaigning was conducted door to door by local activists. When the national intruded on the local it would be through 'whistle stop' tours of party grandees coming to speak to mass rallies around the country.

Significantly, the first era saw no use of 'external' experts such as professional pollsters, media managers, and campaign advisers. Any campaign expertise was strictly 'in house'. Indeed, there was little use of opinion polls at all. Hence, feedback on the party's performance was largely through the 'intuition' and 'feel' of local party leaders and activists (Farrell and Webb, 2002, pp. 104, 105). This lack of 'objective' quantifiable information on what was going on in the electorate could lead to surprise results. One key example of this was the 1945 election in the United Kingdom. Churchill, the charismatic war leader, and incumbent Prime Minister, was facing the efficient organiser of the home front, but also modest and unassuming Labour Party leader, Clement Attlee. The 'popular' feel was that having 'saved' his country from the clutches of Nazism, Churchill would easily defeat Attlee. As Howard (2005, pp. 1–12) describes in his book on the 1945 election, the masses of opinions polls and the close attention that parties, voters, and journalists pay to them was just not a feature of elections at that time. Hence, there was little sign of the electoral earthquake that was about to erupt, with the Labour Party securing a firm majority for the first time in its history. Indeed, the polls that were available were mistrusted and regarded as inaccurate: 'Support for Gallup Polls declined when they made an incorrect calculation about the 1944 American presidential elections' (Howard, 2005, p. 5).

In addition, campaigning and party appeal was based on entrenched social cleavages (Blumler and Kavanagh, 1999, p. 211; Farrell and Webb, 2002, p. 105). This is perhaps the most important feature of the first era. Social cleavages were seen as the basis of the parties' self-identification and ideology as described in Chapter 4. Parties were linked to specific socioeconomic classes and could rely, more or less, on getting the votes of that class. The first era is, therefore, very much the age of the class-mass party (see Chapter 3). Hence, according to Blumler and Kavanagh (1999, p. 212): 'few citizens appeared to sift the arguments concerned, tending to vote instead on group-based loyalties'. This meant that campaigning was less about persuading voters of the attractiveness of a party's policies, and more about mobilising those already sympathetic to the party's 'product'. By 'product' is meant the overall image that a party is trying to convey to voters. This includes its ideology, specific policies, and symbols, as well as the behaviour and public utterances of members, parliamentarians and the party leader.

Lees-Marshment (2001, p. 28) refers to 'product oriented' parties and describes such a party as arguing 'for what it stands for and believes in. It assumes that voters will realise that its ideas are the right ones and therefore vote for it'. In short, in the first era, campaigning is about the mobilisation of existing sympathisers rather than the persuasion of swing voters, of which there is assumed to be very few. The campaign message is, therefore, based on propaganda and even rabble rousing, what Wring (1996, p. 102) refers to as 'the sometimes manipulative appeals of political elites'.

Second Era

The second era, as indicated by Farrell's (1996) term the 'television revolution', was dominated by the rise of television as a common feature in most people's homes in the industrialised world. The centrality of television to this era would suggest that it commenced sometime in the late 1950s and into the 1960s. The rise of television had a number of effects.

First, it saw the early rise of specialists to help parties and individual politicians – party leaders in particular – cope with the new demands of television. A new style of communication was required for television-based campaigning and professionals would now start to play an increasing role in teaching politicians how to look good on television. Indeed, the second era of campaigning saw a rise of public relations specialists generally – not just to cope with television, but also to help parties utilise increasingly sophisticated opinion polling techniques.

Further, the rise of national television made a national campaign necessary – meaning also the imposition of a national message on local campaigns. Messages and themes were planned, tested and refined by central campaign committees with the help of professionals well in advance of the actual election being called. As a result of the rise of the national campaign it became increasingly important for politicians to stick to the agreed national campaign 'script'. Politicians were, therefore, discouraged from 'speaking their mind' unless what was on their mind had been tested for public acceptability in advance (Blumler and Kavanagh, 1999, p. 213).

With the rise of the national campaign came also the rise in prominence of the national leadership and in particularly *the* national leader, whose image had to be carefully crafted and refined. Indeed, the rise of television saw a centralisation of campaigning and of parties more generally. We have just seen how the rise of national television led to the centralisation of campaign planning. Local branches increasingly lost autonomy in this area. In addition, the new specialists needed to cope with television tended to be paid for by the central party. They were, therefore, under the control of the national leadership. In other words, the national leadership was in control of the professionals who were best able to predict what messages were most likely to bring electoral success. These messages were then imposed on local branches and their campaigning. It is, therefore, argued that the second era saw a centralisation of the making of the party's electoral message which by extension also meant a centralisation of parties' policy-making processes.

However, while national television necessitated a national message, national television also made it more difficult to control what messages potential voters were exposed to. Television presented voters with a wider array of views than had previously been the case (Blumler and Kavanagh, 1999, pp. 212–13) – hence parties were no longer the main mediators of political information to their traditional, often class-based, audience. They now had to compete with other parties for 'their' voters' attention and, ultimately, for their loyalty too. Add to that the decline in many traditional class loyalties and we see the beginning of the rise of catch-all parties competing for the attention of voters, based less on intrinsic loyalties and more on the attractiveness of the product being offered.

While these changes had a major impact on political parties, it is also argued that at this time the product was still 'sacrosanct' (Farrell and

Webb, 2002, p. 105). Hence, the message was more or less the same as in the first era, but there was a new belief in the idea that people beyond the traditional audience could be persuaded to 'buy' into the product. This fits with Lees-Marshment's idea of the sales-oriented party which:

> Focuses on selling its argument to voters. It retains its pre-determined product design, but recognises that the supporters it desires may not automatically want it. Using market-intelligence to understand voters' response to its behaviour, the party employs the latest advertising and communication techniques to persuade voters that it is right. A Sales-Oriented Party does not change its behaviour to suit what people want, but tries to make people want what it offers. (Lees-Marshment, 2001, p. 29)

Hence, at this stage professionals are used primarily to design a campaign that will sell the product and help present a party (leader) image that is attractive. However, experts are not yet in charge of designing the overall product.

Third Era

The third era is marked by a number of features. The first is the rise of the Internet. Much has been written about the impact of the Internet on campaigning, but the Internet is still so relatively new and constantly changing that its impact is far from clear. Considering how fast the tools available through the Internet are developing it is uncertain whether there will ever be complete clarity on this issue.

In addition, the third era has seen the rise of the permanent campaign. Parties are now not merely starting to prepare for the campaign some time before the election is called. Rather, they are permanently viewing all their activities through the lens of campaigning demands. Two further features are the continuous rise of campaign professionals and the increasing malleability of the product.

The continuing rise of campaign professionals is said to be having profound effects on party organisations. In the second era external experts were called in to deal with the challenge of new forms of media in the form of television. This has continued with the rise of the Internet. However, with increasingly sophisticated ways of gauging the public mood in the forms of ever more detailed polling techniques, focus groups, and advanced analysis of the relationship between social factors and voting, the external expert has become ever more critical to the success of a party's election campaign. Indeed, the need of parties for highly specialised experts is such that the traditional party organisation is being sidelined (Plasser, 2001, p. 46). According to Farrell and colleagues: 'election campaigns appear to have outgrown the institutional limitations of political parties, requiring a role for political consultants [...] to fill this increasing gap' (Farrell et al., 2001, p. 26). This is supported by Kolodny who argues in the context of the United States that 'if candidates and issue groups believed that their electoral needs could be entirely served by political parties, then there would be no market for a bevy of outside "vendors" such as our contemporary political consultants', however, 'modern campaigning has indeed exceeded the institutional capacity of political parties' (Kolodny, 2000, pp. 110–11). In short, it appears that traditional party organisations simply do not have the ability to cope with modern campaigning without outside help.

Hence, the centralisation of campaigning and party organisations that started in the second era has continued in the third era. However, with the increasing importance of the political consultant, power is not just moving upwards in party organisations to the leadership, but also outwards to these 'for hire' specialists (Gibson and Rommele, 2009, p. 266). If party leaders believe that external experts have the answer to what messages will sell, they may be inclined to give such experts a greater role in the making of the party's message.

This development has led to questions over who is actually in charge of the campaign: parties or external consultants (Farrell and Webb, 2002, p. 106). In a telling piece of research Plasser (2001) found that political consultants, especially in the United States are increasingly seeing party organisations as a hindrance to the effective running of the campaign and as a growing irrelevance. There is a strong sense that the kind of campaigning that the traditional party organisation was capable off – door to door at the local level – is much less useful than was the case in earlier eras of campaigning. What matters is the central campaign run by specialists, delivered through the mass media and centred on the top leadership.

This rising centralisation is well captured by the New Labour pollster Philip Gould who wrote that 'Labour must replace competing existing structures with a single chain of command leading directly to the leader of the party' (Gould, 1998, p. 240). As external expertise becomes increasingly sophisticated, and expensive, the control of the national leadership is enhanced. The central message is carefully honed and passed down the party hierarchy. Deviation from this central line is seen as a major problem with careful attention being given to both responding to external critics and, as importantly, to stamping out internal dissent by '"rubbishing" or marginalizing internal party critics who are "off-message"' (Blumler and Kavanagh, 1999, p. 214).

A final point worth expanding on is the increasing malleability of the product. While the product- and sales-oriented parties in the first and second eras saw the product as more or less fixed, in the third era the product is now also open to change if that is what the voters seem to be asking for – 'the increasing tendency is less one of selling themselves to the voters, but rather one of designing an appropriate product to match voter needs' (Farrell and Webb, 2002, p. 102). In the third age, the so-called market-oriented party: 'designs its behaviour to provide voter satisfaction. It uses market intelligence to identify voter demands, then designs its product to suit them. It does not attempt to change what people think, but to deliver what they need and want' (Lees-Marshment, 2001, p. 30). There is, then, an increasing tendency to see parties as businesses engaged in an attempt to design and produce a product that will attract 'an increasingly fickle audience of voters or consumers' (Gibson and Rommele, 2009, p. 266). There are obviously some limitations to how far a party can move from its original position and still be believable. However, the argument is that parties are increasingly detached from their original ideological origins rooted in societal conflicts and ever more dependent for their policy directions on input from professionals on what will 'sell' in the electoral marketplace.

The limits of change

The idea that parties have moved through three eras of development has gained a considerable amount of currency. A lot of writings on campaigning have at least made a nod in the direction of this view. However, while the three eras view is popular, widely accepted and also has some considerable empirical support, there exist a significant amount of variation and counter trends. The most notable counter trend is the rising awareness of the importance of local campaigning. As we saw above, one of the key trends in the move from the first era through the second to the third is the nationalisation of campaigning, brought about in particular by the rise of national television. Because of this nationalisation it is the national leadership that is important and the local campaign is seen as of secondary importance. However, there is increasing evidence of a continuing and indeed growing awareness of the importance of the local campaign.

One notable contribution to this literature is Marsh's (2004) article 'None of that Post-modern Stuff around Here' which, as the title suggests, is a direct challenge to the themes of the third-era literature. In his article Marsh concludes that:

> Irish elections are certainly not prime examples of the post-modern, post-fordist era of campaigning which some have claimed to see

elsewhere. Personal contact is felt to matter by politicians, and all parties make considerable efforts to knock on as many doors as possible during the weeks of the official campaign [...] the essential style of campaigns remains personal, with individual candidates seeking to make an impact and doing so for the most part by the traditional methods of meeting the folks. (Marsh, 2004, pp. 262–3)

Some of the same trends can be identified in the United Kingdom, normally a country seen as being first when it comes to follow the path of 'Americanisation' – the United States most often being cited as the prime example of third-era campaigning. The counter trend in the United Kingdom is illustrated by a comment made by the former cabinet minister Hazel Blears. In a dig at the then Labour leader and prime minster Gordon Brown's unsuccessful attempt at embracing Internet campaigning through a YouTube video, Blears wrote: 'I'm not against new media. YouTube if you want to. But it's no substitute for knocking on doors or setting up a stall in the town centre.' While Blears' comment was very much part of her personal struggle with a party leader with whom she did not get on, her comment is backed up by a lot of research. It has been argued that the image of the modern electoral professional party as a centrally organized 'army' with local activists taking orders from the national headquarters is misleading when it comes to local campaigning. There is considerable local reluctance to simply follow orders from the centre. Further, it has been suggested that campaigns are more effective when they are locally organized (Whiteley and Seyd, 2003).

Others have also stressed the importance of local campaigning, but have also pointed to the importance of coordination from the centre (Fisher et al., 2005). This is especially the case in the key target seats that a party needs to win or hold in order to win the election overall. It is argued that the national leadership is fully aware of the importance of careful use of local activists in certain key areas and spend a great deal of efforts to get the local campaigning right. Indeed, Fisher and colleagues go so far as to argue that the centrally coordinated local campaign – with activists doing traditional, that is first era, door to door campaigning – is as, or even more, important than the national media campaign that has received so much attention in the third era literature:

there is no doubt that constituency campaigning is now seen as more significant than ever by the parties and possibly even more significant than the national campaign focussed on the mass media. The planning of constituency campaigns has become increasingly integrated into the parties' overall campaign strategy [...] Arguably, then, the campaigns in the constituencies now dominate the parties' overall campaign strategy. The battles that matter are those in the target seats, not the one played out in the national media. (Fisher et al., 2005, p. 18)

The importance of local campaigning has also been recognised elsewhere. There is a longstanding literature from the United States on the role that personal contact and local activism has on turnout at elections (Green and Gerber, 2008). Indeed, it could be argued that the entirety of Barack Obama's road to the White House, from the primaries to both presidential elections, was a lesson in the importance of building grassroots organisations and how such organisations can overcome obstacles such as lack of financial muscle. In his book on the first Obama campaign Plouffe writes:

> Our grassroots supporters again deserve the lion's share of credit. The farther we got from Iowa, the more important our volunteers were. The campaigns in the states were shorter and we had fewer staffers on the ground. The volunteers built our campaigns in the February states and executed incredibly well in the closing weeks. They recruited more help, identified supporters, and made sure people knew where to vote and caucus. (Plouffe, 2009, p. 181)

Later he writes: 'Our secret weapon, day in and day out, was our army of volunteers, real people who brought Obama's message and ideas to their neighbors, co-workers, and fellow citizens, guided by our extraordinary staff' (Plouffe, 2009, pp. 379–80). Plouffe is obviously writing as a firm believer in Obama's message and as someone intimately involved in the campaign, but even ignoring phrases such as 'secret army' and 'extraordinary staff' this seems to be an excellent example of what Fisher and colleagues describe in their work on the importance of centrally coordinated local activism ('army of volunteers' 'guided by our extraordinary staff').

It is true that Obama's campaigns became known for their innovative use of the Internet. However, it is worth noting that it also seems that their use of the Internet was to a large extent about facilitating the growth of a local activists base which could then be encouraged to go out and do the traditional 'shoe leather' work of knocking on doors and getting out the vote. For example, Plouffe notes that 'our website and its social-networking component were heavily trafficked and becoming a real resource for our supporters' (Plouffe, 2009, p. 55).

An appreciation of the importance of local campaigning can also be found in work on Australian elections. In surveys of campaign professionals it was found that such professionals certainly wanted to conduct a modern campaign, but at the same time valued the ability of party organisations to do indispensible local work: 'The Australian example shows that it might be possible to conduct high-tech campaigns on air while valuing the strength of an effective party organization in closely contested marginal seat constituencies' (Plasser, 2001, p. 49). So, there certainly seems to be some evidence suggesting that a number of campaign professionals in the United States see the party organisation as more of a hindrance. However, the examples from the United Kingdom, the Obama campaigns and Australia suggest that the most effective form of campaigning is one that combines a modern professionalised central campaign of the 'third era' kind with centrally coordinated traditional local 'first era' door-to-door activism. Overall this has led Pattie and Johnston (2009, p. 411) to conclude that 'constituency electioneering has become established as an important element of postmodern [that is third era] political campaigning'.

However, there are also variations in the importance of local campaigning in different countries – a variation to some extent based on the political system, and especially the electoral system of a given country. In this context it has been found that direct contact between parties and voters is most notable in elections that use the single member plurality electoral system, for example the United Kingdom and the United States (Karp, Banducci and Bowler, 2008). Here there is far more focus on individual candidates and, therefore, a greater perceived need for candidates to go out and meet the voters and be seen to do so. By contrast in the more party-focused environment of PR electoral systems (especially List PR) there is less pressure for local activists and candidates to go door knocking.

However, there is still some evidence that 'shoe leather' campaigning is also becoming a feature in democracies using proportional representation electoral systems. In Denmark is has been noted in that some parties, especially on the left, have started to focus on getting volunteers out to knock on doors and engage voters face-to-face.

Further, Plasser found that 'third era' campaigning techniques were somewhat unevenly spread across the globe. Professional, marketing and media driven campaigning is at its height in the United States, and is also a strong feature in Europe, West and East, Latin American, Russia and East Asian Democracies (Plasser, 2001, pp. 45–6). By contrast this type of campaigning is much less widespread in Africa and India. Here we still see much more traditional local and personal campaigning techniques dominate, with little professionalization and much less media focus (Plasser, 2001, pp. 50–1). This is perhaps not so surprising. Quite apart from the lower level of television and Internet penetration in these regions, the 'product' that the parties offer is also very different. As Chapter 4 showed Africa is dominated by personal and clientelistic relationships where access to resources through control of the levers of government is much more important than a carefully crafted campaign message derived from detailed study of voter demands. A lot of Indian politics has become very local with a both a lot of small parochial parties and a heavy local orientation in the major parties. There is quite simply neither the means nor the need for third-era style of campaigning in India or democratic states in Africa the way there is in certain other democracies.

Drivers of change

It is now worth considering what drives change. Three driving forces will be considered. First, as is discussed in both Chapter 3 and Chapter 4, underlying societal changes have had a major impact on the life of parties, and are also an important factor in understanding campaigning change. Second, technology has played a major role. As was observed earlier, one of the main causes of the rise of campaign professionals was the appearance of new communications technologies which parties needed help utilising. However, it has also been pointed out that sometimes parties operating in similar social and technological environments will adopt modern campaign techniques to different degrees (Gibson and Rommele, 2001). Hence, as a third issue we need to look at party-specific factors.

Social changes

Chapter 3 and Chapter 4 show the intricate connection between political parties and underlying social forces. Indeed, one of the main features of the party-politics literature is the connection between society and parties – their ideology, organisation and behaviour. Hence, if those forces change, so will political parties – including how they campaign.

The main social changes that are of relevance to party organisational change relate to the decline of traditional political cleavages, especially class. As voters increasingly become divorced from traditional societal conflicts they start voting according to a wider and more amorphous set of concerns. This means that parties can no-longer rely on traditional conflicts to predict voting patterns. As Hindess argued: 'it is [...] becoming increasingly difficult to support one of the other major party on the basis of class loyalty – to support Labour because one is working class, or the Conservatives because one is not' (Hindess, 1971, p. 10). Hence, it is no longer enough to merely mobilise already sympathetic voters. It is necessary to also persuade them of the virtues of the party's position, as was seen in the move from first- to second-era campaigning.

However, 'persuading' requires radically different methods than 'mobilisation'. In order to be able to persuade voters to vote for a particular party, that party needs to find out what voters will find persuasive. That in turn leads to a massive increase in the need for information about the demands and wishes of voters, something that requires expert help, hence the rise of professionalization (Smith, 2009, p. 556). The argument, therefore, goes that societal changes were one of the main factors in the rise of a new form of party employing new forms of campaigning techniques: 'the catch-all party emerge[d] from – and to suit – a specific form of society' (Smith, 2009, p. 559).

Technological change

A significant part of what has encouraged or forced changes in the way parties campaign is related to technological change. It is true to point out that technological change clearly is not the entire explanation. This has been acknowledged by Farrell and Webb, who adopt what they refer to as 'soft technological determinism' (Farrell and Webb, 2002, p. 103). That is, technology is part of the explanation for change, but only one part.

New technology has provided means by which parties can gather increasing amounts of information, as well as ever more sophisticated ways of analysing it.

In addition, first radio, and most significantly television and the Internet provided parties with both a vastly increased potential for powerful campaigning strategies, but also a challenge in how to best utilise that potential. Hence, technology provided new ways of campaigning; utilising those new ways required experts; failing to utilise these new ways meant electoral defeat if rivals were better or faster at using new methods. At the same time the spread of telephones and later the Internet made questionnaire polling far easier than it had been in the past (again with the help of experts – Twyman, 2008). The rise of ever more powerful personal computers made the analysis of such data both faster and more sophisticated. In short, technological change provided parties with many opportunities for more effective campaigning, but at the same time also created challenges and dangers – challenges in getting the most out of the technology; and dangers if the technology was used badly, such as a bad performance on television or YouTube, or by reacting slower than rivals. As Kirchheimer pointed out, the adoption of new ways of doing campaigning is a competitive phenomenon: 'A party is apt to accommodate to its competitor's successful style because of hope of benefits or fear of losses on election day' (Kirchheimer, 1966, p. 188). Hence, successful use of a certain type of technology is likely to increase demand for that technology, which brings us to the other side of the equation – party-specific issues affecting changes in campaigning.

Party-specific issues

There are clearly major factors that have encouraged and sometimes forced changes in how parties operate. However, not all parties react the same way to these outside forces. At a national level it may be possible to explain variations between countries based on their relative technological and social context. Hence, it is perhaps not surprising that for example Africa and India should be using methods more associated with the first and possibly second eras of campaigning compared to say the United States or Europe. Considering the much lower level of technological penetration in Africa and India – such as television and PC ownership and access to the Internet – the availability of certain campaigning techniques will simply be that much lower. However, these factors do not explain why we sometimes find parties in the same political system adopting different campaigning techniques from across the three eras. In order to understand such differences we need to look at party specific factors (Gibson and Rommele, 2001). It has been suggested that a number of key factors may help explain why a party becomes inclined to adopt new approaches.

First, it is argued that a major motivating factor in adopting a new approach to campaigning will be if the party's primary goal is no-longer being met (Gibson and Rommele, 2001, p. 36). If that is the case the party will be motivated to change its behaviour to turn around its fortunes. Good examples of this would be the US Democrats under Bill Clinton, the UK Labour Party in the mid-1990s when Tony Blair became leader, and the UK Conservative Party under David Cameron. In this context, suffering a string of heavy defeats is likely to trigger some serious soul-searching in a party, which may lead to new campaigning techniques being adopted. This is especially the case if such defeats lead to a change of leadership bringing with it new approaches and ideas.

Another factor which is likely to have a significant impact on campaign innovation is having a healthy bank balance (Gibson and Rommele, 2001, p. 37). Hiring the professionals that are necessary for utilising many modern campaign strategies is only likely to happen if there are substantial resources in place – such help does not come cheap. Intuitively this does make sense. If you do not have money to buy the expensive equipment and services seen as necessary for modern campaigning, then you will not get very far in that direction. However, at the same time, as the first Obama campaign illustrated, operating a tight budget can itself be a source of innovation. Plouffe writes that:

> During the general election, on a conference call we held with labor leaders, one of Clinton's big labor supporters who had spent millions on her behalf in the primary derided our belief and trust in volunteers. He insisted that we needed to pay people to do things like door-knocking and phone calls [...] 'Well, our volunteers certainly did a number on you in the primary.' I reminded him. He was one of many who, even after witnessing the endgame, discounted our grassroots strategy in favor of the old dusty playbook. (Plouffe, 2009, p. 182)

Nevertheless, having said that, money does allow the use of certain approaches that would not otherwise be possible. A major element in Plouffe's description of the first Obama campaign is how they built up of a solid donor base and beat fundraising targets and records. Innovation driven by scarce resources is fine, but having lots of resources is arguably even better.

In addition, Gibson and Rommele (2001) argue that a party which has 'existing norms of internal hierarchy' – or in other words, a tradition of strong leadership, will find it easier to adopt the top-down approach seen as central to second- and third-era campaigning. Conversely, parties with long histories of internal opposition to leadership control will find it more difficult to accommodate the strategic swiftness and hierarchical organisational structure associated with third-age modern profession-alised campaigning. This is a theme also evident in connection with the challenges of intra-party democracy in policy making as we saw in Chapter 7. A good example of this issue is the UK Labour Party. One of the reasons why Gould's 'single chain of command' line (Gould, 1998, p. 240) was so controversial ('This offended everybody' (Gould, 1998, p. 240)) was the Labour Party's long history of formal (if not actual) adher-ence to internal democracy.

Finally, it is argued that a right-wing party is more likely to be sympa-thetic to 'the principles of marketing and use of outside consultancy firms underpinning professionalized campaigning, than a left wing party' (Gibson and Rommele, 2001, p. 37). Marketing, a quintessential free market capitalist pursuit, perhaps comes easier to a party of the right than the left.

The overall conclusion is, therefore, that the most likely adopter of modern campaigning techniques is a 'well-funded, mainstream, right-wing party with significant resources and a centralized internal power structure that has recently suffered a heavy electoral defeat and/or loss of governing status' (Gibson and Rommele, 2001, p. 37).

Impact of changes

From the above outline of the changes that have happened to election campaigning, it should be fairly clear that these changes are likely to have had significant organisational implications for the parties involved.

When looking at the changes wrought by the development in campaigning it is worth noting that there seems to be a close connection between the three eras of campaigning and party types. As Smith (2009, pp. 557–8) points out there is a great deal of overlap between the description of campaigning in the first era – targeting specific social groups and reliance on a mass membership organisation – and the literature on the mass party. Similarly, second- and third-era campaigning overlaps with the literature on the catch-all and electoral professional party types. Hence, many of the changes associated with the move from first-, to second- and to third-era campaigning are dealt with in Chapter 3 and will not be repeated here. However, one issue will be dealt with here. There is a potentially significant problem in combining three central elements of third-era campaigning: 1) the increased centralisation of the party organisation associated with campaign modernisation; 2) the central role played by local campaigning in modern elections; and 3) the challenge of retaining and incentivising members (see Pettitt, 2012a).

There is a significant debate over whether internal party democracy is a good thing or not for political parties and democracy generally as we saw in Chapter 7. However, there are reasons to believe that having influence on the direction of a party is a central motivating factor in party member activism (Whiteley and Seyd, 2002). At the same time Lilleker (2005) suggests that there are severe challenges in combining modern political marketing with internal democracy. This is to some extent a longstanding issue. As is described in Chapter 7, one of the key challenges of building internal party democracy is that while the wheels of democracy often move slowly, the electoral market can move very quickly indeed. There is, then, an unresolved paradox at the heart of modern campaigning: Modern, third-era, campaigning requires a great deal of speed, centralisation, and local participation. Yet there is a clash between speed and centralisation on the one hand, and motivating people to be not only members of a party, but also to be active, something which requires giving them a sense of ownership of the organisation. How can central control of an organisation be combined with, at the very least, a *feeling* of widespread ownership?

This is a problem that does not seem to have been solved by any modern party. The UK Labour Party saw both a significant increase in centralisation and a rise in membership in the late 1990s. However, since about 2001, the membership rise has turned into a massive decline. Once the Labour Party was in government and started doing things the sense of ownership that was part of the 1990s rise very quickly dissipated. On the other side of the Atlantic Obama was able to build an impressive grassroots organisation during his first presidential primary and general election campaigns. Arguably though this was partly because he was a relatively unknown quantity and people were, therefore, able to fill in the blanks as they saw fit (Pettitt, 2012a). To some extent he was able to repeat that feat in 2012, although the earlier enthusiasm has certainly faded. There is currently no straightforward solution to this problem. Only a growing awareness that modern campaigning requires local volunteer participation and that such participation requires incentives – ideally, it has been argued, through giving activists a sense of ownership of the product being sold on the door step (Pettitt, 2012a). How this can be achieved in a centralised organisation is currently an unanswered question.

Financing

If there is one thing that most scholars and practitioners can agree on in the rise of modern professionalised campaigning, then it is the fact that such activities are expensive. Hence the last issue the chapter will deal with is the issue of party financing. This is an area which, as Fisher and Eisendtadt (2004, p. 619) point out, is somewhat under-researched. This may be partly explained by the fact that apart from when it sparks a major scandal, which party financing has a tendency to do, it is also an area which it can be difficult to learn very much about.

Often parties are required by law to open their accounts to public scrutiny, especially if, as is increasingly the case, the state has a role to play in the funding of parties. Even so, parties tend to be reluctant to talk too much about their finances and their donor base. Indeed, it has been pointed out that one of the costs of a high level of accountability and transparency in party financing is that it can scare off potential donors (Fisher and Eisenstadt, 2004, p. 621). Parties are not popular and being too closely associated with them could bring bad publicity for the donors – and possible accusations of favouritism and even corruption.

However, money is central to the life of parties: The expense of modern campaigning has already been mentioned. In addition, parties need money to maintain their organisations in-between elections. This will certainly cost less than the capital intensive weeks leading up to an election, but as we saw above, one of the characteristics of third-age campaigning is its permanency. In other words, even if the permanent campaign may vary in intensity it will still consume money even at its less active stages. Further, all but the most amorphous party organisations will maintain some form of permanent presence in the form of national and regional offices in-between elections. This is particularly the case the closer a party is to the mass party model with is large membership base. Hence, parties need money and the amount they have and the way they get it is of key importance for how democracy operates.

Hence, party financing is important for a number of reasons. First, while having local volunteer activists is important even, or perhaps especially, in modern campaigning, there are few things that volunteers can offer that cannot also be bought with money (Fisher and Eisenstadt, 2004, p. 619). That means that unequal funding streams have the potential to result in unequal power. Unequal power is not necessarily a problem in democracy – after all, that is a normal aspect of politics. However, if some parties are permanently better funded than others that could be a problem for the fair competition between them. In other words, money can result in an uneven playing field, which has been one of the arguments for increased state funding (van Biezen, 2004, p. 703).

Second, where parties get their money from has a significant impact on politics. As described in Chapter 3 the mass party was defined by its close relationship with civil society. Unlike the cadre party and its few but wealthy supporters, the mass party relied on thousands of small contributions (Duverger, 1964, p. 63). In return for their membership subscription the members were given a stake in the party, its ideological development and policy stance (even if that stake was often more imagined than real – see Chapters 3 and 7). Hence, the mass party was a key part of civil society and served as a bridge between citizens and politicians. However, one of the key issues in modern party politics is the decline of the mass-party model. In its stead has come party organisational forms that are defined more by their relationship with the state than the people (van Biezen and Kopecky, 2007, pp. 236–7) and this is exemplified by the changing nature of party funding. Rather than the multitude of many small contributions, parties are increasingly relying on fewer big donations, in the manner of the cadre party, and state funding as exemplified by the cartel party model. These two funding streams have profound implications for the role of parties in democratic states.

One of the implications of fewer large donations is that the sources of these donations, be they companies, organisations or rich individuals, may want something in return for their largesse. Hence, there is a fear that parties may favour those who fund them over other, less well-off elements in society (Fisher and Eisenstadt, 2004, p. 620; Hopkin, 2004, pp. 632–4). There is, then, a fear that some people may buy influence for their particular point of view, potentially to the detriment of the majority of the population, what West (2000) has referred to as 'check- (or cheque-) book' democracy. There is then a worry about favouritism and even outright corruption. This latter issue, outright corruption, has frequently had a severe impact on the politics of democratic states. Italy saw massive changes in its political landscape due to corruption scandals emerging in the early 1990s. The reputation of Germany's 'unification' Chancellor Helmut Kohl was largely destroyed due to funding irregularities during his time as leader of the CDU. Funding scandals involving the French president Sarkozy dominated political news in France for several months in 2010.

One possible solution to special interests buying influence through donations to parties is state funding, which is indeed an increasing feature of democratic states (see van Biesen; 2004; van Biezen and Kopecky, 2007). If the state is the main source of funding there is some guarantee that special interests will not buy influence and much greater transparency in the raising and spending of financial resources can be achieved. However, there is also a downside to state funding. One of the main trends in party development (see Chapter 3) is the way parties are becoming ever more absorbed by the state:

> Parties have traditionally been understood in terms of their permanent linkage with society and their temporal linkage with the state. Parties neither depended on their state for their resources and legitimacy nor were they managed or controlled by the state. Recent processes of organization-building and organizational adaptation, however, have reversed these patterns [...] parties are now perhaps best understood in terms of their temporal linkage with society and their more permanent linkage with the state. (van Biezen and Kopecky, 2007, p. 237)

Research has shown that state funding for parties is steadily increasing, and in new democracies has started out at a much higher level than in more established democracies (see van Biezen 2004; van Biezen and Kopecky, 2007). This means that the state has a much greater control over the internal life of parties through the creation of monitoring mechanisms for ensuring the legitimate use of state funds. In addition, parties are increasingly cut off from society as they now have an alternative source of income, as argued in the 'cartel party' literature (see Chapter 3). State and special interest funding of political parties, therefore, seem to have important implications for the functioning of democracy.

Indeed, Hopkin argues that the mass-party way of funding political parties is normatively more attractive than the alternatives (such as state funding or major donors – either external to the party or internal as with Berlusconi's Forza Italia). However, somewhat pessimistically, he also argues that the mass party model of funding is 'utopian' (Hopkin, 2004, p. 646).

Hence, the funding of political parties is an issue that is central to the workings of democracy in many ways, and seems to be an area that deserves much more attention that it is currently getting.

Conclusion

Even though there is some disagreement in the literature over the exact nature of how campaigning has changed, there is no doubt that it is changing under the accumulated pressure of social and technological developments. It is equally clear that this change is having a major impact on how parties operate and how they are funded. Hence, a concern with how election campaigns are won is not just about understanding what works and what does not, but also about understanding the changing relationship between parties and wider civil society.

Chapter 9

Government

One of the defining features of a democratic state is the free competition for government power. In modern democracies that competition is centred on political parties. When citizens vote they do so mainly to determine which party's or parties' politicians will be able to enter government office. By and large, voters tend to be concerned more with the party affiliation of a particular government minister, rather than his or her individual qualities. In short, the long-term job security of any minister is determined by the fate of their party, not their individual (in-)competence. It is, therefore, important to understand how party politics interacts with how governments are formed.

Getting into government is arguably *the* most ambitious, difficult and costly goal a party can have. The benefits of government office in terms of being able to shape society in a certain direction are huge. However, being in government also carries a high price. Winning elections costs money; will involve painful compromises; and government responsibility inevitably means getting the blame for any number of sins. This means that not all parties desire to enter government office, at least in the short term. That will be the topic of the next section. Having explored the path a party takes towards government ambition the chapter will then look at how parties get into government with a particular focus on coalition formation. The chapter will finish by looking at what parties get out of government participation in terms of ministerial portfolios.

Deciding to aim for government office

One of the definitions of a political party explored in Chapter 1 was as an organisation dedicated to acquiring control of the levers of government. This would suggest that based on some views of political parties, their main goal is acquiring government power. However, in this book the definition used is that a party is a body of people fielding candidates for publically elected legislative assemblies. Why they do that is then left open. That would suggest that gaining government power will be only one among several possible goals. Indeed, the whole idea of focusing the definition of a party on the electoral aspect is that the ultimate goal behind entering legislative assemblies may be many and varied.

It was also argued in Chapter 1 that the idea of a party as a unified rational actor is only a convenient shorthand, and a slightly misleading one at that (Laver and Shepsle, 1999). A party is made up of many internal actors, each of which may have different and contradictory goals. This is exemplified by the idea of curvilinear disparity (see Chapter 7). Strøm (1990) argues that parties generally pursue a combination of three goals: office (generally seen as being executive office, but could also be legislative office); policy realisation; and votes. No goal is ever pursued to the complete exclusion of the other two, but rather a party will strike a balance between the three. It is worth noting that Strøm's model is zero-sum, which means that the pursuit of one goal will mean that less attention can be given to the other two. Hence, the pursuit of office will lead to losses elsewhere, and depending on a number of factors, a party may decide that the pursuit of office is not worth the costs, at least in the short term. Getting into government will, therefore, only be one element in a complicated mix of goals with associated costs and benefits attached. Indeed, goals will change over time as the result of external and internal stimuli (Harmel and Janda, 1994). In short, when considering the issue of government ambition in the context of party politics we will first have to consider what leads a party to pursue that goal in the first place.

It is rare that a party will pursue one of Strøm's three goals to the exclusion of the others, but one may at various times weigh more heavily than the others. Hence, government is not the only goal a party will pursue. Virtually any party that won more than 50 per cent of the seats in its country's parliament would use that power to take control of the levers of power. However, in many countries achieving more than 50 per cent of seats is all but impossible for a single party. Hence, to enter government would require making deals with other parties, something that would entail compromise and, therefore, sacrifices. Even in country where parties routinely win 50+ per cent of seats, this electoral success will involve making sacrifices to achieve a sufficiently broad electoral appeal. A number of factors will influence the extent to which a party is willing to make the sacrifices necessary to enter government.

Perhaps the most important factor in explaining a party's government ambitions is its origins. As we saw in Chapter 3, a party's characteristics depend more upon its history, especially on how the organisation originated and how it consolidated, than upon any other factor. So, Duverger's cadre parties (see Chapter 3) could be argued to have the pursuit for government office written into their organisational DNA. These parties, emerging from loosely organised individuals, where wholly and exclusively focused on acquiring office for their own benefits and for the benefit of their local supporters. We are here primarily talking about parties of relatively old origins such as liberal and conservative parties in for example the United Kingdom, United States, France and Scandinavia. These parties started out as office-seeking groups in parliament. Only as a result of the extension of the franchise in the late 1800s and early 1900s were they forced to add on extra-parliamentary organisations to assist with office seeking in a changed electoral environment. Such parties, therefore, never really made a decision to pursue government office, but rather were 'born' to do so.

Something similar can be said of traditional working-class centre-left social democratic and labour parties. These parties were created specifically with the purpose of defending the interests of the working class. They were also founded on the basic idea that government office would be the best way of realising that goal. This is exemplified by the British Labour party of which Attlee wrote in 1937 that a 'further characteristic of the British [socialist] movement has been its practicality [...] From the first, British Socialists have taken their share wherever possible in the responsibility of Government' (Attlee, 1937, p. 30). In short, these parties were also created with government office in mind from the very beginning. Duverger notes of the French Socialist Party that 'the party aims at the political education of the working class, at picking out from it an elite capable of taking over the government and the administration of the country' (Duverger, 1964, p. 63). As with the earlier liberal and conservative parties, government ambition was a written into these parties from the beginning.

It is true that this government ambition has at times been less strong for some social democratic parties. Several have at various times been marked by the presence of strong radical socialists groupings within them. These groupings frequently had far less government oriented priorities than the rest of their party, and were instead much more focused on ideological ends. The government-leaning orientation of social democratic leaders would lead to charges of ideological betrayal from the radical elements in the party and bouts of internal struggle. Many of these radical socialist elements left their mother parties to form communist parties in the wake of the 1917 Russian Revolution. Nevertheless, despite the presence of such radicals, social democratic parties have, like the older liberal and conservative parties, still tended to be government oriented from birth.

However, the picture is much more varied and changeable for many, often small, but frequently critically placed, newer parties. It has been argued that party systems since the 1960s have been marked by the rise of a large number of new parties (Deschouwer, 2008, p. 1). These parties were created to champion new political cleavages (see Chapter 4), revive old allegedly neglected issues, 'purify' existing ideologies from the compromises of the old parties (Deschouwer, 2008; Lucardie, 2000) or were guided by somewhat more amorphous 'anti-establishment' rhetoric (Bolleyer, 2008, p. 31). In short, many of these parties had far more policy oriented stances and, at least to start with, saw government ambition as selling out to the old establishment. These parties, therefore, have a far more complicated relationship with government participation than the older 'built for office' parties of the centre right and the centre left that preceded them.

Many factors will have an impact on if and when a party, primarily oriented towards policy realisation rather than office, will still at some point decide to actively pursue government participation. One such factor is how a party weighs the costs and benefits of being in government, which are many and varied. The benefits of being in government are pretty straightforward and can be summarised as 'power' and 'resources'. Governments usually hold the initiative when it comes to legislation. Even in democracies with strong traditions of negotiation between government and opposition, it is usually the bills proposed by the executive that get most of the attention and have the highest likelihood of making it onto the statute books. The opposition is often limited to amending government initiatives at best or impotent rhetoric at worst. Being in government also gives access to the many resources of the state which can be used to strengthen a party's organisation and as patronage for supporters. Having civil servants to help with the details of policy proposals is also a great boon for parties. Katz and Mair's (1995) cartel thesis is an example of the importance of access to government resources and is based on the idea of certain parties trying to monopolise access to those resources (see Chapter 3). In addition, as is explored in Chapter 4, in many African democracies, having access to the resources of the state to be used as patronage for supporters is far more important than ideology-driven policy realisation. Finally, there are many smaller perks of being in government, including chauffeur driven cars, big offices in ministry buildings, and the prestige of representing one's country at international summits.

However, there are also many costs associated with being in government. The primary cost is perhaps that with power comes responsibility. Not necessarily meaning that there is an expectation that power should be wielded responsibly (even if that is normatively desirable), but rather in the sense that when things go wrong it is usually the government which gets the blame. Indeed, even if things are not particularly going wrong, being responsible for allocating limited resources will always involve disappointing someone, somewhere which may then lead to the withdrawal of electoral support. The longer a party remains in government the more decisions it will have to make and the more people it will disappoint.

In addition, Strøm (1990, p. 573) argues that voters will usually value consistency between policy pronouncements by a party and what it then actually does. However, being in government can constrain a party's freedom of action with may mean that it is forced to deviate from what they announced they would do, thus putting off voters. One example of this is the Danish government after the 2011 election. In order for the Social Democrats and the smaller Socialist People's Party to form a government they needed the Social Liberals onboard. That involved a number of compromises which led to accusations that the Social Democrats and the Socialist People's Party had broken their pledges from before the election. Even if these accusations are not necessarily entirely accurate they stuck, resulting in very poor opinion poll showings for the Social Democrats and the Socialist People's Party (see Figure 9.1). There is then an unavoidable electoral cost to being in government. This is further illustrated by Johnston and Pattie (2008) who show that challenger parties get more votes for their campaign spending than incumbent parties. Put slightly simplistically, votes 'cost' more for incumbent parties than for opposition parties.

Further, it has been argued that being in government requires more in the way of internal discipline than being in opposition (Pettitt, 2012a, see also Chapter 7). It is more difficult for a party in government to tolerate internal dissent than it is for a party in opposition, if nothing else because a governing party is likely to have more media attention than an opposition party. Journalists will usually see any sign of disagreement as a 'good story' and present it in dramatic terms. Hence, disagreement in a governing party is much more likely to be covered in the press than disagreement in an opposition party. However, clamping down on dissent usually brings with it a backlash somewhere down the line from those who have been affected, leading to further negative media coverage.

Also, any form of office holding by a party will generate intra-organisational pressures. Any party with both parliamentary and an extra-parliamentary sections will have to manage the relationship between the two, something which has often proven itself to be difficult. Entering government means adding an additional layer (government ministers) that has to be managed. Now it is not just a matter of having to manage the relationship between party organisation and parliamentary party. Instead it is a tri-party relationship between party organisation, parliamentary party and government ministers. Managing this relationship has often proven too much, especially for organisationally 'immature' young parties (Bolleyer, 2008).

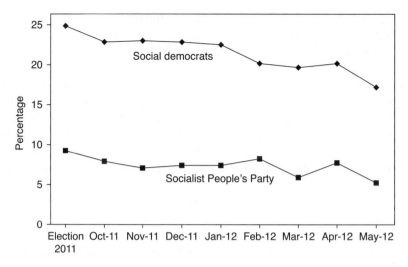

Figure 9.1   *Support for the Social Democrats and the Socialist People's Party in Denmark after the 2011 election*

Source: DR (Danish Broadcasting Corporation) http://www.dr.dk/nyheder/politik/meningsmaalinger (accessed 21 November 2013).

A final problem of incumbency worth mentioning is the danger of becoming part of the very establishment that many young parties were created to fight. Especially parties of the far right have been based on more or less vague anti-establishment, anti-politician, even anti-party sentiments – generally speaking on an opposition to 'normal' politics. Joining a government is likely to be seen by some as a sign that a given party has become part of 'normal' politics, which may serve to alienate core supporters – a group that for a fringe party is likely to be fairly small in the first place (Bolleyer, 2008, p. 31). Arguable this is what happened to the Freedom Party of Austria (*Freiheitliche Partei Österreichs*) when they were in government 2000–05. After gaining significantly in the polls in 2000 the party proceeded to tear itself apart over the next five years under the pressure of being in government.

An important point to consider when analysing how parties will weigh the pros and cons of government office is the type of democracy a party operates in – here taken to mean where a country sits on the spectrum between consensus and majoritarian democracy (Lijphart; 1984; 1999). Consensus democracies tend to be dominated by multi-party systems, coalition and/or minority governments. Hence power is shared between several parties and the opposition is likely to have a fairly significant level of influence, either by bargaining with minority governments or through a powerful committee system. In majoritarian democracies on the other

hand power tends to be concentrated in single-party majority governments and the opposition is often more or less completely excluded from
legislative influence. As Sartori (2005, p. 308) writes:

> In the two-party context 'winning' means a plurality, and whoever
> does not win a plurality simply loses. In the more-than-two party
> system, instead, winning means gaining votes or seats – and, further-
> more, a party may be more interested in winning in terms of posi-
> tioning than in terms of returns. And there is a world of difference
> between the winner-takes-all and the greater-share notions of winning.

In a two-party majoritarian style democracy a party can either win and
have influence, or lose and be impotent. In a multi-party consensus style
democracy on the other hand the political game is about manoeuvring for
a share of power which can come in many forms other than government
office. Hence, the further towards the consensus end of the spectrum a
country is the more power the opposition will have and the less attractive
government will be for a largely policy oriented party. If policy goals can
to a significant extent be realised in opposition there is less reason to pay
the costs of being in government (Bolleyer, 2008; Strøm, 1990).
Therefore, opposition will be a much more attractive option in a consensus democracy than a majoritarian democracy. One particularly
extreme example of this was Denmark in the 1980s where the centre-
right minority government effectively ceded control of certain areas of
foreign policy to the opposition (Damgaard and Svensson, 1989). The
government was repeatedly defeated on matters of foreign policy, but did
not see that as sufficiently important to warrant calling an election. At
the same time the opposition, which was split between the left and the
right, could not get together on a motion of no confidence in the government. Hence, the government continued, but with the opposition effectively making policy on certain matters.

Nevertheless, regardless of how much legislative influence the opposition has, the government will more often than not still be able to exert a
significantly greater control over politics in a given country than the
opposition. As was argued earlier, legislative initiative usually rests with
the government. So, while the opposition parties may have significant
power to amend legislation being proposed by the government, they are
still reacting to a government-controlled agenda, rather than taking independent initiatives. In addition, the detailed implementation of policy is
done by the government (Bolleyer, 2008) and any negotiations on the
international scene are also usually done by government ministers.

This leads to the second reason why policy-focused parties may
decided to adopt a more government office oriented approach: failure to

influence policy when in opposition. A consistent failure to achieve a satisfactory level of policy influence would encourage a policy-oriented party to seek greater policy influence through government office. In addition, what counts as a 'satisfactory' level of policy influence may well change over time. The longer a party is in opposition the less satisfying amending government initiatives may get. For a young party lesser changes may be enough, but over time this may lose its appeal as frustration at the limitations of opposition sets in.

Getting into government – coalitions

Even if a party has been moving in a government-seeking direction that is only the first step on an often long and difficult road towards actually achieving government office. Just as the political system will have an impact on the decision to aim for government office, so it will have an impact on the process of getting into government.

In a majoritarian democracy the process of acquiring government office is usually exceedingly simple, as suggested by Sartori above: typically, a party simply has to win a majority of the seats and then form a single-party majority government. While simple, it is obviously also easier said than done, and usually an option open only to the two main parties in the typical two-party system of a majoritarian democracy.

However, in a great many democracies, such overall single-party majorities are a rarely or never occurring event. This is particularly the case in the context of increased electoral volatility and fragmentation experienced in virtually all democratic states since about the 1960s (De Winter and Dumont, 2006, p. 175). In the light of the relative rarity of overall single-party majorities in many democracies, coalition building became of crucial importance (Warwick and Druckman, 2006, p. 635). The question then is which parties get to join a given coalition. Understanding coalition formation is an area of significant and ongoing debate. Much effort has been invested in trying to come up with models that would predict what kind of coalition would be formed and which parties would be included after a given election result. These attempts at explaining and predicting coalition formations have become increasingly sophisticated both theoretically and methodologically, but have also met with widespread failure in actually explaining real world coalition formation (De Winter and Dumont, 2006, pp. 177, 184). However, the ability to predict possible coalitions would be a very powerful tool in analysing the politics of a country. Being able to predict the most likely governing parties after an election would have significant value to both those involved in politics and those writing about it in either academia or the press. It is, therefore, an important debate in party politics, and thus deserves attention.

Many attempts at explaining coalition formation have been highly influenced by game theory (De Winter and Dumont, 2006; Riker, 1962; Von Neumann and Morgenstern, 1953). The theoretical basis of much of this literature has been that party leaders act as rational individuals seeking to maximise their utility. Taking that as a foundation it is hoped that it will be possible to predict the kinds of decisions party leaders will make when negotiating coalition agreements. This game theoretical approach has over the years produced a large number of suggestions for what 'rational' coalitions will look like. Figure 9.2 shows a hypothetical election result in a 100 seat parliament and the possible coalition combinations for each proposition.

The most basic proposition is the need for a 'winning' coalition. This proposition is based on the idea that only a majority government will survive. No rational office-seeking politician would allow themselves to be excluded from government by a minority (De Winter and Dumont, 2006, p. 176). In other words, *any* combination of parties that result in a majority would be a rational possibility. This proposition has a number of problems when encountering the real world. First, it results in a very

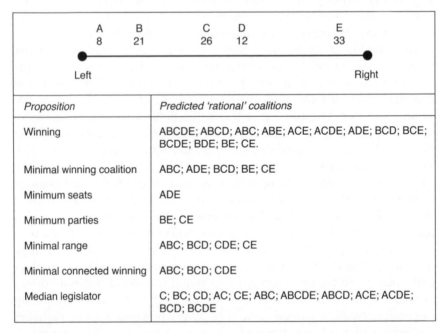

Proposition	Predicted 'rational' coalitions
Winning	ABCDE; ABCD; ABC; ABE; ACE; ACDE; ADE; BCD; BCE; BCDE; BDE; BE; CE.
Minimal winning coalition	ABC; ADE; BCD; BE; CE
Minimum seats	ADE
Minimum parties	BE; CE
Minimal range	ABC; BCD; CDE; CE
Minimal connected winning	ABC; BCD; CDE
Median legislator	C; BC; CD; AC; CE; ABC; ABCDE; ABCD; ACE; ACDE; BCD; BCDE

Figure 9.2   *Coalitions in a minority situation for hypothetical 100-seat legislature*

Source: Modified from De Winter and Dumont (2006, p. 176).

large number of possibilities as illustrated by Figure 9.2. Further, it is based on the erroneous assumption that all parties are government seeking, which would exclude the possibility of a minority government being supported by other parties. As we saw above not all parties are government seeking. Some parties are happy to stay in opposition and let a minority government survive in return for policy concessions. Indeed, a significant proportion of governments are minority governments (Woldendorp, Keman and Budge, 2000, p. 86). Finally, the proposition is 'policy blind' (De Winter and Dumont, 2006, p. 176) in that it ignores the fact that parties from opposite ends of the ideological spectrum are unlikely to want to work together.

The problems associated with the very simple 'winning' proposition led to the idea of a 'minimal winning coalition'. This proposition is based on the idea that as the spoils of office are limited (such as the number of ministerial portfolios) parties will want to avoid any surplus members that are not needed in terms of reaching a majority (Von Neumann and Morgenstern, 1953; Riker, 1962). Again only majority coalitions are assumed to be able to survive. As with the 'winning' proposition there are a fairly large number of possible 'rational' options which limits the predictive value of the model. It repeats the erroneous 'only majority governments' and the policy blindness of the 'winning' proposition.

A development of the 'minimal winning' proposition is the 'minimum seats' proposition. This proposition assumes that if a *formateur* (the party leader tasked with trying to put a coalition together) has a choice between two parties to reach a majority (which is again assumed to be necessary) he/she will choose to work with the smaller one (Riker, 1962). This idea derives from the so-called Gamson's law (see below) which stipulates that a party will be able to demand a share of portfolios equal to the share of seats they bring to the coalition. Hence, a *formateur* will naturally go for the 'cheapest' coalition partner. Of all the predictions proposed by the various models this is the one that has produced only one prediction based on the hypothetical election result. However, as with the previous propositions it is policy blind and the predicted 'rational' coalition contains both the far right and the far left, not a likely scenario in real world coalition building.

A further development of the 'minimum' approach is the 'minimum parties' proposition. This proposition stems from the idea that negotiations will go smoother the fewer actors are involved in negotiations. Hence, a smaller number of parties will make for easier negotiations than a larger number of parties. This proposition and the related minimum seats proposition have reduced the number of predictions. However, empirical research has also shown that this reduction in the number of predicted coalitions was also accompanied by a reduction in the 'success rate in predicting the actual governments' (De Winter and Dumont, 2006, p. 177; see also Browne, 1973).

The next proposition is also a 'minimal' approach, but this time one that takes into account ideology. The 'minimal range' proposition proposes that parties forming coalitions will want to achieve the smallest ideological range of parties (even if they are not necessarily next to one another). The need for an overall majority is still assumed. While the inclusion of ideology is an improvement, the proposition still assumes the need for a majority. In addition, as we saw in Chapter 4, ideology is not a straightforward issue. Two parties may sit next to each other on one ideological cleavage, but far apart on another. Then there is the problem of areas of the world where traditional Western European notions of ideology do not apply. It would be difficult to apply minimal range to, say, the African context where issues not directly related to traditional notions of ideology separate political parties.

A development on 'minimal range' is the 'minimal connected winning' proposition. It adds the extra requirement that there will be no gaps between the parties (Axelrod, 1970; De Winter and Dumond, 2006). This may occasionally require a surplus party which is not needed to reach an overall majority, but is required to plug a gap between two other parties. This proposition makes the issue of ideology more acute. While 'connected' parties may make sense on a one-dimensional ideological spectrum, it is very difficult to operationalise in a multi-dimensional ideological space. While two parties may be close on one dimension, they may very well differ on the other as argued earlier.

Another approach that takes a step away from the 'minimum' idea and its assumption that only majority governments will survive is the 'median legislator' proposition. This proposition works with the idea that the median party can be a 'policy dictator' (see De Winter and Dumont, 2006, p. 177; and Laver and Schofield, 1990). The argument is that the party in the ideological mid-point can never be faced with a hostile majority on its right or its left. Neither the parties on the right-of-centre nor on the left-of-centre have enough seats for an overall majority without the party in the middle. Exactly because the centre party will never face a majority against it, assuming that the left-of-centre and the right-of-centre will find it impossible to co-operate, it could potentially form a viable minority coalition. While this proposition does not necessarily help very much in predicting a likely coalition it does help explain the existence of minority governments. Unless the parties to the right and to the left of a minority government containing the median legislator can agree to defeat the government, which considering their inevitable ideological differences will be difficult, a minority government can survive (Laver and Schofield, 1990). Indeed, empirical research has shown that the majority of coalitions contain the median party (De Winter and Dumont, 2006, p. 185n3).

Factors impacting on coalition formation

While all these propositions have resulted in numerous testable predictions and have become increasingly theoretically and methodologically sophisticated, they have also somewhat failed in actually predicting real world coalitions with any great success. De Winter and Dumont write that 'the empirical results remain modest' (2006, p. 177) and that models 'aggregating current knowledge still do not manage to predict correctly more than half of the coalitions actually formed in the real world' (p. 184).

This should perhaps not be too surprising. Coalition formations are affected by numerous factors that are both difficult to formalise in general models and are also sometimes unique to a particular country, party, time or set of individuals. The problem of dealing with ideology and especially multi-dimensional ideological spaces has already been touched upon in Chapter 4. In addition a few other major problems are worth mentioning.

The first issue is the impact of institutions – in the sense of regular patterns of behaviour and rules and regulations of the game rather than merely 'bronze plaque on the door' institutions – on coalition building. Most countries will have more or less formalised rules for which party leader gets to take on the role as *formateur* first. Obviously, the choice of who gets to try to build a coalition first will be an important factor in explaining which parties end up in a coalition (see, for example, Diermeier and Merlo, 2004, p. 795). In some countries it tends to be the leader of the largest party who is given the opportunity first (Diermeier and Merlo, 2004, p. 795). In others it is the incumbent prime minister who is given the chance.

Another issue is the coalition potential of a party – or the lack thereof (see Chapter 2). It has been argued that the coalition potential of a party should be broken down into two elements: government relevance and government potential (Bolleyer, 2008, p. 25). Government relevance is influenced by whether a party is 'needed' for a coalition in terms of its seat share and its 'programmatic compatibility' with other parties. This element is covered by several of the propositions in Figure 9.2. However, government potential in this context is far more subtle and is not always something a party can control on its own. Government potential in this sense is assigned to a party by the other parties in a system. It is essentially about whether others are willing to work with a given party or not.

Some parties may be regarded as being 'unfit to govern', often for ideological reasons (Mattila and Raunio, 2004, p. 265). Examples include the old Italian communist party which, despite significant electoral success was kept away from government power by the other parties (Newell, 2010). The former Danish Prime Minister, Poul Nyrup Rasmussen, once described the far right Danish People's Party as being 'not house trained' (see http://politiken.dk/politik/ECE1112637/roede-vaelgere-enige-med-nyrup-df-er-ikke-stuerent). The idea of a *cordon sanitaire* has been used to describe the process of centre-left and centre-right parties trying to exclude radical parties on their flanks from influence (Coffe, 2008, p. 181). Olsen (2010) describes how the Norwegian Socialist Party had to go through a number of internal changes before it was ready to consider joining a social democratic led coalition government. However, just as importantly both the Social Democrats and the other potential coalition partner, the Centre Party, had to go through a fairly long process before they were willing to cooperate with the socialists. Finally, Christensen (2010) argues that the main barrier to the coalition participation for the Danish Socialist People's Party was the members of the centrist Social Liberals who were not keen on letting the Socialist People's Party near government responsibility. Hence, the lack of government potential will frequently throw out coalition options which the models would regard as 'rational'. Government potential is very difficult to include in abstract general models as it varies massively from country to country and over time.

A final problem, related to the above issue of government potential is the very human trait of personal likes and dislikes. Coalition bargaining is heavily influenced by the personal interaction between individual actors, something that abstract and general models will find very difficult to deal with. This impact of the personalities of party leaders can be illustrated by the failure of the Danish Social Democrats to form a coalition government after the 1990 election. Despite being the biggest party and achieving its best result in decades, the then leader of the Social Democrats, Svend Auken, was unable to form a coalition because the leader of their traditional partners, the Social Liberals, did not trust Auken and refused to work with him (Buksti, 2005). Auken was subsequently ousted by Poul Nyrup Rasmussen, who then went on to form a coalition with the Social Liberals in 1993. No general model would be able to incorporate such interpersonal matters, which is part of the explanation of the limited success of abstract models in coping with real-world coalition formation.

An additional issue is the link between gaining government power and the actual election result. As Sartori pointed out (above) winning in a majoritarian democracy generally means winning an overall majority of the seats and then acquiring exclusive control over the levers of government. However, when it comes to minority and coalition governments the link between electoral success and acquiring government power is much less clear. Indeed, it has been found that electoral success is not a very good predictor of who gets into government office (Mattila and Raunio, 2005, pp. 266–7). Gaining seats in an election does in fact not make it more likely that a party will be able to enter government – quite the opposite. In a study of 18 democracies between 1948 and 1979 Rose and Mackie (1983) discovered that about 65 per cent of governing parties had lost votes in the previous election. This was backed up by a study conducted by Muller and Strøm (2000) who found that between 1945 and 2000 only about 36 per cent of governing parties had gained votes at the most recent election. Finally, Budge and Keman (1990) showed that, of the parties with the greatest electoral gains in an election, less than half were subsequently able to join the governing coalition. Hence, being the greatest 'winner' in electoral terms is not a good predictor of who would be acquiring government office. This should not necessarily be a surprise given what has been noted earlier about government office not necessarily being a party's primary goal and issues surrounding 'government potential'. The one area where gaining seats did seem to have an impact was in becoming the *formateur*. It has been found that gaining seats in an election had a positive impact on a party's leader's chances of becoming *formateur* (Warwick, 1999).

What all this shows is that getting into government is not a straightforward process, and is dependent on much more than merely gaining seats and making up the numbers for a majority.

Portfolio allocation

Once a group of parties are in a position to form a coalition the next step will be to determine who get what posts in the new government – that is, portfolio allocation. Clearly, the main point of getting into government is getting to control government ministries – especially those covering issues close to a party's ideological heart. Exactly which positions go to which parties will be a matter of negotiation and party preferences in each country and at each election. That part is, therefore, not easy to generalise about. What is possible to generalise about is how *many* ministries each party gets to control – or in other words the share of portfolios each party will get. One of the most important developments in this area is what has been referred to as 'Gamson's law' (Frecette, Kagel and Morelli, 2005).

Gamson wrote that: 'any participant will expect others to demand from a coalition a share of the payoffs proportional to the amount of resources which they contribute to a coalition' (Gamson, 1961, p. 376). That is, if a party provides one-third of the seats in a coalition they will expect to get one-third of government portfolios. The reason why this has been labelled a 'law' is that this does appear to be the case with almost complete accuracy (Browne and Franklin, 1973). That this should be the case has been somewhat of a puzzle (Warwick and Druckman, 2006). One of the reasons why the accuracy of Gamson's Law is so surprising is that it could be argued that a 'smaller party that is pivotal to a host of coalitions' (Warwick and Druckman, 2006, p. 660) would be able to demand a greater than proportional share of the portfolios in return for supporting one possible coalition over another. In short, why should a king maker party not demand a price for choosing one king over another? However, this does not appear to be the case.

One possible answer to the Gamson's law puzzle is that parties are seeing the longer term and not just focusing on the immediate coalition negotiations. If a king maker party demands more than its 'fair share' of portfolios, measured by what share of the seats it brings to the coalition, it may have an impact on a party's chances next time round where it may no longer be in a king maker position. 'Unfair' demands could make a party a less desirable coalition partner in the long run. In other words, negotiating hard after one election may reduce a party's government potential after the next election.

Whatever is the case, as it stands Gamson's law 'is an empirical relationship still deserving of its law-like status – but in acute need of a firm theoretical foundation' (Warwick and Druckman, 2006, p. 660) – that is, we know it happens, but not why.

It is worth mentioning that while size may not make a big difference to a party's chances of getting into government, it does make a difference to its chances of getting the post of chief executive (Prime Minister). De Winter and Dumont (2006, p. 182) found that in about 80 per cent of cases the largest party in a coalition will get the chief executive portfolio.

Conclusion

It should by now be clear that getting into government is a very complicated process for a party. It first has to want government power, and once in that position it has to overcome a number of hurdles to achieve that goal. In addition, winning/losing in terms of seat shares may not be a good predictor of a party's chances of getting into government. However, party size does make a difference to how much it will get out of being in government. A greater share of the seats means greater rewards in the shape of a greater share of portfolios. Hence even in a consensus democracy, vote and seat shares still matter, but in very different ways to a majoritarian democracy. In short, a party's road to government can be long and convoluted and will be affected by numerous factors, many beyond its control.

The Internationalisation of Party Politics

This book has so far focused mainly on party politics as it has played out on the national stage. However, to complete the picture it is worth looking beyond the nation state. Indeed, political parties have long endeavoured to engage with politics beyond the national. This is not just in the sense that, to be credible all parties need to have something to say about the foreign policy of the state in which they are operating. There is more to it than that. Parties have in various ways tried to go beyond the national, not just in terms of their policies, but also in how they work as organisations. The internationalisation of party politics has a long history. The creation of various international affiliations between parties goes back to the 1800s. Further, in 1983 Goldman wrote (perhaps somewhat prematurely as we shall see) that there were tendencies in evidence which 'taken together, appear to predict the emergence of a transnational or world party system' (p. ix). This chapter will first look at the earliest and longest running attempt at internationalising party politics: party internationals. It will then consider Europarties in the context of the European Union. Having looked at these two examples of organisational internationalisation it will look at how parties have responded to the issue of globalisation. Finally, it will look at the internationalisation of campaign consultancy.

Party Internationals

There have been many attempts at building forms of permanent international co-operation between parties. This has been particularly popular on the left-wing where many socialist parties and, especially, communist parties have seen themselves as part of a world-wide movement. However, other party families have also worked to build international structures for the pursuit of common ideals.

The First, Second, Fourth and Socialist Internationals

The left-wing in party politics has a long, and largely unsuccessful, history of trying to build international cooperation in the name of the working class solidarity. The First International (or the International Workingmen's Association) was created in London in 1864 and lasted until 1876. It worked as a forum for various left-wing groups and was supposed to lead to a common direction for left-wing parties. However, it collapsed under the weight of internal disagreements over policy and strategy. Karl Marx played a significant role in the First International and was very much involved in the disagreements which eventually led to its demise.

The idea of international socialist cooperation was revived in organisational form in 1889 with The Second International. The Second International is noted for making 1 May the International Workers' Day, starting in 1889, to commemorate the so-called 1886 Haymarket Massacre in Chicago. It also instigated 8 March as International Women's Day, first observed in 1910. However, like the First International it was marked by disagreement between the national member organisations and it finally collapsed in 1916 as socialist, social democratic and labour parties overwhelmingly failed to oppose national involvement in the First World War (fought, obviously, overwhelmingly by working class soldiers on all sides). The various left-wing parties largely supported the war effort of their respective governments.

The Third International (also known as the Communist International or Comintern) will be dealt with separately below.

In 1938 Leon Trotsky founded the Fourth International as an alternative to the Stalinist Comintern. The Fourth International never received much support from the rest of the left-wing and remained largely isolated. The Fourth International suffered from increasing divisions and splits starting just a few years after its creation. By the 1960s the splits had become terminal with several independent and mutually warring organisations claiming the Fourth International's mantle – some of which continue to lead a ghostly half-life on the fringes of political life even today.

If there is one lesson to be learnt from the various left-of-centre Internationals it is the near impossibility of achieving close cooperation between national parties in the absence of strong incentives to overcome disagreements. Such incentives might include access to legislative power or funds as is the case in the European parliament which, as we shall see, has led to increasingly institutionalised forms of transnational party formations. In the absence of such incentives international cooperation on anything more than the most superficial level has proven well-nigh impossible, certainly for the left-of-centre which is in any case prone to disagreements and splits.

However, the idea of international left-wing cooperation has not died and is currently represented by the Socialist International created in 1951 (see http://www.socialistinternational.org). The Socialist International currently serves as an umbrella organisation for 163 centre left socialist, labour and social democratic parties. The Socialist International is to a certain extent built like a national party which typically (see Chapter 1) has a 'congress' as its highest authority to which 'local' fees paying 'branches', that is, national parties, can send delegates. In the Socialist International's statutes the Congress is described as 'the supreme body'. The Congress elects the president of the Socialist International as well as the Vice-Presidents, the Secretary General, and is the only body that can change the organisation's statutes. However, apart from those very specific organisational powers there is not much to indicate what 'supreme body' actually means. There is certainly no indication that the Socialist International has any power, or indeed, desire to impose any policy or ideological line on the national member parties. Nevertheless, it no doubt serves as a useful forum for communication between the member parties. The Socialist International also has 'consultative status' in the United Nations. However, there is no claim that the Socialist International is aiming to be a transnational party, but rather an umbrella group for networking and sharing experience and developing more or less specific ideas for promoting social democracy.

The Liberal International

The Liberal International was created in 1947 and serves much the same purposes as the Socialist International. It seems to share the Socialist International's relatively limited practical impact on the day-to-day lives of its membership parties. It functions mostly as a networking facility with an additional think-tank function – that is, as with the Socialist International, but from a liberal perspective, it has the purpose of developing and promoting a certain set of standpoints. It is also an interesting example of the standard liberal reaction to globalisation (see Chapter 4): 'Liberals believe that the poverty of large parts of the world can be alleviated through freedom to travel and to trade and to this end are committed to the further opening of "western" markets for products from the developing world.' (http://www.liberal-international.org/editorial.asp?ia_id=508). That is, a theoretical commitment to the view that globalization is a good thing and greater openness and integration are beneficial for all nations.

The Liberal International seems even more loosely organized than the Socialist International. While the Socialist International has a set of statutes available on their website, vague and unarticulated as they are, there is no such equivalent for the Liberal International. So, the Liberal International has an important symbolic role, but it shares the limited practical role of the Socialist International.

International Democratic Union

This association of conservative and Christian democrat parties completes the set of contemporary internationals. It was founded in 1983 by several leading right-wing leaders including Margaret Thatcher, Helmut Kohl and George Bush Sr. Its website (http://www.idu.org/history.aspx) has probably the best description of the most important purpose that these party internationals serve:

> the IDU provides a forum in which Parties holding similar beliefs can come together and exchange views on matters of policy and organisational interest, so that they can learn from each other, act together, establish contacts and speak with one strong voice to promote democracy and centre-right policies around the globe.

Although this is taken from the International Democratic Union's website it could serve as a good description of what the other international are trying to achieve. The International Democratic Union does have a set of rules (Bylaws) available on their website (http://www.idu.org/structure.aspx), suggesting at least some form of formal structure. What is important to note is that at the 'Party leaders conference' decisions have to be taken unanimously. What is referred to as 'recommendations' can be passed by a three-quarters majority, but even then parties which have expressed a 'dissenting opinion' are not covered by such 'recommendations'. This is indicative of the limited organisational ambitions of the International Democratic Union, a feature it shares with the other contemporary internationals. These are *not* 'world parties' in the making, but loose networks of like-minded organisations geared towards the exchanging of ideas and experience.

Communist International (Comintern)

If the organisational ambitions of the main centre-left and centre-right internationals have been and remain somewhat limited, the original purpose of The Communist International was the polar opposite. Comintern was established in 1919 and dissolved on the orders of Stalin in 1943 in an effort to placate the concerns of his Western allies during a critical phase of the Second World War. The idea behind the Comintern was nothing less than the creation of a world communist party. Comintern had it headquarters in Moscow and each of the national parties linked to it were regarded and encouraged to behave as 'local' branches or sections. This was the first and only attempt at creating a genuine world party (Thorpe, 1998, p. 637), and is thus worthy of attention. It illustrates the challenges involved in such a project, and is, therefore, important to our understanding of why no successful world party exists. The extent to which Comintern was actually able to operate as a single party – that is, its ability to truly control the behaviour of the national member parties – has been the subject of a longstanding, and it seems still ongoing debate. Three broad strands exist in this debate:

1   The so called 'orthodox' standpoint (Thorpe, 1998, pp. 637–8; Trapeznik, 2009, p. 125) argues that the national parties were little more than the willing and obedient tools of Moscow (see Draper, 1957; Pelling, 1958). This stance would suggest that Comintern was a successful world party. It was a view particularly popular with anti-communists during the Cold War (Thorpe, 1998, p. 637). Obviously in the charged atmosphere of the Cold War if one could paint Western communists as tools of Moscow that would undermine the legitimacy of these parties.

2   The orthodox view was challenged by 'revisionists' (Thorpe, 1998; Trapeznik, 2009). The revisionist position was the polar opposite of the orthodox view and argued that most members of Communist parties outside the Soviet Union were largely divorced from the machinations between the leadership of Comintern and national communist leaders (Macintyre, 1980). What mattered was not what went on between national party leaders and Comintern, but what communists did at the local level, far from both national leaders and Moscow.

3   Challenging both position are the 'post-revisionists' (Thorpe, 1998, p. 638; Trapeznik, 2009, p. 126). In essence the post-revisionist view is placed somewhere in between the orthodox and revisionist view. Authors in the post-revisionist vein (such as Isserman, 1982) argue that Comintern's influence is often exaggerated, but at the same time, it would be wrong to assume that Comintern did not have an impact on the day-to-day workings of Western communists.

Sadly it appears that most scholarship on Comintern has been, and to a certain extent still is, dominated by this division with its roots in the Cold

War. Hence, any wider party-politics lessons from Comintern tend to be lost in point scoring between left-wing and right-wing scholars. Overall, it is probably fair to say that Comintern was a failure. There were no successful Communist takeovers during its lifetime. Directives from Moscow frequently put national communist parties in positions where they were pushing enormously unsuccessful policy positions – most notably 'class against class' from 1928 until 1935. The class against class policy, part of the so called Third Period, held that anyone not a communist was an enemy of the working class, including social democrats and labour parties which were labelled 'social fascists'. National communist parties were, therefore, directed to attack centre-left parties as vigorously as right-wing parties. Some have argued that this led the German communists to ignore the rise of the Nazi party and partially aided the collapse of the Weimar Republic and the rise of Hitler. In addition, a number of Western communists living in the USSR were executed during Stalin's purges in the 1930s. Hence, Comintern, as the only real attempt at a true world party, not only failed in its stated purpose of promoting a world communist revolution, it can be said to have actively undermined this goal.

However, while a lot of the work on Comintern may to an extent be undermined by ideological blinkers it is still worth exploring some of the reasons behind the failure of Comintern, as it has lessons for other efforts at building transnational parties.

Essentially, Comintern failed because of two major problems which will face any attempt at building transnational parties: national distinctiveness and maintaining discipline around a central policy line.

As hinted at above, the attempts at imposing a central policy line from Moscow at times had the effect of damaging the efforts of local parties. Class against class led to the isolation of communists from their potential allies in other left-wing parties and thus managed to split the left, something which could only help the centre-right (Beckett, 1995; Jacobsen, 1996). The policy of attacking all non-communists certainly made sense in a communist one-party state such as the Soviet Union, but in democratic countries it was counter-productive. When the policy was suddenly reversed in 1935 after its abject failure, most catastrophically in Germany, the damage caused by an inappropriate policy was exasperated by the loss of credibility when national parties were instructed to turn 180 degrees – from attacking 'social fascists' to calling for 'united front' cooperation with other left-of-centre parties. Hence, Comintern illustrated with painful clarity the damage that a lack of consideration of local factors can cause. Policies dreamed up in Moscow failed miserably in states which were culturally and politically radically different from the Soviet Union.

The second problem was how to ensure that national parties followed the line laid down by the Comintern leadership. Thorpe (1998) argues that Comintern found it particularly difficult to keep national parties in democratic countries under control. As long as national communist leaders were beyond the physical grasp of the Soviet regime, Comintern had to rely on other means of persuasion. Money was certainly a major factor, particularly where the local party's membership was relatively modest. One good example of this was the Communist Party of Great Britain (CPGB). In 1927 the CPGB's membership was less than 8,000. That year it received from Comintern £21,000 for running the organisation and a further £18,000 to support a newspaper project. In comparison the Labour Party had a membership, direct and indirect (that is, trade union members), of 3,293,615 and an income of £55,708. In short with a tiny fraction of the Labour Party's membership the CPGB had finances equal to about 70 per cent of Labour's. The threat to withdraw that sum from the CPGB was a major leverage in the relationship between Moscow and the British 'branch'. However, in, for example, France where the communist party membership was vastly bigger and local resources therefore much greater, such a threat would be much less severe.

Ultimately, a party could be excluded from the Communist International the way an individual member or a local branch can be excluded from a national party. For an individual member or even a whole branch in a national context such exclusion can be devastating in terms of electoral success. There is virtually no place in electoral politics for non-party independents and the loss of party affiliation will almost invariably mean the loss of any electoral office previously held once the next election comes around. However, for a national section of a 'world party' that is much less relevant. Indeed, as was shown above, anti-communists used Comintern connections as a rod with which to beat Communist parties. Hence, apart from the loss of Comintern income, exclusion was probably not a very effective threat. Indeed, it could be argued that the European far left did much better outside the Comintern than inside it as illustrated by the notable electoral successes of the so-called Eurocommunists in the post-war period. Further, while Comintern could offer little more than financial support to its 'members', the national parties, at least where they were electorally successful, could offer Comintern influence on the politics of non-Communist countries. It might, therefore, be argued that Comintern needed the national parties more than the national parties needed Comintern.

In short, this first experiment in building a world party was largely unsuccessful, but provided it is given more non-partisan attention might be able to yield useful insights into the challenges of managing transnational parties.

Europarties

That brings us to the most successful example of cross-national party cooperation in existence so far: Europarties. The Europarties represent the only example of truly transnational party organisations in the world today. Since Comintern, they are the only party organisations that go beyond the political context of a single country. Since 1979, there has been a gradual, if incomplete, emergence of recognisable political party organisations within the European Union.

That this should be so is hardly surprising. Once direct elections were introduced in 1979, the European Parliament became the only supranational directly elected assembly in the history of democratic politics. This meant that for political parties, defined as organisations fielding candidates for publically elected assemblies, transnationalism now made sense, especially once the EU made party funding available.

The Development of Europarties

This does not mean that their development has been straightforward or that there are now fully fledged EU wide political parties the way we see them at a national level. The process is still very much ongoing and still has a considerable way to go. The emergence of Europarties can be traced back to at least the 1970s (see Table 10.1). A notable limiting factor in the development of Europarties was that no European treaty made mention of parties until the Maastricht Treaty of 1993. This ought not in and of itself be an insurmountable factor. Many national constitutions do not mention parties at all, although parties do then tend to be recognised in 'normal' legislation. What is now the EU did not recognise the existence of Europarties until 1993, and while the recognition in 1993 was rather vague and aspirational it did set in motion a series of changes that brought into existence an embryonic Europe-wide party system.

The Maastricht Treaty contains the so-called party article (Hertner, 2011, p. 326; Johansson and Raunio, 2005, p. 515), officially called Article 138a, which reads: 'Political parties at the European level are important as a factor for integration within the Union. They contribute to forming a European awareness and to expressing the political will of the citizens of the Union' (see http://eur-lex.europa.eu/en/treaties/dat/11992M/htm/11992M.html#0001000001).

While this was a major advance from previous treaties, where no mention of political parties is made at all, it should also be immediately evident that Article 138a is almost entirely vacuous and of very little

Table 10.1   *Brief description of existing Europarties*

Name	Year Created	Comments	Website
European People's Party	1976	The party is made up of the main centre-right conservative and Christian democratic parties in the EU member states. It has a strongly federal slant. As of 2011 it has 75 full, associate or observer members across 39 EU and non-EU countries.	http://www.epp.eu/
Party of European Socialists	1974	Represents the centre-left social democratic/labour tradition. PES allows members of national parties to sign up as something akin to a individual membership PES, labelled 'PES Activists' (http://www.pes.org/en/pes-activists). As of 2011 PES had 28 full members, 10 associate members, and 5 observer members).	http://www.pes.org/
European Liberal Democrats and reform Party	1976	Is made up of centre-right liberal parties. The party consists of 55 national parties from EU and non-EU countries. As with the PES individuals can join the party as an 'associate member' (http://www.eldr.eu/associate).	http://www.eldr.eu/en/index.php
European Green Party	1984	Is made up of 34 national Green parties. According to its website it is possible to join the European Green Party, although it is not entirely clear how.	http://europeangreens.eu/
Party of the European Left	2004	The Party of the European Left essentially consists of parties situated to the left of the main centre-left social democratic and labour parties. It contains much of what is left of European communism (e.g., the French Communist Party) as well as some East European parties with their roots in the former Soviet Bloc communist parties. It has 27 member parties and also allows for individual party membership (http://www.european-left.org/english/about_the_el/individual_members/)	http://www.european-left.org

European Democratic Party	2004	Is a pro-EU party situated on the centre-right. Its MEP co-operate with the MEPs from the Liberal Democrats and Reform Party, but the two Europarties remain separate entities. It is a relatively small party with 12 national party members (2011).	http://www.pde-edp.net/main/_pde/index.jsp
European Free Alliance	1994	The European Free Alliance is made up of 40 regionalist and separatist parties, very much representing 'the periphery' in the 'national revolution' political cleavage (see Chapter [ideology]).	http://www.e-f-a.org/home/
EU Democrats	2004	This is a very small Euro-sceptic (or 'Euro-realist' according to their website) group. Several of its national members are unaffiliated to any national party.	http://www.eudemocrats.org/eud/index.php
Alliance of European Conservatives and Reformists	2009	Represents Euro-sceptic conservative parties, most notably the British Conservative Party. It is made up mainly of East European parties with a very right wing and highly euro-sceptic profile. It is one of the smallest groups with only 11 national members.	http://aecr.eu/
European Christian Political Movement	2009	Is a Christian right wing and Euro-sceptic group to the right of the European People's Party. Unusually it is not associated with any of the groups in the European parliament and according to their website seems to be made up largely of NGO (including one from the USA). Indeed, it does not even appear to have any MEPs.	http://www.ecpm.info/en/

practical value. It did however open the door for further developments, by constituting what Johansson and Raunio (2005) call an 'incomplete contract'. Europarties were able to capitalise on the opening provided by the party article in the Maastricht Treaty to develop an increasingly significant role in the European Union system. Over the next 10 years after the Maastricht Treaty the existing Europarties successfully argued for a more prominent role. A major result of this was that the Nice Treaty, signed in 2001 and coming into force in 2003, made provisions for European funding of Europarties via the European Parliament's budget (see Siglas et al., 2010, p. 6). Because funding was now going to be made available to Europarties it was necessary to define what a Europarty actually looks like in practice. According to a regulation issued in 2003 a Europarty was defined as follows:

> A political party at European level shall satisfy the following conditions:
>
> a) it must have legal personality in the Member State in which its seat is located;
> b) it must be represented, in at least one quarter of Member States, by Members of the European Parliament or in the national Parliaments or regional Parliaments or in the regional assemblies, or it must have received, in at least one quarter of the Member States, at least three per cent of the votes cast in each of those Member States at the most recent European Parliament elections;
> c) it must observe, in particular in its programme and in its activities, the principles on which the European Union is founded, namely the principles of liberty, democracy, respect for human rights and fundamental freedoms, and the rule of law;
> d) it must have participated in elections to the European Parliament, or have expressed the intention to do so. (see http://eur-lex.europa.eu/LexUriServ/LexUriServ.do?uri=CELEX:32003R2004:EN:NOT)

At first European funding could not be used for election campaigning, but that was changed in time for the 2009 European Parliament elections (Hertner, 2011, p. 327). The availability of funding had a major impact on the development of Europarties, formalising those already in existence and encouraging the creation of new ones. By the 2009 elections there were a total of 10 Europarties (see Table 10.1 and Gagatek, 2009, p. 16).

It is important to note that Europarties are not the same as the formal groups in the European parliament even though they are linked (see Figure 10.1 and Gagatek, 2009, p. 13; and Hertner, 2011, p. 323). For example the Party of European Socialists is linked to the 'Group of the

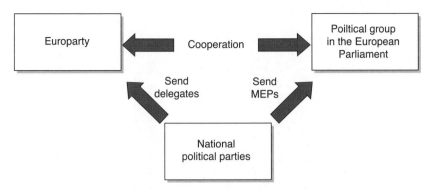

Figure 10.1   *Relations between Europarties and European Parliament Groups*

Source: Modified from Gagatek (2009, p. 13).

Progressive Alliance of Socialists and Democrats'. Where a Europarty does have links with a European Parliament group – which tends to be the norm – the two do work very closely together.

Hence, in the 'three faces of parties' framework (see Chapter 1) the European Parliament group is the party in public office, the national parties are the party on the ground and the Europarties are the party in central office. However, this picture is somewhat confused by the fact that some Europarties have started adding a separate individual membership organisation as mentioned in Table 10.1 – hence some Europarties have two forms of party on the ground. However, the 'individual membership' organisations are very weakly developed.

Limits to the development of Europarties

It would, therefore, be fair to say that Europarties have made considerable strides since the introduction of direct elections to the European Parliament in 1979. From being little more than very loose associations of national parties, they have now developed into formal organisations with legal recognition from the European Union, independent legal 'personalities' in the countries where they are registered and an independent budget.

There are however, also notable limitations to their institutionalisation. Table 10.2 outline some of the key features of the parties whose statutes are available on their websites. As we can see the power structures of all five parties in the table are not very articulated. In some of the party statutes it is specified that the Congress is the highest authority, but there is little indication of what that means in practice. Sanctions in the

Table 10.2   *Key organisational features of Europarty statutes*

| Name | Key features of party statutes | | |
	Highest decision-making body	Sanctions against members	Nature of decision making
Party of European Socialists	The congress – little detail of what that means in practices.	Membership can be suspended by the Presidency. Requests for lifting of suspension can be made to the Presidency and rejections of such requests appeal to the Congress. Members can be excluded by a qualified (75 per cent) majority of Congress.	'Efforts shall be made to establish broadest possible measure of agreement'. Administrative and organisational matters can be made by a simple majority. Political decisions require a qualified majority of 75 per cent. A party is not bound by a decision made by qualified majority if it declares itself unable to do so before the vote is taken.
European Liberal Democrats and Reform Party	Not specified	Members can be expelled by the Council with ⅔ majority.	Decisions at conference can be made with a simple majority and are binding on all members, including those absent and dissenting.
European Green Party	Not specified	Membership of a national party can be decided by ⅔ majority in the Council. Expulsion requires ¾ majority.	Decisions in the Council requires ⅔ majority.

European Democratic Party	'The congress has the most extended powers for the attainment of the purpose of the association'	Exclusion of a member party can happen by a ⅔ majority of the Council.	Congress decisions are taken by a simple majority and a binding on all members including those who voted against or abstained. Changes to the statutes require ¾ majority.
European Christian Political Movement	'The general assembly is the general meeting by law. All powers in the association not conferred on the board by law or in this charter shall vest in the General Assembly.'	Exclusion possible but process not specified.	Not specified.

Sources: European People's Party http://www.epp.eu/; The Party of European Socialists (PES) http://www.pes.org/; Alliance of Liberals and Democrats for Europe Party http://www.eldr.eu/en/index.php; European Green Party http://europeangreens.eu/; European Left http://www.european-left.org/; European Democratic Party http://www.pde-edp.net/main/_pde/index.jsp; European Free Alliance http://www.e-f-a.org/home/; EUD http://www.eudemocrats.org/eud/index.php; AECR (Alliance of European Conservatives and Reformists) http://aecr.eu/;European Christian Political Movement http://www.ecpm.info/en/ (accessed 21 November 2013).

form of a suspension of membership and expulsion exist in all parties. However, in several of the parties there are requirements for qualified majorities and in the Party of European Socialists decisions do not apply to members who have declared before a vote that they cannot abide by them. Notably the Liberals and the European Democratic Party both have clauses stating that all members are bound by decisions regardless of whether they agree with them or not. This makes those two parties the most institutionalised of the five. However, across the statutes of the five parties, institutionalisation is relatively low and power structures are left fairly vague. Hence, judging by their statutes Europarties still fall short of the institutionalisation of many national parties. Despite the fact that some Europarties now allow for direct individual membership, rather than merely indirect via national parties, the important players are overwhelmingly the leaders of national parties and there is very little direct contact between Europarties and European voters.

Further, there may be doubts about the extent to which Europarties can be regarded as 'proper parties' based on the definition of a political party adopted in this book (that is, as organisations fielding candidates). As of the 2009 European Parliament election none of the parties fielded candidates under their own name. All candidates in the European elections in 2009 stood under the banner of national parties, with the exception of the short-lived and largely unsuccessful Libertas party (Gagatek, 2009, p. 10). In short, European elections are still national elections with a European outcome (Gagatek, 2009, p. 9). The result obviously affects the composition of the European Parliament, but it is fought on national issues and by national parties. One prime example of this is the adoption of Europarty election manifestos. All the Europarties adopted manifestos in the lead up to the 2009 European elections. Indeed, some parties went through quite extensive consultation processes in making their manifesto. However, while some of these manifestos were adopted in their entirety by a few national parties or partly incorporated in national manifestos, they were to a very large extent ignored. So, despite the fact that Europarties now have their own campaign funds and can therefore provide election materials to national parties, this is only rarely utilised by the national parties. Campaigns remain overwhelmingly national affairs focused on issues related to national rather than EU politics (Gagatek, 2009; Hertner, 2011; Siglas et al., 2010).

There are many reasons for the limited development of Europarties. However, two can be singled out as being of particular importance: the difference between the nature of European Union politics and the nature of national politics; and the problem of national peculiarities.

It is true that the European Union political system can be said to have a separation of powers similar to that found to varying degrees at the national level. So, the European Union has a legislature, an executive and a judiciary. However, unlike most parliamentary democracies there is very little link between legislative elections and the formation of the executive (Day, 2005, p. 4; Gagatek, 2009, pp. 20–1; Lightfoot, 2006, p. 304). The executive office in the European Union, in the form of the European Commission and the Council of Ministers, is only open to national parties, not Europarties. The composition of the Commission and the Council of Ministers is determined by the outcomes of national elections, not election to the European Parliament. Europarties have very little impact on the makeup of the Commission and none at all on the Council of Ministers. European Commissioners are appointed by national governments; and the Council of Ministers is made up of ministers from national governments. It is true that the European Parliament has a role in approving commissioners, but that is very far from the influence that a national parliament has on the composition of a national government. As a result, and in contrast to the national politics of European states, there is very little in the way of a government/opposition dynamics in the European Parliament. After a European Parliament election it may be possible to say that either the left or the right has won or lost based on how many seats the two wings won. However, 'winning' in this sense does not give the winner the right to put their people on the Commission or the Council of Ministers. Indeed, the Commission is supposed to be non-partisan and is very little affected by European Parliament election outcomes. Hence, unlike elections fought at the national level, European Elections are not fought on the record of the incumbent executive. That means that by default European Elections tend to be fought on the basis of the performance of national governments, and therefore on national issues, and in the context of national party politics. Europarties, and indeed European Union issues, are, therefore, often largely ignored in European Parliament elections. There is then little reason for national parties to follow the lead of Europarties when it comes to deciding the themes of the campaign. If Europarties cannot effectively control the campaign themes of their national 'branches' they are never going to be fully fledged parties.

Added to that is the problem of dealing with many different national contexts. As was explored in the context of Comintern, the imposition of a supranational set of policies from some distant centre, which is likely to be ignorant or uncaring about local circumstances, is unlikely to be electorally beneficial. This problem has affected the formation of Europarty election manifestos. They have to avoid being too specific in order to not render themselves irrelevant to local circumstances. However, this has often meant that Europarty manifestos have been driven by the lowest common denominator and have ended up being very vague and lacking in substance. Europarties have struggled to find a balance between being too specific and too vague and have so far not managed to find a solution. Other, that is, than leaving policy development to the national parties, thus yet again illustrating the problem of creating meaningful supranational parties.

In short, while Europarties have certainly come a long way since 1979, and have seen an acceleration in their development since the early 1990s they are still a long way off being anything near as important as national parties. Indeed, it is perhaps unlikely that they will ever reach that stage. Having said that, Europarties are still developing and their future trajectory is far from certain.

Parties and globalization

It is clear from the above that party politics has a significant, if also very under-developed international element. This under-development of the international aspect of party politics is particularly noteworthy considering how much the study of so many other areas of politics has been dominated by issues surrounding globalisation. It would be fair to say that in most areas of politics the term globalisation has become a major, if often also overhyped, area of concern and study. In both teaching and research the idea that politics is becoming ever more interconnected across national borders has gained a big following and has had a huge impact on what is researched and taught. Degree courses with 'international' and/or 'global' in the title have been attracting students in ever greater numbers, which in turn has led many university departments to focus greater and greater attention on this area in terms of teaching and new hires.

It is obviously the study of international relations, and related fields, such as national security and political economy, which have been the most affected by this trend. However, it has also affected the study of national politics. The national is increasingly seen as declining in importance compared to the global. Many civil society organisations, especially those dealing with civil rights and environmental concerns, have embraced globalisation in a major way. Political parties, however, have remained relatively unaffected by this growing infatuation with globalisation. Both in their activities and in the academic study of them, parties have remained steadfastly national: 'Hardly anyone is talking about globalization in the context of political parties. Political parties have, to a large extent, remained limited to the national spheres' (Sehm-Patomäki and Ulvila, 2007, p. 1). This is not to say that parties have remained completely ignorant of globalization. In terms of their policy, parties have had to react. Broadly speaking the reaction of political parties to globalization can be divided into three main trends:

First, many free-market liberal parties have embraced globalization as a more or less unreserved good. The free movement of everything – finance, goods, services and labour – across borders has, at least officially been welcomed and encouraged in the formal policy stance of free market supporting parties. Many conservative parties have also embraced this trend. Indeed it was Margaret Thatcher of the British Conservative Party who popularised the term TINA (There Is No Alternative) in the context of economic liberalisation. It is true that most conservative parties have limited their enthusiasm for globalisation to certain aspects of 'low' politics (social and economic issues) and have resisted it in 'high' politics (most issues related to traditional sovereignty – such as national security and border control). Likewise, the free movement of labour has been noticeably less popular among conservative, and indeed many liberal, parties than the free movement of goods, finance and services. Nevertheless, in policy terms, parties of the right with strong laissez faire elements have by and large embraced globalization as both inevitable and beneficial.

Second, the social democratic centre-left parties have, on the whole, displayed noticeably less enthusiasm for globalization in their policy stances than the free-market right. However, most social democratic and labour parties have to a large extent bought into the idea of TINA, and have approached the issue with the view that if one cannot beat it one might as well make the most of it. Hence, social democratic parties have mostly adopted a moderate pro-globalisation stance. This approach has gone the furthest in the 'Third way' stance of Tony Blair and Gerhard Schroder – even though the latter was somewhat less eager than the former. Indeed, Blair and Schroder's attempt at a common approach to modernising social democracy can be seen as an example of the internationalisation of party politics. However, the fact that their project never went very far is illustrative of the limits of this internationalisation.

Third, outright opposition to globalization tends to be limited to the fringes of most party systems. Most far-right and far-left parties have taken a very national, even nationalistic, approach, of opposing globalization in all its forms – usually by opposing the lowering of taxes and cutting of social services and the free movement of labour (the far right fears the dilution of the national spirit by foreigners; the far left fears foreign, and often un-unionized, workers will undercut wages). This links back to the discussion in Chapter 4 where we saw that some parties have taken on the mantle of protectors of those who seem to be losing out under globalisation.

However, while policies have been affected by globalization, it has had virtually no impact on parties organisationally. There are no global parties and few transnational parties, with the partial exception of the Europarties.

According to some, this failure to react organisationally to globalisation represents a failure on behalf of parties to move with the times: 'political parties have for the most part retained a now obsolete statist-territorialist-nationalist modus operandi' (Scholte, 2007, p. 12). This is in sharp contrast with both state institutions and non-party civil society organisations, both of which have made considerable strides in engaging with globalised politics. According to some authors this is a deficiency that is in urgent need of being rectified. What we need, according to Scholte (2007, p. 13) is 'more globally oriented political parties'. Scholte suggest a number of things parties could do to rectify the lack of party politics engagement with globalisation (2007, pp. 23–30):

- Educate the general public about the importance and impact of globalisation.
- Use government power to improve the democratic elements in global governance.
- Scrutinise state policies on global governance issues.
- Engage directly with global governance bodies, such as the WTO, the World Bank and the IMF, the way many NGOs with a global slant have done.
- Promote greater global equality on the basis that only people with a certain minimum of resources can engage meaningfully in democratic processes.
- Move beyond the idea that 'the people' to be represented are only the people of a single territorial state. Instead parties should start to cater to supraterritorial types of demos.

Leaving aside the issue of the pure practicality of doing these things, there are two major issues with Scholt's proposals for a globalisation of party politics. The first problem is that some of the issues he raises are clearly of a left-wing slant. It would not be too much to say that a significant section of the political spectrum has no interest in a more equal redistribution of global resources. Most parties of liberal, conservative or nationalist persuasion would see no benefit in such a project. His remedies, therefore, speak to a particular normative position and not to 'parties' as a group. It might well be argued that left-wing parties ought to think more about global democracy and equality and have failed in properly promoting this agenda by focusing on national rather than global governance. However, many parties have as their main founding goals the promotion of *national* and not global interests. Hence, his criticism of 'parties' as a whole are in fact much more relevant for parties of the left than parties of the right.

Scholte, therefore, neglects to recognise that parties have a plethora of goals, only some of which may be undermined by parties' lack of engagement with global governance. Indeed, many party goals would run completely counter to his remedies. Hence, the problems he identifies and the remedies he proposes speak to *some* parties of a particular ideological makeup. He does not speak of all parties.

The second problem is linked to the very nature of what a political party is. This is related to a question raised, but never answered, by Patomäki and Teivainen (2007, p. 95): 'the fact that there are no global elections or parliaments may indicate that building party-like transnational organs is a relatively unattractive idea. What is the point if we cannot win elections?' In the Introduction to this book it was argued that the definition which best captured what a party is, is as an organisation which fields candidates under a common name for publically elected assemblies. This is what separates parties from other groups in civil society. Parties do many other things than field candidates – seek power, pursue ideological goals, strive for access to wealth or the personal aggrandisement for its leader(s). As was explored in Chapter 1 most such goals are shared by everything from guerrilla groups and terrorist organisations to NGOs. The fielding of candidates is what differentiates parties from the many other organisations around them that they may share traits with. There are, as Patomäki and Teivainen point out, no global elected assemblies. Hence, a key problem with Scholte's argument, that there is a need for more globally oriented parties, is that there is nothing for parties, as parties, to be oriented towards. For some parties, as seekers of certain policy goals, there may well be a call for a more global mode of operating. However, that very much depends on the specific goals being pursued by a party – goals which are as varied as parties are numerous.

Hence, truly global parties are only relevant in the context of global publicly elected assemblies, of which there are none; or in the context of specific policy goals which will only speak to some parties. The very definition of a party would, therefore, explain why both the organisational work of parties and the study of them have remained focused on the national. The lack of globalisation of party organisations cannot, therefore, be seen as a sign of parties failing. At most it can be seen as a failure of *some* parties to effectively pursue specific policy goals.

The internationalisation of campaign consultancy

While parties as organisations have remained overwhelmingly national in their operation, there is one area where there has been a significant internationalisation – the use of campaign consultants. Since the late 1960s, campaign consultants have increasingly worked abroad (Farrell, 1998; Plasser, 2000). This has been particularly the case for consultants normally based in the United States, a country often seen as being at the cutting edge of 'modern' campaigning. The International Association of Political Consultants had 110 members on its 2010 list of members. Of these 36 (about 33 per cent) claim to have some level of international experience. Of those 36, 22 come from the United States.

There are many reasons why consultants might have an incentive to go abroad. One driving force, particularly relevant for US-based consultants, is that there is a significant oversupply of political consultants in the American market. According to Plasser (2000, see also Farrell, 1998) there is a glut of campaign consultants operating in the domestic consultancy market in the United States, which means that the competition for contracts is fierce. Many consultants may, therefore, be tempted to try to tap new markets outside the United States.

In addition there seems to be a growing demand for consultants who are perceived as being able to provide the latest in campaigning knowhow. Techniques found to be successful in one country, often first in the United States, attract attention in other countries where parties seek to gain an advantage over domestic opponents. This in turn will drive a domestic arms races further pushing up demand for expertise. As Duverger argued in connection with the mass-party and Kirchheimer for the catchall party, the reason why these models spread from their specific origins to the rest of the party system was because they were successful – and success breeds demand. The same is the case for successful campaigning methods and consultants deemed able to teach such methods to their clients.

Further, many long-established democracies have implemented democratic assistance programmes to new democracies (Farrell, 1998, p. 173; Plasser, 2000, pp. 36–7), especially since the end of the Cold War. This has often been in the form of financial aid, which has allowed parties in newly democratic countries to buy in expert help.

There is some disagreement about what exactly the effects are of this internationalisation of campaign consultancy. In essence the disagreement is focused on whether what we are seeing is a process of Americanisation or modernisation (Swanson and Mancini, 1996; see Figure 10.2). In the Americanization view other countries are converging on the American model. By contrast the modernisation view is that all countries are simply moving towards ever more 'modern' campaign techniques, albeit with the United States in the lead.

Which of these views is more accurate is not clear. As was explored in Chapter 8 the debate over the exact nature of modern campaigning and what direction it is going in is very much an ongoing affair.

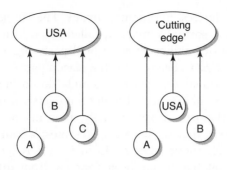

Figure 10.2   *Americanisation vs. Modernisation*

There are also several factors that limit the spread of American/new techniques. One issue is that not all techniques 'travel' very well. Especially techniques which rely on a certain level of technological penetration, that is, access to the Internet or television ownership, will be virtually useless in many developing countries. Hence, many of the lessons from Barack Obama's first presidential campaign, which saw heavy use of web sites to coordinate local volunteers, will not be relevant in many new democracies in, for example, Africa. In addition, in countries where the focus of campaigning is on parties rather than individual candidates, the demand for consultants will be lower. Where individual candidates are responsible for their own campaigning as it the case in the United States, there will be a much larger demand for consultants than in countries where a single-party campaign headquarter hires consultants to work on a fairly centralised national campaign. Imagine a country of 100 parliamentary seats and five parties. That will mean 500 candidates. In a party-oriented system each party's head office would be in charge of hiring consultants. There would, therefore, be five clients. In a candidate-focused system there would be 500 potential clients. Clearly, the political system will make a difference to how much demand there is for the work of consultants.

However, regardless of these limitations there can be no doubt that the internationalisation of campaign consultancy is a trend that is likely to continue. In ever-more-competitive electoral markets, parties will want to make use of every trick to beat their opponents. Inspiration for such tricks is likely to increasingly come from abroad.

Conclusion

The internationalisation of party politics is not an area that has received very much attention. This is partly because it is an area that parties have not shown a great interest in organisationally. The one serious attempt to create a true world party, Comintern, failed in no little part due to the inherent problems of building international party organisations. Indeed, there are good reasons to believe that the reason parties have not internationalised organisationally is that they simply do not need to. There are no international assemblies elected under a universal franchise except for the European Parliament. Unsurprisingly, it is in connection with the European Parliament that we have seen the most advanced development of functioning international parties. Even here it is only on a regional scale, and the result has so far been very far from fully formed party organisations seen at the national level. Nevertheless, parties have still been impacted by internationalisation, especially when it comes to policy stances and campaigning. The internationalisation of campaign consultancy is an area that is likely to continue to attract attention, even as other aspects of party organisations remain resolutely national.

Chapter 11

The Future of Party Politics

This final chapter will look at the future of the academic study of party politics and consider what the big areas of research are. It will also try to evaluate one of the big questions in party politics: are parties as a collective in crisis?

Future direction in the study of political parties

The study of party politics is a very active and growing field. This section will look briefly at what is going on in research in each of the areas covered by this book.

There is little to suggest that Sartori's model of party systems is about to be challenged. It has, as could be expected, been criticised, but no one has come up with a scheme that has seriously looked to undermine Sartori's dominance. The discipline seems relatively content with his scheme and mostly uses it as the starting point for research, if not explicitly, at least implicitly. As Bardi and Mair write, there has been 'almost no substantial innovation since the publication of Sartori's classic work in 1976' (2008, p. 148). So, the main concern in the field of party systems is not defining them. Instead the focus is on: a) what drives party system formation and change; and b) developing better ways of calculating party system fragmentation. As was explored in Chapter 2 what drives the formation of one party system rather than another is not clear, and this lack of clarity has had the effect of spawning a growing literature. This has also been driven by the emergence of new democracies in Eastern Europe, Africa and East and South East Asia since the end of the Cold War. These areas have provided rich soil for examining how party systems emerge and stabilise (or fail to stabilise). So, for example Croissant and Volkel (2012) consider the formation of party systems in East and South East Asia; Rose and Mishler (2010) explore the lack of stability in Russia's party system; Mozaffar and Scarritt (2005) examine the reason behind the low fragmentation, yet high volatility in African party systems. Another area that has received attention is calculating the fragmentation of party systems. Laakso and Taagepera's (1979) approach to calculating the effective number of parties is popular and widely accepted, but has also

202 Contemporary Party Politics

received considerable critical attention. Both the emergence and stability of party systems and approaches to counting parties and measuring fragmentation are likely to continue to be the subject of scholarly concern.

The issue of how parties are developing is certainly an area that could be said to be the foundational concern of the party politics field. However, more specifically the 'party types' literature is an area of continuous growth. As was shown in Chapter 3 there is a steady stream of suggestions for new party types. While the cadre to catch-all development is more or less accepted, there seems to be no consensus on what has happened since. The competition to be Kirchhemimer's successor is certainly fierce. Most new suggestions do not get much attention, but some such as Katz and Mair's cartel party generate considerable debate.

The reasons for this proliferation of new types compared to the relatively straightforward cadre to catch all development are not entirely clear. As was discussed in Chapter 3, the proliferation of new party types since Kirchheimer's work could be down to one of two explanations. First, it may be that democracy, and therefore party organisations have become more complex – thus giving rise to many more new party types than was previously the case. Second, there may just be that many more people doing work on party organisations and, therefore, there is much more focus on the small differences between parties as new scholars find their individual niche. Whichever is the case, the development of new party types is likely to continue.

The issue of ideology is an area that is dominated by the efforts of trying to understand what the end of the Cold War and the seeming victory of liberalism and the rise of globalisation are doing to the distinctiveness of political parties. There is a strong sense that many parties seem to be converging on a liberal free-market standpoint. However, there is also a considerable amount of work being done on the rise of parties challenging the status quo, especially on the far right. The far left is still struggling to re-define itself in the wake of the collapse of Communism, but the far right seems to have found rich soil among the 'losers' from globalisation, most prominently illustrated by the strong, if also uneven, rise of anti-immigration parties in many countries. However, one area which perhaps deserves far more attention than it has been receiving is what ideology means in party political terms outside Europe. As we saw in Chapter 4 many of the models developed to understand party ideology have their origins in Western Europe. They do not always travel very well outside Europe and there seems to be a need to develop models that can cope better with the ideological foundations of political parties more widely. The case of African parties suggests that the very idea of ideology may not be easily applied to parties in certain political contexts. This would seem to be a research agenda with a rich potential.

Party membership is not only a topic receiving considerable attention in the academic literature, it is also the subject of a great deal of soul-searching and agonising both in academia and among political parties. The cause of this soul-searching and agonising is the widespread decline in party membership numbers experienced by a great many parties. The idea that the mass-membership party is, or perhaps increasingly was, the 'normal' and also the most desirable form of party organisation means that the decline of party membership organisations is viewed with particular trepidation. There, then, seems to be three main areas active in party-membership research.

The first is research into the trends in membership numbers. That this area of research should continue despite the generally agreed conclusion that numbers are going down is driven by two issues. The first is that there are still parties where numbers are not going down, but up, or at least merely fluctuating. Identifying which parties are resisting the general trend will allow scholars to study them to identify what allows them to resist decline. The second is that, as was pointed out in Chapter 5, the extent to which mass-membership organisations were 'normal', as opposed to a temporary phase, may have been exaggerated. The more data is available the easier it is to understand the long-term developments of membership organisations.

The second main area of research into party members is to understand what drives decline. This is exemplified by Whiteley and Seyd's (2002), work based on membership surveys. Using that data they have tried to establish whether the decline is driven by long-term societal change, or shorter-term party-specific issues (that is, party leaders no longer seeing membership recruitment and retention as a priority).

The third area of research in relation to party members is focused on better understanding the members that are left. Who are this dwindling minority of people who insist on holding on to what some regard as an anachronistic form of political engagement? What are their beliefs; their social, educational and employment backgrounds; what are their ideological beliefs; and to what extent do they differ from non-member citizens?

Candidate selection procedures are a very active area of research. It is an area that is broadly speaking of interest to two groups of scholars. One group consist of those who want to know something about the balance of power between the three faces of parties. As was argued in Chapter 6, candidate selection is an enormously important area of party life and understanding who controls it will tell us an awful lot about who has the power in a party. In addition, candidate recruitment is of great interest to those who want to understand the under-representation of certain groups in society, most notably women. It is probably in the area of gender studies that we are seeing the most active research agenda on this topic at the moment. Women make up more than half of the world's population, yet are massively under-represented in almost all democratically elected parliaments. This is obviously a major problem for the democratic world and more than warrants the attention devoted to this area of research. This research agenda promises to continue to grow.

The issue of who controls policy making in political parties is a somewhat under-researched area. In 2002 Scarrow et al. (2002, p. 144) wrote that 'for all the importance of party programmes to democratic theory and practice, we still know very little about where these programmes come from, and particularly about the role of intra-party democracy in the process'. Even now this still broadly holds true. There have been several recent studies of intra-party democracy, including of Denmark (Pedersen, 2010), Sweden (Loxbo, 2013) and comparing Denmark and the United Kingdom (Pettitt, 2012b). However, there is still no major comparative study to draw general conclusion across several cases about wider patterns of who controls policy making. This is an area that holds a lot of potential for further research. As was explored in Chapter 7, the normative side of the argument, that is, *should* parties be internally democratic, has been relatively settled on the 'yes' side. It seems that, generally speaking, democracy is seen as a 'good thing' and something to be encouraged including within political parties.

One area that has received a lot of attention and that continues to be very active is election campaigning and how this is affecting party organisations. That this should receive as much attention as it does is hardly surprising considering how important elections are to the very foundations of what a party is about: the presenting of candidates in elections. One area that has seen a lot of interest is the re-emergence of local campaigning and with it the return in importance of having a local volunteer base to rely on at election time. It is very likely that this will be a topic that will continue to receive more attention as data becomes available from future elections.

As we saw in Chapter 9 the research on coalition formation has a long history and a steadily expanding literature. It has been argued that significant success in predicting coalition formation remains somewhat elusive, but this will no doubt be an area where people will continue to refine the predictive tools. One research agenda which has seen considerable growth is recent years is how parties usually regarded as being on the fringes of the political system cope with entering government for the first time. A lot of attention has been focused on understanding the price that the parties of the far right and the far left have to pay for government participation. This is a research agenda that will no doubt continue for as long as parties previously regarded as being beyond the pale are given the opportunity to enter government.

205 The Future of Party Politics

The internationalisation of party politics is probably the least developed area in terms of research that has been covered in this book. This is partly because party politics are overwhelmingly focused on domestic politics. This is especially so when looking at the organisational side of party politics. There are no world parties, and the only really international parties are the Europarties linked to the European parliament. However, Europarties have only emerged fairly recently. Hence, research on them is also at an early stage. Nevertheless, Europarties will no doubt provide a longstanding rich vein of research as they continue to develop. Another area that will also continue to provide rich research pickings will be the increasing internationalisation of campaign consultancy. Parties have been seeking inspiration from likeminded partners internationally and this is only likely to intensify. The ways in which this intensification manifests itself and the consequences will almost certainly be one of the major research agendas in the coming decades. What is not likely to happen is the appearance of truly international parties. Without the existence of popularly elected international assemblies outside the European Union, parties simply have no incentive to develop their organisation in an international direction. International cooperation between parties is likely to be limited to knowledge exchange, especially in the area of election campaigning.

Are parties in crisis?

It is possible to argue that political parties have never been more significant than they are now. As a collective they constitute the most important and powerful type of political organisation in the world. No democratic country has been able to do without them, and with the rise of new democracies in Eastern Europe, Africa and Asia they have continued their dominance. Modern democracy is and continues to be party democracy, a fact confirmed in every single post-1989 democracy. Throughout the democratic world the path to political power is exclusively through a political party. Despite considerable anti-party feelings in most democratic countries, independents have nowhere made significant gains. For anyone with political ambitions in democratic societies the means to realising those ambitions was, is and is likely to continue to be a political party. There is currently no viable alternative to party democracy, and thus Schattschneider's claim that democracy is unthinkable save in term of political parties, cited at the very beginning of this book, holds as true today as it did then.

However, there are also serious claims of party weakness both in the academic literature and in the media. Broadly speaking these claims can be summarised under three headings: unpopularity; shrinking member-ship organisations; and disengagement.

It certainly is true that political parties are unpopular. That was evident from the data presented in the Introduction. However, it is also true that parties have always been viewed with suspicion. Their unpopu-larity is, therefore, not something particularly new. It is also true that political parties are losing members, sometimes at a significant rate. This has been cited as one piece of evidence for the idea that political parties are now in crisis. It is important though to keep in mind the argument made in Chapter 5 that mass-membership organisations should not nec-essarily be viewed as the normal state of affairs for political parties. Indeed, the high point of the mass-membership party was a fairly brief period immediately after the Second World War.

What may well be true is that parties are struggling to maintain their engagement with voters. Lawson's view of the failure of linkage and the cartel party argument that political parties are withdrawing into the state (see Chapter 3) do seem to have some merit. Mair's (2006) claim that contemporary democracy is witnessing a mutual withdrawal, of citizens into private life or short-term forms of political engagement and of politi-cians into the institutions of the state is backed up by considerable evi-dence.

The question then is: are parties in crisis? At the most fundamental level, based on the definition of what a political party is laid out in the introduction to this book, the answer must be no. If we see a party as being defined as an organisation that presents candidates to publically elected assemblies then parties are, as was argued above, stronger than ever. There is no evidence to suggest that parties are being threatened by a rise in non-party independents. In addition there is little evidence to make us believe that modern representative democracy is likely to turn in a more direct democracy direction, bypassing political parties. Parties make the most sense in a representative democracy where they are the main and even only suppliers of representatives. If a more direct form of democracy was to emerge, parties would potentially have much less justi-fication for their existence. However, such a change is not in evidence.

The extent to which parties are in crisis must, therefore, be related to the other tasks that they perform in modern democracy. Ignazi (1996, p. 550) argues that the idea of a crisis of party is mainly related to the crisis of a certain *type* of party, that is, the Duvergerian mass party. As should be clear from both Chapter 3 on the development of parties through several stages/types and Chapter 5 on party members, the mass-party model is not 'normal'. It is, or was, depending on how far one thinks the decline has gone, one temporary stage in the continual development of political parties. Modern democracy, and indeed society as such, is not static, but continually evolving, and that includes party organisations. The leaders of the old cadre parties may well have regarded the rise of the mass party as a sign of a crisis of party and even of democracy. That certainly seems to have been Ostrogorski's stance. Ostrogorski did not have a problem with organised groups in parliament, but was notoriously suspicious of permanent organisations outside parliament. To him the rise of the mass party was a sign of crisis and decline of the old, and better, order based on cadre parties. We now seem to be seeing a repeat of that view: that new forms and types of party organisations are evolving that are seen as inferior to what came before, that is, the mass party.

So, yes: parties are changing. They always have and they always will. Just as human society is not static so parties are continually evolving as they react to and influence changes in their environment. There is no 'normal' or 'standard' model for what a party looks like and against which changes can be evaluated. They are, however, many normative ideas of what parties *ought* to look like and what is currently happening to parties may well deviate from some of those norms. Especially if they rest on ideas derived from the mass-party model of party organisation.

In short, the answer to the question of whether parties are in crisis relies on normative ideas of what a party *should* look like – normative ideas that are inherently and unavoidably contested. Because these ideas are contested the question of whether parties are in crisis or not cannot really be settled objectively. Indeed the question has been with us for as long as political parties have been the subject of academic study and public debate. Parties as such show no signs of disappearing or reaching some stable form and consequently will, therefore, continue to generate research and disagreement. The one thing that can be said then, is that party politics as an academic discipline is in rude good health, and that most other questions regarding parties, including their supposed crisis, is a matter for continuing debate.

Bibliography

African National Congress (2012) *African National Congress Constitution*, Johannesburg, African National Congress.

Aldrich, John Herbert (2011) *Why Parties: A Second Look*, Chicago, University of Chicago Press.

American Political Science Association Committee on Political Parties (1950) *Towards a More Responsible Two-Party System*, New York, Rinehart.

Amery, L. S. (1947) *Thoughts on the Constitution*, Oxford, Oxford University Press.

Amery, L. S. (1964) *Thoughts on the Constitution*, London, Oxford University Press.

Ashworth, T. R. and H. P. C. Ashworth (1901) *Proportional Representation Applied to Party Government: A New Electoral System*, London, Swan Sonnenschein.

Attlee, Clement (1937) *The Labour Party in Perspective*, London, Victor Gollancz.

Axelrod, Robert (1970) *Conflict of Interest*, Chicago, Markham.

Bacharatz, Peter and M. S. Baratz (1963) 'Decisions and non-decisions: an analytical framework', *American Political Science Review*, 57, 632–42.

Bardi, L. and P. Mair (2008) 'The parameters of party systems', *Party Politics*, 14, 2, 147–66.

Basedau, Matthias and Alexander Stroh (2009) 'Ethnicity and party systems in Francophone Sub-Saharan Africa', *GIGA Working Paper*, 100, May 2009, Hamburg, GIGA.

Beckett, Francis (1995) *Enemy Within: The Rise and Fall of the British Communist Party*, London, John Murray.

Beer, Samuel H. (1965) *Modern British Politics: A Study of Parties and Pressure Groups*, London, Faber and Faber.

Benoit, Kenneth and Michael Laver (2006) *Party Policy in Modern Democracies*, London, Routledge.

Berntson, Lennart (1974) *Politiska partier och sociala klasser: En analys av partiteoren i den moderna statskunskapen och marxismen*, Lund, Cavefors Bokforlag.

Bille, Lars (1997) *Partier i forandring*, Odense, Odense Universitetsforlag.

Bille, Lars (2001) 'Democratizing a democratic procedure: myth or reality? Candidate selection in Western European parties', *Party Politics*, 7, 3, 363–80.

Blau, Adrian (2008) 'The effective number of parties at four scales: votes, seats, legislative power, executive power', *Party Politics*, 14, 2, 167–87.

Blondel, Jean (1968) 'Party systems and patterns of government', *Canadian Journal of Political Science*, 1, 2, 180–203.

Blumler, J. and D. Kavanagh (1999) 'The third age of political communication: influence and features', *Political Communication*, 16, 3, 209–30.

Bochel, John and David Denver (1983) 'Candidate in the Labour Party: what the selectors seek', *British Journal of Political Science*, 13, 1, 45–69.

Bolleyer, Nicole (2008) 'The organizational costs of public office', in K. Deschouwer (ed.), *New Parties in Government*, London, Routledge, 17–41.

Brass, Paul (1966) *Factional Politics in an Indian State*, Oxford, Oxford University Press.

Browne, Eric (1973) *Coalition Theories: A Logical and Empirical Technique*, London, Sage.

Browne, Eric and Mark Franklin (1973) 'Aspects of coalition payoffs in European Parliamentary democracies', *The American Political Science Review*, 67, 2, 453–69.

Budge, Ian and Hans Keman (1990) *Parties and Democracy: Coalition Formation and Government Function in Twenty States*, Oxford, Oxford University Press.

Buksti, Jacob (2005) *Ånden fra finderup: formandsopgøret i Socialdemokratiet 1992*, Copenhagen, Aschehoug.

Burke, Edmund (1981) 'Thoughts on the cause of the present discontents', in Paul Langford (ed.), *The Writings and Speeches of Edmund Burke: Volume 2: Party Parliament and the American Crisis, 1766–1774*, Oxford, Clarendon Press, 251–322.

Burnell, P. (2001) 'The party system and party politics in Zambia: continuities past, present and future', *African Affairs*, 100, 399, 239–63.

Carty, R. Kenneth (2004) 'Parties as franchise systems: the stratarchical organizational imperative', *Party Politics*, 10, 1, 5–24.

Cecil, Hugh (1912) *Conservatism*, London, Williams and Norgate.

Christensen, Dag (2010) 'The Danish Socialist People's Party: still waiting after all these years', in Jonathan Olsen, Michael Koß and Dan Hough (eds), *Left Parties in National Governments*, Basingstoke, Palgrave Macmillan, 121–37.

Clapham, Christopher (1996) *Africa in the International System: The Politics of State Survival*, Cambridge, Cambridge University Press.

Clark, Peter and James Wilson (1961) 'Incentive systems: a theory of organizations', *Administrative Science Quarterly*, 6, 2, 129–66.

Coffe, H. (2008) 'Social Democratic parties as buffers against the extreme right: the case of Belgium', *Contemporary Politics*, 14, 2, 179–95.

Colomer, Josep (2005) 'It's parties that choose electoral systems (or Duverger's law upside down),'*Political Studies*, 53, 1, 1–21.

Conservative Party (2012) *Guide to Becoming a Conservative MP*, London, The Conservative Party.

Croissant, Aurel and Philip Vokel (2012) 'Party system types and party system institutionalization: comparing new democracies in East and Southeast Asia', *Party Politics*, 18, 2, 235–65.

Cowley, Philip (2005) *The Rebels: How Blair Mislaid His Majority*, London, Politico's.

Cutts, David, Sarah Childs and Edward Fieldhouse (2005) '"This is what happens when you don't listen"', *Party Politics*, 14, 5, 575–95.

Daalder, Hans (1992) 'A crisis of party?', *Scandinavian Political Studies*, 15, 4, 269–88.

Dahlerup, Drude (2001) *Men kvinderne vil jo ikke selv: diskurs omkring betydningen af køn ved danske kommunevalg*, Aalborg, Aalborg Universitet GEP-Tekstserie No. 2.

Damgaard, Erik and Palle Svensson (1989) 'Who governs? Parties and policies in Denmark', *European Journal of Political Research*, 17, 6, 731–45.

Day, Stephen (2005) 'Developing a conceptual understanding of Europe's transnational political parties (with a specific focus on the Party of European Socialists)', *Journal of Contemporary European Studies*, 13, 1, 59–77.

De Winter, Lieven and Patrick Dumont (2006) 'Parties into government: still many puzzles', in Richard S. Katz and Willian Crotty (eds), *Handbook of Party Politics*, London, Sage, 175–88.

Deschouwer, Kris (2008) 'Comparing newly governing parties', in K. Deschouwer (ed.), *New Parties in Government*, London, Routledge, 1–16.

Diermeier, Daniel and Antonio Merlo (2004) 'An empirical investigation of coalitional bargaining procedures', *Journal of Public Economics*, 88, 3–4, 783–97.

Dominguez, Casey (2005) 'Does a house divided really fall? A test of the consequences of party unity around Primary candidates', Paper presented at the annual meeting of the Midwest Political Science Association, Palmer House Hilton, Chicago, Illinois, 7 April.

Downs, Anthony (1957) *An Economic Theory of Democracy*, New York, Harper and Brothers .

Draper, Theodore (1957) *The Roots of American Communism*, New York, Viking Press.

Dunleavy, Patrick (1991) *Democracy, Bureaucracy and Public Choice*, New York, Harvester.

Duverger, Maurice (1964) *Political Parties: Their Organization and Activity in the Modern State*, London, Methuen.

EIU (2011) *The Democracy Index 2011: Democracy under Stress*, London, Economist Intelligence Unit.

Eldersveld, Samuel (1964) *Political Parties: A Behavioural Analysis*, Chicago, Rand McNally.

Epstein, Leon (1967) *Political Parties in Western Democracies*, New York, Praeger.

Epstein, Leon (1980) *Political Parties in Western Democracies*, New Brunswick, Transaction Publishers.

Evans, Elizabeth (2008) 'Supply and demand: women candidates and the Liberal Democrats', *British Journal of Politics and International Relations*, 4, 10, 590–606.

Farrell, David (1996) 'Campaign strategies and tactics', in Lawrence Leduc, Richard Niemi and Pippa Norris (eds), *Comparing Democracies: Elections and Voting in Global Perspective*, Thousand Oak, Sage, 156–81.

Farrell, David (1998) 'Political consultancy overseas: the internationalization of campaign consultancy', *PS: Political Science and Politics*, 31, 2, 171–6.

Farrell, David and Paul Webb (2002) 'Political parties as campaign organizations', in Russel Falton and Martin Wattenberg (eds), *Parties Without Partisans: Political Change in Advanced Industrial Democracies*, Oxford, Oxford University Press, 102–28.

Farrell, David, Robin Kolodny and Stephen Medvic (2001) 'Parties and campaign professionals in a digital age: political consultants in the United States and their counterparts overseas', *The Harvard International Journal of Press/Politics*, 6, 4, 11–30.

Fisher, J. and T. Eisenstadt (2004) 'Introduction: comparative party finance', *Party Politics*, 10, 6, 619–26.

Fisher, Justin, David Denver, Edward Fieldhouse, David Cutts and Andrew Russell (2005) *Constituency Campaigning in the 2005 British General Election*, Paper prepared for the Annual Conference of the PSA Specialist Group on Elections, Public Opinion and Parties, Essex, September.

Franceschet, Susan (2005) *Women and Politics in Chile*, Boulder, Lynne Reinner.

Frechette, G., J. Kagel and M. Morelli (2005) 'Nominal bargaining power, selection protocol, and discounting in legislative bargaining', *Journal of Public Economics*, 89, 8, 1497–517.

Freire, A (2008) 'Party polarization and citizens' left-right orientation', *Party Politics*, 14, 2, 189–209.

Gagatek, Wojciech (2009) *European Political Parties as Campaign Organisations: Toward a Greater Politicisation of the European Parliament Elections*, Brussels, Centre for European Studies.

Gallagher, Michael (1985) *Political Parties in the Irish Republic*, Manchester, Manchester University Press.

Gallagher, Michael (1988) 'Introduction', in Michael Gallagher and Michael Marsh (eds) *Candidate Selection in Comparative Perspective: The Secret Garden of Politics*, London, Sage, 1–19.

Gallagher, Michael and Michael Marsh (eds) (1988) *Candidate Selection in Comparative Perspective: The Secret Garden of Politics*, London, Sage.

Gallagher, Michael and Paul Mitchell (2008) 'Appendix B: Indices of fragmentation and disproporitonality', in Michael Gallagher and Paul Mitchell (eds), *The Politics of Electoral Systems*, Oxford, Oxford University Press, 598–606.

Gallagher, Michael, Michael Laver and Peter Mair (2011) *Representative Government in Modern Europe*, Maidenhead, McGraw Hill.

Gamson, William (1961) 'A theory of coalition formation', *American Sociological Review*, 26, 3, 373–82.

Giddens, Anthony (1998) *The Third Way: The Renewal of Social Democracy*, Cambridge, Polity.

Giddens, Anthony (2000) *The Third Way and Its Critics*, Cambridge, Polity.

Gerring, John (1998) *Party Ideologies in America, 1828–1996,* Cambridge, Cambridge University Press.

Gibson, Rachel and Andrea Rommele (2001) 'Changing campaign communications: A party centered theory of professionalized campaigning', *Harvard International Journal of Press/Politics*, 6, 4, 31–44.

Gibson, Rachel and Andrea Rommele (2009) 'Measuring the professionalization of political campaigning', *Party Politics*, 15, 3, 265–93.

Goldman, Ralph (1983) *Transnational pparties: Organizing the World's Precincts*, New York, University Press of America.

Gould, Philip (1998) *The Unfinished Revolution: How the Modernisers Saved the Labour Party*, London, Abacus.

Gray, John (1997) *Is Conservatism Dead?*, London, Profile Books.

Green, Donald and Alan Gerber (2008) *Get out the Vote: How to Increase Voter Turnout*, Washington, DC, The Brookings Institute.

Grum, John G. (1958) 'Theories of electoral systems', *Midwest Journal of Political Science*, 2, 4, 357–76.

Gutmann, Amy and Dennis Thompson (1996) *Democracy and Disagreement*, Cambridge, MA, The Belknap Press of Harvard University.

Hansen, Bernhard and Karina Pedersen (2003) 'Medlemsrollen og det interne partidemokrati', in Lars Bille and Jørgen Elklit (eds), *Partiernes Medlemmer*, Aarhus, Aarhus Universitets Forlag, 103–31.

Hardgrave, Robert and Stanley Kochanek (2008) *India: Government and Politics in a Developing Nation*, Boston, Thomson Wadsworth.

Harmel, Robert and Kenneth Janda (1994) 'An integrated theory of party goals and party change', *Journal of Theoretical Politics*, 6, 3, 259–87.

Haupt, Andrea B. (2010) 'Parties' responses to economic globalization. What is left for the Left and right for the Right?', *Party Politics*, 16, 1, 5–27.

Hazan, Reuven and Gideon Rahat (2010) *Democracy within Parties: Candidate Selection Methods and their Political Consequences*, Oxford, Oxford University Press.

Heidar, Knut (2006) 'Party membership and participation', in Richards S. Katz and William Crotty (eds), *Handbook of Party Politics*, London, Sage, 301–15.

Heidar, Knut and Jo Saglie (2002) *Hva skjer med Partierne?*, Oslo, Gyldendal.

Hertner, Isabelle (2011) 'Are European election campaigns Europeanized? The case of the Party of European Socialists in 2009', *Government and Opposition*, 46, 3, 321–44.

Hindess, Barry (1971) *The Decline of Working Class Politics*, London, MacGibbon and Kee.

Hinnfors, Jonas (2006) *Reinterpreting Social Democracy: A History of Stability in the British Labour Party and the Swedish Social Democratic Party*, Manchester, Manchester University Press.

Hoffman, David (1961) 'Intra-party democracy: a case study', *The Canadian Journal of Economics and Political Science*, 27, 2, 223–35.

Hofstadter, Richard (1948) *The American Political Tradition and the Men Who Made It*, New York, A. A. Knopf.

Hopkin, J. (2001) 'Bringing the members back in? Democratizing candidate selection in Britain and Spain', *Party Politics*, 7, 3, 343–61.

Hopkin, J. and Paolucci, C. (1999) 'The business firm model of party organization: cases from Spain and Italy', *European Journal of Political Research*, 35, 3, 307–39.

Hopkin, K. (2004) 'The problem with party finance: theoretical perspectives on the funding of party politics', *Party Politics*, 10, 6, 627–51.

Hough, Dan, Michael Koß and Jonathan Olsen (2007) *The Left Party in Contemporary German Politics*, London, Palgrave Macmillan.

Howard, Norman (2005) *A New Dawn: The General Election of 1945*, London, Politico's.

Ignazi, Piero (1996) 'The crisis of parties and the rise of new political parties', *Party Politics*, 2, 4, 549–66.

Inglehart, Ronald (1977) *Silent Revolution: Changing Values and Political Styles among Western Politics*, Princeton, Princeton University Press.

Isserman, Maurice (1982) *Which Side Were You On? The American Communist Party During the Second World War*, Middletown, Wesleyan University Press.

Jacobs, Herbert (1962) 'Internal recruitment of elected officials in the US – a model', *The Journal of Politics*, 24, 4, 703–16.

Jacobsen, Kurt (1996) *Aksel Larsen – en politisk biografi*, Copenhagen, Vinderose.

Johansson, Karl and Tapio Raunio (2005) 'Regulating Europarties: cross-party coalitions capitalizing on incomplete contracts', *Party Politics*, 11, 5, 515–34.

Johnston, Ron, and Charles Pattie (2008) 'How much does a vote cost? Incumbency and the impact of campaign spending at English general elections', *Journal of Elections, Public Opinion and Parties*, 18, 2, 129–52.

Karp, Jeffery, Susan Banducci and Shaun Bowler (2008) 'Getting out the vote: party mobilization in a comparative perspective', *British Journal of Political Science*, 38, 1, 91–112.

Katz, Richard S. (1986) 'Party government: a rationalistic conception', in Francis G. Castles and Rudolf Wildenmann (eds), *Visions and Realities of Party Government*, New York, Walter de Gruyter, 31–50.

Katz, Richard S. (1997) *Democracy and Elections*, London, Oxford University Press.

Katz, Richard S. and Robin Kolodny (1994) 'Party organizations and an empty vessel: parties in American politics', in Richard Katz and Peter Mair (eds), *How Parties Organize: Change and Adaptation in Party Organizations in Western Democracies*, London, Sage, 23–51.

Katz, Richard S. and Peter Mair (eds) (1992) *Party Organizations: A Data Handbook*, London, Sage.

Katz, Richard and Peter Mair (1993) The evolution of party organizations in Europe: the three faces of party organization', *The American Review of Politics*, 14, 593–617.

Katz, Richard and Peter Mair (1995) Changing models of party organization and party democracy: the emergence of the cartel party', *Party Politics*, 1, 1, 5–28.

Katz, Richard S. and Peter Mair (2002) The ascendency of the party in public office: party organisational changes in twentieth-century democracies', in Richard Gunther, Jose Ramon Montero and Juan J. Linz (eds), *Political Parties: Old Concepts and New Challenges*, Oxford, Oxford University Press, 113–36.

Kennedy, Fiachra, Pat Lyons and Peter Fitzgerald (2006) 'Pragmatists, ideologues and the general law of curvilinear disparity: the case of the Irish Labour Party', *Political Studies*, 54, 4, 786–805.

Kirchheimer, Otto (1966) 'The transformation of the Western European party', in Joseph LaPalombara and Myron Weiner (eds), *Political Parties and Political Development*, Princeton, Princeton University Press, 177–200.

Kitschelt, Herbert (1989) 'The internal politics of parties: the laws of curvilinear disparity revisited', *Political Studies*, 37, 3, 400–21.

Kittilson, M, and S. Scarrow (2003) 'Political parties and the rhetoric and realities of democratcization', in B. E. Cain, R. J. Dalton and S. Scarrow (eds), *Democracy Transformed? Expanding Political Opportunities in Advanced Industrial Democracies*, Oxford, Oxford University Press, 59–80.

Kolodny, Robin (2000) 'Electoral partnerships: political consultants and political parties', in A. Thuber and Candice Nelson (eds), *Political Consultants in Elections*, Washington DC, Brookings Institute Press, 110–32.

Krook, Mona Lena (2010a) 'Beyond supply and demand: a feminist-institutionalist theory of candidate selection', *Political Research Quarterly*, 63, 4, 707–20.

Krook, Mona Lena (2010b) 'Why are fewer women than men elected: gender and the dynamics of candidate selection', *Political Studies Review*, 8, 2, 155–68.

Kriesi, Hanspeter (1998) 'The transformation of cleavage politics: the 1997 Stein Rokkan lecture', *European Journal of Political Research*, 33, 2, 165–85.

Kriesi, Hanspeter, Edgar Grande, Romain Lachat, Martin Dolezal, Simon Bornschier and Timotheos Frey (2006) 'Globalization and the transformation of the national political space: six European countries compared' *European Journal of Political Research*, 45, 6, 921–56.

Krishna, Gopal (1967) 'One party dominance: development and trends', in Rajni Kothari (ed.), *Party System and Election Studies*, Mumbai, Allied Publisher, 133–56.

Laakso, M. and R. Taagepera (1979) '"Effective" number of parties: a measure with application to Western Europe', *Comparative Political Studies*, 12, 1, 3–27.

Labour Party (2013) *Labour Party Rule Book 2013*, London, The Labour Party.

Laffin, Martin, Eric Shaw and Gerald Taylor (2005) 'The Labour Party and devolution', *Economic and Social Research Council's Devolution and Constitutional Change Programme* Briefing No. 14, January.

Laponce, J. A. (1981) *The Topography of Political Perceptions*, Toronto, University of Toronto Press.

Laver, Michael and Norman Schofield (1990) *Multiparty Government: The Politics of Coalition in Europe*, Oxford, Oxford University Press.

Laver, Michael and Kenneth Shepsle (1990) 'Government coalitions and intraparty politics', *British Journal of Political Science*, 20, 4, 489–507.

Lawless, Jennifer and Richard Fox (2005) *It Takes a Candidate: Why Women Don't Run For Office*, Cambridge, Cambridge University Press.

Lawless, Jennifer and Richard Fox (2010) *It Still Takes a Candidate: Why Women Don't Run For Office*, Cambridge, Cambridge University Press.

Lawson, Kay (1988) 'When linkage fails', in Kay Lawson and Peter Merkl (eds), *When Parties Fail: Emerging Alternative Organizations*, Princeton, Princeton University Press, 3–12.

Laybourn, Keith (2001) *A Century of Labour: A History of the Labour Party*, Stroud, Sutton.

LeDuc, Lawrence (2001) 'Democratizing party leadership selection', *Party Politics*, 7, 3, 323–42.

Lees-Marshment, Jennifer (2001) *Political Marketing and British Political Parties: The Party's Just Begun*, Manchester, Manchester University Press.

Lightfoot, Simon (2006) 'The consolidation of Europarties? The "party regulation" and the development of political parties in the European Union', *Representation*, 42, 4, 303–14.

Lijphart, Arend (1984) *Democracies: Patterns of Majoritarian and Consensus Government in Twenty-One Countries*, New Haven, Yale University Press.

Lijphart, Arend (1999) *Patterns of Democracy: Government Forms and Performance in Thirty-Six Countries*, New Haven, Yale University Press.

Lilleker, Darren (2005) 'The impact of political marketing on internal party democracy', *Parliamentary Affairs*, 58, 3, 570–84.

Lipset, Seymour M. and Martin Rokkan (1967) *Party Systems and Voter Alignments*, New York, Free Press.

Lipson, Leslie (1964) *The Democratic Civilization*, Oxford, Oxford University Press.

Loxbo, Karl (2013) 'The face of intra-party democracy: leadership autonomy and activist influence in the mass party and the cartel party', *Party Politics*, 19, 4, 537–54.

Lucardie, P (2000) 'Prophets, purifiers and prolocutors: towards a theory on the emergence of new parties', *Party Politics*, 6, 2, 175–85.

Lundell, Krister (2004) 'Determinants of candidate selection: the degree of centralization in comparative perspective', *Party Politics*, 10, 1, 25–47.

MacDonald, J. R. (1909) *Socialism and Government*, London, Independent Labour Party.

Macintyre, Stuart (1980) *A Proletarian Science: Marxism in Britain, 1917–1933*, Cambridge, Cambridge University Press.

Mair, Peter (2003), 'Political parties and democracy: what sort of future?', *Central European Political Science Review*, 4, 13, 7–15.

Mair, Peter (2006) 'Ruling the void: the hollowing of Western democracy', *New Left Review*, 42, 25–51.

Mair, Peter and Cas Mudde (1998) 'The party family and its study', *Annual Review of Political Science*, 1, 211–29.

Manning, Carrie (2005) 'Assessing African party systems after the Third Wave', *Party Politics*, 11, 6, 707–27.

Margetts, Helen (2001) 'The cyber party', paper presented at the ECPR Joint Sessions of Workshops, Grenoble, 6–11 April.

Mattila, Mikko and Tapio Raunio (2004) 'Does winning pay? Electoral success and government formation in 15 West European countries', *European Journal of Political Research*, 43, 2, 263–85.

Marsh, Michael (2004) 'None of that post-modern stuff around here: grassroots campaigning in the 2002 Irish General Election', *British Elections and Parties Review*, 14, 245–67.

May, John D. (1973) 'Opinion structure of political parties: the special law of curvilinear disparity', *Political Studies*, 21, 2, 135–51.

McKenzie, Robert (1963) *British Political Parties*, London, Mercury Books.

McKenzie, Robert (1982) 'Power in the Labour Party: the issue of intra-party democracy', in Dennis Kavanagh (ed.), *The Politics of the Labour Party*, London, George Allan and Unwin, 191–201.

Michels, Robert (1915) *Political Parties: A Sociological Study of the Oligarchical Tendencies of Modern Democracy*, New York, Hearst's International Library Company.

Miliband, Ralph (1958) 'Party democracy and parliamentary government', *Political Studies*, 6, 2, 170–4.

Mill, John Stuart (1994) *Principles of Political Economy*, Oxford, Oxford University Press.

Mozaffar, S. and J. Scarritt (2005) 'The puzzle of African party systems', *Party Politics*, 11, 4, 399–421.

Muller, Wolfgang and Kaare Strøm (2000) 'Conclusion: cabinet governance in Western Europe', in Wolfgang Muller and Kaare Strøm (eds), *Coalition Government in Western Europe*, Oxford, Oxford University Press, 403–30.

Murray, Rainbow (2010) *Parties, Gender Quotas and Candidate Selection in France*, Basingstoke, Palgrave Macmillan.

Murray, Rainbow, Mona Lena Krook and Katherine Opello (2012) 'Why are gender quotas adopted? Party pragmatism and parity in France', *Political Research Quarterly*, 65, 3, 529–43.

New Patriotic Party of Ghana (2009) *Constitution of the New Patriotic Party*, Accra North, New Patriotic Party of Ghana.

Newell, James L. (2010), *The Politics of Italy: Governance in a Normal Country*, Cambridge, Cambridge University Press.

NIMD (2004) *Internal Party Democracy: The State of Affairs and the Road Ahead – Results of the Mini-Survey Commissioned by NIMD Knowledge Centre*, The Hague, NIMD.

Niven, Favid (1998) 'Party elites and women candidates: the shape of bias', *Women and Politics*, 19, 2, 57–80.

Norris, Pippa (1995) 'May's law of curvilinear disparity revisited: leaders, officers, members and voters in British political parties', *Party Politics*, 1, 1, 29–47.

Norris, Pippa (1997) 'Introduction: theories of recruitment', in Pippa Norris (ed.), *Passages to Power: Legislative Recruitment in Advanced Democracies*, Cambridge, Cambridge University Press, 1–14.

Norris, Pippa (2002) 'Campaign Communications', in Lawrence Le Duc, Richard G. Niemi and Pippa Norris (eds), *Comparing Democracies*, 2nd edn., London, Sage, 127–47.

Norris, Pippa (2006) 'Recruitment', in Richard S. Katz and William Crotty (eds), *Handbook of Party Politics*, London, 89–109.

Norris, Pippa and Joni Lovenduski (1993) *Gender and Party Politics*, London, Sage.

Norris, Pippa and R. Mattes (2003) 'Does ethnicity determine support for the incumbent party?', *KSG Working Papers Series* No. RWP03-009.

Norris, Pippa, Elizabeth Vallence and Joni Lovenduski (1992) 'Do candidates make a difference? Gender, race, ideology and incumbency', *Parliamentary Affairs*, 45, 4, 496–517.

Obama, Barack (2006) *The Audacity of Hope: Thoughts on Reclaiming the American Dream*, Edinburgh, Canon Gate Books.

Obler, Jeffery (1974) 'Intraparty democracy and the selection of parliamentary candidates: the Belgian case', *British Journal of Political Science*, 4, 2, 157–84.

Olsen, Jonathan (2010) 'The Norwegian Socialist Left Party: office-seekers in the service of policy?', in Jonathan Olsen, Michael Koß and Dan Hough (eds), *Left Parties in National Governments*, Basingstoke, Palgrave Macmillan, 16–32.

Olson, Mancur (1965) *The Logic of Collective Action: Public Good and the Theory of Groups*, Cambridge, Harvard University Press.

O'Neill, Michael (2000) 'Preparing for power: the German Greens and the challenge of party politics', *Contemporary Politics*, 6, 2, 165–84.

Ostrogorski, M. (1902) *Democracy and the Organization of Political Parties*, London, Macmillan & Co.

Panebianco, Angelo (1988) *Political Parties: Organization and Power*, Cambridge, Cambridge University Press.

Patomäki, Heikki and Teivo Teivainen (2007) 'Researching global political parties', in Katarina Sehm-Patomäki and Marko Ulvila (eds), *Global Political Parties*, London, Zed Books, 92–113.

Pattie, Charles and Ron Johnston (2009) 'Still talking, but is anyone listening? The changing face of constituency campaigning in Britain, 1997–2005' *Party Politics*, 15, 4, 411–34.

Pedersen, Helene Hedboe (2010) 'Differences and changes in Danish party organisations: central party organisations versus parliamentary party group power', *The Journal of Legislative Studies*, 16, 2, 233–50.

Pedersen, Karina and Bernhard Hansen (2003) 'Partimedlemmernes aktivitet', in Lars Bille and Jørgen Elklit (eds), *Partiernes Medlemmer*, Aarhus, Aarhus Universitetsforlag, 73–102.

Pedersen, Mogens N. (1989) 'En kortfattet oversight over det danske partisystems udvikling', *Politica*, 21, 3, 265–77.

Pettitt, Robin T. (2007) 'Challenging the leadership: the party conference as a platform for dissenting membership voice in British and Danish parties of the left', *Scandinavian Political Studies*, 30, 2, 229–48.

Pettitt, Robin T. (2012a) 'Internal party political relationship marketing: encouraging activism amongst local party members', in Jennifer Lees-Marshment (ed.), *Routledge Handbook of Political Marketing*, Abingdon, Routledge, 137–50.

Pettitt, Robin T. (2012b) 'Exploring variations in intra-party democracy: a comparative study of the British Labour Party and then Danish Centre-Left', *British Journal of Politics and International Relations*, 14, 4, 630–50.

Pelling, Henry (1958) *The British Communist Party: A Historical Profile*, London, A. and C. Black.

Plasser, F. (2000) 'American campaign techniques worldwide', *The Harvard International Journal of Press/Politics*, 5, 4, 33–54.

Plasser, F. (2001) 'Parties' diminishing relevance for campaign professionals', *Harvard International Journal of Press/Politics* 6, 4, 44–59.

Plouffe, David (2009) *The Audacity to Win: The Inside Story and Lessons of Barack Obama's Historic Victory*, London, Viking Penguin.

Poguntke, Thomas (2001) 'From nuclear building sites to cabinet: the career of the German Green Party', *Keele European Research Unit Working Paper 6*.

Popkin, Samuel (1991) *The Reasoning Voter*, Chicago, University of Chicago Press.

Puhle, Hans-Jürgen (2002) 'Still the age of catch-allism?: *Volksparteien* and *Parteienstaat* in crisis re-equilibration', in Richard Gunther, Jose Ramon Montero and Juan J. Linz (eds), *Political Parties: Old Concepts and New Challenges*, Oxford, Oxford University Press, 58–83.

Ranney, Austin (1962) *The Doctrine of Responsible Party Government: Its Origins and Present State*, Urbana, University of Illinois Press.

Ranney, Austin (1981) 'Candidate selection', in David Butler, Howard Penniman and Austin Ranney (eds), *Democracy at the Polls*, Washington DC, American Enterprise Institute, 75–106.

Reinhardt, Gina and Jennifer Victor (2008) *Competing for the Platform, the Politics of Interest Group Influence on Political Platforms*, paper presented to the 105th Annual Meetings of the American Political Science Association, Toronto.

Richards, Paul (2000) *Is the Party Over? New Labour and the Politics of Participation*, London, Fabian Society.

Riker, William (1962) *The Theory of Political Coalitions*, New Haven, Yale University Press.

Riker, William (1982) 'The two-party system and Duverger's Law: an essay on the history of political science', 76, 4, 753–66.

Rommele, Andrea, David M. Farrell and Piero Ignazi (2005) 'Preface', in Andrea Rommele, David M. Farrell and Piero Ignazi (eds), *Political Parties and Party Systems: The Concept of Linkage Revisited*, London, Praeger, vii–x.

Rose, Richard and Thomas Mackie (1983) 'Incumbency in government: asset or liability?', in Hans. Daalder and Peter Mair (eds), *Western European Party Systems: Continuity and Change*, London, Sage, 115–37.

Rose, Richard and William Mishler (2010) 'A supply-demand model of party-system institutionalization: the Russian case', *Party Politics*, 16, 6, 801–21.

Rousseau, Jean Jacques (1966) *The Social Contract and Discourses*, London, Everyman's Library.

Russell, Meg (2005) *Must Politics Disappoint?*, London, Fabian Society Pamphlet no. 614.

Sartori, Giovanni (2005) *Parties and Party Systems: A Framework for Analysis*, Colchester, ECPR Press.

Scarrow, Susan E. (1996) *Parties and Their Members: Organizing for Victory in Britain and Germany*, Oxford, Oxford University Press.

Scarrow, Susan E. (2002) *Perspectives on Political Parties: Classic Readings*, Basingstoke, Palgrave Macmillan.

Scarrow, Susan E (2005) *Implementing Intra-Party Democracy*, Washington, DC, The National Democratic Institute for International Affairs.

Scarrow, Susan E. (2006) 'The nineteenth-century origins of modern political parties: the unwanted emergence of party-based politics', in Richard S. Katz and William Crotty (eds), *Handbook of Party Politics*, London, Sage, 16–24.

Scarrow, Susan E. and Burcu Gezgor (2010) 'Declining memberships, changing members? European political party members in a new era', *Party Politics*, 16, 6, 823–43.

Scarrow, Susan E., Paul Webb and David M. Farrell (2002) 'From social integration to electoral contestation: the changing distribution of power within political parties', in Russell J. Dalton and Martin P. Wattenberg (eds), *Parties without Partisans: Political Change in Advanced Industrial Democracies*, Oxford, Oxford University Press, 129–56.

Schattschneider, E. E. (1942) *Party Government*, New Brunswick, Transaction Publishers.

Schattschneider, E. E. (1960) *The Semi-Sovereign People: A Realist View of Democracy in America*, New York, Holt, Rinehart and Winston.

Scholte, Jan (2007) 'Political parties and global democracy', in Katarina Sehm-

Patomäki and Marko Ulvila (eds), *Global Political Parties*, London, Zed Books, 12–38.

Schumpeter, Joseph A. (1976) *Capitalism, Socialism and Democracy*, London, Routledge.

Sehm-Patomäki, Katarina and Marko Ulvila (2007) 'Introduction', in Katarina Sehm-Patomäki and Marko Ulvila (eds), *Global Political Parties*, London, Zed Books, 1–11.

Seyd, Patrick (1987) *The Rise and Fall of the Labour Left*, London, Macmillan.

Seyd, Patrick (1999) 'New parties/new politics?: A case study of the British Labour Party', *Party Politics*, 5, 3, 383–405.

Seyd, Patrick and Paul Whiteley (2002) *New Labour's Grassroots: The Transformation of the Labour Party Membership*, Basingstoke, Palgrave Macmillan.

Seyd, Patrick and Paul Whiteley (2004) 'British party members: an overview', *Party Politics*, 10, 4, 355–66.

Shugart, M. S. (2008) 'Comparative electoral systems research: the maturation of a field and new challenges ahead', in Michael Gallagher and Paul Mitchell (eds), *The Politics of Electoral Systems*, Oxford, Oxford University Press, 25–56.

Siglas, Emmanuel, Monika Mokre, Johannes Pollak, Peter Slominski and Jozef Batora (2010) *Democracy Models and Parties at the EU Level: Empirical Evidence from the Adoption of the 2009 European Election Manifestos*, Recon Online Working Paper 2010/13.

Smith, Jennifer (2009) 'Campaigning and the catch-all party: the process of party transformation in Britain', *Party Politics*, 15, 5, 555–72.

Spirer, Herbert F. and Louise Spirer (1991) 'The use of statistics: Bismarck, sausages and policy', *American Journal of Economics and Sociology*, 50, 3, 347–50.

Stanyer, James (2001 *The Creation of Political News: Television and British Party Political Conferences*, Brighton, Sussex Academic Press.

Strøm, Kaare (1990) 'A behavioural theory of competitive political parties', *American Journal of Political Science*, 34, 2, 565–98.

Studlar, Donlev T. and Ian McAllister (1991) 'Political recruitment to the Australian legislature: towards an explanation of women's electoral disadvantages', *The Western Political Quarterly*, 44, 2, 467–85.

Svåsand, L. (2008) *Internal Party Democracy: The Case of the United Democratic Front in Malawi*, paper presented to Nordic Political Science Association Convention, Tromsø.

Swanson, David and Paolo Mancini (1996) *Politics, Media and Modern Democracy: An International Study of Innovations in Electoral Campaigning and their Consequences*, Westport, Greenwood Publishing Group.

Taagepera, R. (2003) 'Arend Lijphart's dimensions of democracy: logical connections and institutional design', *Political Studies*, 51, 1, 1–19.

Taagepera, R. and B. Grofman (1985) 'Rethinking Duverger's Law: predicting the effective number of parties in plurality and PR systems – parties minus issues equal one', *European Journal of Political Research*, 13, 341–52.

Teorell, Jan (1999) 'A deliberative defence of intra-party democracy', *Party Politics*, 5, 3, 363–82.

Thorpe, Andrew (1998) 'Comintern "control" of the Communist Party of Great Britain', *The English Historical Review*, 113, 452, 637–62.

Trapeznik, Alexander (2009) 'The Comintern and the Communist Party of New Zealand', *Journal of Cold War Studies*, 11, 1, 124–49.

Twyman, Joe (2008) 'Getting it right: YouGov and online survey research in Britain', *Journal of Elections, Public Opinion and Parties*, 18, 4, 343–54.

van Biezen, Ingrid (2004) 'Political parties as public utilities', *Party Politics*, 10, 6, 701–22.

van Biezen, Ingrid and Petr Kopecky (2007) 'The state and the parties: public funding, public regulation and party patronage in contemporary democracies', *Party Politics*, 13, 2, 235–54.

van Biezen, Ingrid, Peter Mair, and Thomas Poguntke (2011) 'Going, going, ... gone? The decline of party membership in contemporary Europe', *European Journal of Political Science*, 51, 1, 24–56.

Verney, Douglas (2004) 'How has the proliferation of parties affected the Indian Federation: a comparative approach', in Soya Hasan, E. Sridharaan and R Sudarshan (eds), *India's Living Consitution*, Delhi, Permanent Black, 134–58.

von Beyme, Klaus (1985) *Political Parties in Western Democracies*, Aldershot, Gower.

Von Neumann, John and Oskar Morgenstern (1953) *Theory of Games and Economic Behaviour*, Princeton, Princeton University Press.

Ware, Alan (1979) *The Logic of Party Democracy*, London, Macmillan.

Ware, Alan (1996) *Political Parties and Party Systems*, Oxford, Oxford University Press.

Warwick, Paul (1999) 'Ministerial autonomy or ministerial accommodation? Contested bases of government survival in parliamentary democracies', *British Journal of Political Science*, 29, 2, 369–94.

Warwick, Paul (2002) 'Toward a common dimensionality in West European policy spaces', *Party Politics*, 8, 1, 101–22.

Warwick, Paul V. and James N. Druckman (2006) 'The portfolio allocation paradox: an investigation into the nature of a very strong but puzzling relationship', *European Journal of Political Research*, 45, 4, 635–65.

Weber, Max (1990) 'The advent of plebiscitarian democracy', in Peter Mair (ed.), *The West European Party System*, Oxford, Oxford University Press, 31–7.

Weinberg, Martha (1977) 'Writing the Republican platform', *Political Science Quarterly*, 92, 4, 655–62.

West, Darrell (2000) *Checkbook Democracy: How Money Corrupts Political Campaigns*, Boston, Northeastern University Press.

White, John K. (2006) 'What is a political party?', in Richard S. Katz and William Crotty (eds), *Handbook of Party Politics*, London, Sage, 5–15.

Whiteley, Paul (2011) 'Is the party over? The decline of party activism and membership across the democratic world', *Party Politics*, 17, 1, 21–44.

Whiteley, Paul and Patrick Seyd (2002) *High-Intensity Participation: The Dynamics of Party Activism in Britain*, Ann Arbor, University of Michigan Press.

Whiteley, Paul and Patrick Seyd (2003) 'How to win a landslide by really trying: the effects of local campaigning on voting in the 1997 British general election', *Electoral Studies*, 22, 2, 301–24.

Whitfield, Lindsay (2009) '"Change for a better Ghana" – party competition, institutionalization and alternation in Ghana's 2008 elections', *African Affairs*, 108, 433, 621–41.

Widtfeldt, Anders (1997) *Linking Parties with People?: Party Membership in Sweden 1960–1994*, Göteborg, Göteborg University.

Williams, Michelle (2009) 'Kirchheimer's French Twist: a moden of the catch-all thesis applied to the French case', *Party Politics*, 15, 5, 592–614.

Witcover, Jules (2003) *Party of the People: A History of the Democrats*, New York, Random House.

Woldendorp, Jaap, Hans Keman and Ian Budge (2000) *Party Govcernment in 48 Democracies (1945–1998)*, Dordrecht, Kluwer Academic Publishers.

Wolf, Frieder Otto (2003) 'Whatever happened to the German Greens?', *Red Pepper*, August 2003, online at: http://www.redpepper.org.uk/whatever-happened-to-the-german/.

Wolinetz, Steven B. (2002) 'Beyond the catch-all party: approaches to the study of parties and party organizations in contemporary democracies', in Richard Gunther, Jose Ramon Montero and Juan J. Linz (eds), *Political Parties: Old Concepts and New Challenges*, Oxford, Oxford University Press, 136–65.

Wring, Dominic (1996) 'Political marketing and party development in Britain: a "secret" history', *European Journal of Marketing*, 30, 10/11, 92–103.

Yishai, Yael (2002) 'Bringing society back in: post-cartel parties in Israel', *Party Politics*, 7, 6, 667–87.

Young, Lisa and William Cross (2002) 'The rise of plebiscitary democracy in Canadian political parties', *Party Politics*, 8, 6, 673–99.

Index

221